Contents

Introduction to Astrology *by Kim Rog...*

    Planets: The First Building Block 4

    Signs: The Second Building Block 10

    Houses: The Third Building Block 15

    Aspects and Transits: The Fourth Building Block 18

    Retrograde Planets 23

    Moon Void-of-Course 24

    The Moon's Influence 25

    The Moon Through the Signs 26

2021 Eclipse Dates 30

2021 Retrograde Planets 31

2021 New and Full Moons 32

2021 Planetary Phenomena 33

2021 Weekly Forecasts
    by Michelle Perrin, aka Astrology Detective 35

Finding Opportunity Periods *by Jim Shawvan*. 75

Business Guide 81

Calendar Pages 83

    How to Use Your *Daily Planetary Guide* 83

2021 Calendar with Aspects and Opportunity Periods
    by Paula Belluomini. 84

World Time Zones 190

World Map of Time Zones 191

2021 Ephemeris Tables 192

The Planetary Hours 204

Table of Rising and Setting Signs 205

Blank Horoscope Chart. 206

Introduction to Astrology

by Kim Rogers-Gallagher

Your horoscope is calculated using the date and time you were born from the perspective of your birth location. From this information, a clock-like diagram emerges that shows where every planet was located at the moment you made your debut. Each chart is composed of the same elements, rearranged, so everyone has one of everything, but none are exactly alike. I think of planets, signs, houses, and aspects as the four astrological building blocks. Each block represents a different level of human existence.

The eight planets along with the Sun and Moon are actual physical bodies. They represent urges or needs we all have. Chiron also falls into this category. The twelve signs of the zodiac are sections of the sky, and each is 30 degrees. The signs describe the behavior a planet or house will use to express itself. The twelve houses in a chart tell us where our planets come to life. Each house represents different life concerns—values, communication, creativity, and so on—that we must live through as life and time progress.

Basically, aspects are angles. Some of the planets will be positioned an exact number of degrees apart, forming angles to one another. For example, 180 degrees is a circle divided by two and is called an opposition. A square is 90 degrees and divides the circle by four. A trine is 120 degrees and divides the circle by three, and so forth. Aspects show which planets will engage in constant dialogue with one another. The particular aspect that joins them describes the nature of their "conversation." Not all planets will aspect all other planets in the houses.

Planets: The First Building Block

Each planet acts like the director of a department in a corporation, and the corporation is, of course, you. For example, Mercury directs your Communications Department and Jupiter oversees your Abundance and Growth Department. When you have the need to communicate, you call on your Mercury; when it's time to take a risk or grow, you use your Jupiter. Let's meet each of the planets individually and take a look at which job duties fall under each planet's jurisdiction.

The Sun

Every corporation needs an executive director who makes the final decisions. The Sun is your Executive Director. The Sun in your chart is your core, your true self. Although each of the planets in your chart is important in its own right, they all "take their orders," figuratively speaking, from the Sun.

Everyone's Sun has the same inner goal: to shine. The house your Sun is in shows where you really want to do good, where you want to be appreciated and loved. Your Sun is your inner supply of pride and confidence, your identity. The Sun is you at your creative best, enjoying life to the fullest.

The Sun shows the focus of the moment, where the world's attention will be directed on that particular day. In fact, in horary and electional astrology, the two branches that pertain most to timing and prediction, the Sun represents the day, the Moon the hour, and the Midheaven the moment. In the physical body, the Sun rules the heart, upper back, and circulatory system.

The Moon

Speaking of the Moon, a good place to meet her and begin to understand her qualities is by the water on a clear night when she's full. Whether you're looking up at her or at that silvery patch she creates that shivers and dances on the water, take a deep breath and allow yourself to be still. She represents the soft interior of each of us that recalls memories, fears, and dreams.

She's a lovely lady who oversees the Department of Feelings; she's the bringer of "moods" (a great Moon word). Her house and placement in your chart reveal how your intuition works, what your emotional needs are, and how you want your needs met. She is the ultimate feminine energy, the part of you that points both to how you were nurtured and to how you will nurture others. In the body, the Moon has jurisdiction over the breasts, ovaries, and womb. She also rules our body fluids, the internal ocean that keeps us alive.

Mercury

☿ Back when gods and goddesses were thought to be in charge of the affairs of humanity, Mercury shuttled messages between the gods and mortals. In today's world, Mercury is the computer, the telephone, and the internet. He's the internal computer that constantly feeds you data about the world. His position and house in your chart show how you think and reason, and how you express yourself to others. You'll recognize him in your speech patterns, in your handwriting, and in the way you walk, because moving through your environment means communicating with it. He operates through your five senses and your brain, and makes you conscious of opposites—light and dark, hot and cold, up and down. He's what you use when you have a conversation, exchange a glance, gesture, or interpret a symbol. Mercury represents the side of you living totally in the present.

If you've ever tried to collect mercury after it escaped from a broken thermometer, you've learned something about Mercury. Just as your Mercury never stops collecting data, those tiny beads you tried so hard to collect brought back a bit of everything they contacted—dog hair, crumbs, and grains of dirt. In the body, Mercury also acts as a messenger. He transmits messages through his function as the central nervous system that lets your eyes and hands collaborate, your eyes blink, and breathing continue.

Venus

♀ Venus spends her energy supplying you with your favorite people, places, and things. If you want chocolate, music, flannel sheets, or the coworker you've got a mad crush on, it's your Venus that tells you how to get it. Venus enjoys beauty and comfort. She shows how to attract what you love, especially people. When you're being charming, whether by using your manners or by adorning yourself, she's in charge of all behavior that is pleasing to others—social chitchat, smiles, hugs, and kisses. Whenever you're pleased, satisfied, or content enough to purr, it's your Venus who made you feel that way. Since money is one of the ways we draw the objects we love to us, she's also in charge of finances. Venus relates to your senses—sight, smell, taste, touch, and sound—the body's receptors. After all, it's the senses that tell us what feels good and what doesn't. Venus responds to your desire for beautiful surroundings, comfortable clothing, and fine art.

Mars

♂ Mars is in charge of your Self-Defense and Action Department. He's the warrior who fights back when you're attacked—your own personal SWAT team. Your Mars energy makes you brave, courageous, and daring. His placement in your chart describes how you act on your own behalf. He's concerned only with you, and he doesn't consider the size, strength, or abilities of whomever or whatever you're up against. He's the side of you that initiates all activity. He's also in charge of how you assert yourself and how you express anger.

"Hot under the collar," "seeing red," and "all fired up" are Mars phrases. Mars is what you use to be passionate, adventurous, and bold. But he can be violent, accident-prone, and cruel, too. Wherever he is in your chart, you find constant action. Mars pursues. He shows how you "do" things. He charges through situations. This "headstrong" planet corresponds to the head, the blood, and the muscles.

Jupiter

♃ Jupiter is called "the Greater Benefic," and he heads the Department of Abundance and Growth. He's the side of you that's positive, optimistic, and generous. He's where you keep your supply of laughter, enthusiasm, and high spirits. It's Jupiter's expansive, high-spirited energy that motivates you to travel, take classes, and meet new people. Wherever he is in your chart is a place where you'll have an extensive network of friends and associates—folks you can visit, count on, and learn from. Jupiter is the side of you that will probably cause you to experience the "grass is greener" syndrome. Your Jupiter is also what you're using when you find yourself being excessive and wasteful, overdoing, or blowing something out of proportion. Words like "too" and "always" are the property of Jupiter, as are "more" and "better." In general, this planet just loves to make things bigger. In the body, Jupiter corresponds with the liver, the organ that filters what you take in and rids your body of excess. Jupiter also handles physical growth.

Saturn

♄ Saturn represents withholding and resistance to change. He heads the Boundaries and Rules Department. Locate Saturn in your chart to find out where you'll build walls to keep change out, where you may segregate yourself at times, where you'll be most likely to say no. Your Saturn is the authority inside you, the spot where you may inhibit or stall yourself throughout life—most often because you fear failure and would rather not act at all than act inappropriately. This planet teaches you to respect your elders, follow the rules, and do things right the first time. Wherever Saturn is in your chart is a place where you'll feel respectful, serious, and conservative. Your Saturn placement is where you'll know that you should never embellish the facts and never act until you're absolutely sure you're ready. Here is where you won't expect something for nothing. Saturn is also where you're at your most disciplined, where you'll teach yourself the virtues of patience, endurance, and responsibility. Because this planet is so fond of boundaries, it's also the planet in charge of organization, structures, and guidelines. In the physical body, Saturn correlates with the bones and the skin, those structures that hold your body together.

Uranus

♅ There's a spot in everyone's chart where independence is the order of the day, where rules are made specifically to be broken, and where personal freedom is the only way to go, regardless of the consequences. Here's where you'll surprise even yourself at the things you say and do. Meet Uranus, head of the Department of One Never Knows, the place in your chart where shocks, surprises, and sudden reversals are regular fare.

Your Uranus energy is what wakes you up to how confined you feel, breaks you out of the rut you're in, and sets you free. He's a computer wizard and involved in mass communications. Where he's strong in your chart, you will be strong, too. Here is where you'll have genius potential, where you'll be bold enough to ignore the old way to solve a problem and instead find a whole new way. Major scientific and technological breakthroughs like the space program and the internet were inspired by Uranus. In the body, Uranus rules the lower part of the legs, including the calves and ankles, and he co-rules with Mercury the central nervous system.

Neptune

Next time you hear yourself sigh or feel yourself slip into a day-dream, think of Neptune. This is the planet in charge of romance, nostalgia, and magic. Although her official title is head of the Department of Avoidance and Fantasy, she's also one of the most creative energies you own. Wherever she is in your chart is where you're psychic. It's also where you're capable of amazing compassion and sensitivity for beings and creatures less fortunate than yourself. It's where you'll be drawn into charity or volunteer work because you realize that we're all part of a bigger plan, that there are no boundaries between you and what's out there.

This combination of sensitivity and harsh reality doesn't always mix well. This may also be a place where you'll try to escape. Sleep, meditation, and prayer are the highest uses of her energies, but alcohol and drugs are also under her jurisdiction. Neptune's place in your chart is where you're equally capable of fooling all of the people all of the time, and of being fooled yourself. In the body, Neptune and the Moon co-rule fluids. Neptune also has a connection with poisons and viruses that invisibly infiltrate our bodies and with the body's immune system, which is how we keep our barriers intact.

Pluto

Pluto is head of the Department of Death, Destruction, and Decay. He's in charge of things that have to happen, and he disposes of situations that have gone past the point of no return, where the only solution is to "let go." He also oversees sex, reincarnation, recycling, regeneration, and rejuvenation. Pluto's spot in your chart is a place where intense, inevitable circumstances will arrive to teach you about agony and ecstasy. Pluto's place in your chart is where you'll be in a state of turmoil or evolution, where there will be ongoing change. This is the side of you that realizes that, like it or not, life goes on after tremendous loss. It is the side of you that will reflect on your losses down the road and try to make sense of them. Most importantly, since

Pluto rules life, death, and rebirth, here's where you'll understand the importance of process. You'll be amazingly strong where your Pluto is—he's a well of concentrated, transforming energy. In the body, Pluto is associated with the reproductive organs since here is where the invisible process of life and death begins. He is also in charge of puberty and sexual maturity. He corresponds with plutonium.

Signs: The Second Building Block

Every sign is built of three things: an element, a quality, and a polarity. Understanding each of these primary building blocks gives a head start toward understanding the signs themselves, so let's take a look at them.

The Polarities: Masculine and Feminine

The words "masculine" and "feminine" are often misunderstood or confused in the context of astrology. In astrology, masculine means that an energy is assertive, aggressive, and linear. Feminine means that an energy is receptive, magnetic, and circular. These terms should not be confused with male and female.

The Qualities: Cardinal, Fixed, and Mutable

Qualities show the way a sign's energy flows. The cardinal signs are energies that initiate change. Cardinal signs operate in sudden bursts of energy. The fixed signs are thorough and unstoppable. They're the energies that endure. They take projects to completion, tend to block change at all costs, and will keep at something regardless of whether or not it should be terminated. The mutable signs are versatile, flexible, and changeable. They can be scattered, fickle, and inconstant.

The Elements: Fire, Earth, Air, and Water

The fire signs correspond with the spirit and the spiritual aspects of life. They inspire action, attract attention, and love spontaneity. The earth signs are solid, practical, supportive, and as reliable as the earth under our feet. The earth signs are our physical envoys and are concerned with our tangible needs, such as food, shelter, work, and responsibilities. Air signs are all about the intellectual or mental sides of life. Like air itself, they are light and elusive. They love conversation, communication, and mingling. The water signs correspond to the emotional side of our natures. As changeable, subtle, and able to infiltrate as water itself, water signs gauge the mood in a room when they enter, and operate on what they sense from their environment.

Aries: Masculine, Cardinal, Fire

♈ Aries is ruled by Mars and is cardinal fire—red-hot, impulsive, and ready to go. Aries planets are not known for their patience, and they ignore obstacles, choosing instead to focus on the shortest distance between where they are and where they want to be. Planets in Aries are brave, impetuous, and direct. Aries planets are often very good at initiating projects. They are not, however, as eager to finish, so they will leave projects undone. Aries planets need physical outlets for their considerable Mars-powered energy; otherwise their need for action can turn to stress. Exercise, hard work, and competition are food for Aries energy.

Taurus: Feminine, Fixed, Earth

♉ Taurus, the fixed earth sign, has endless patience that turns your Taurus planet into a solid force to be reckoned with. Taurus folks never, ever quit. Their reputation for stubbornness is earned. They're responsible, reliable, honest as they come, practical, and endowed with a stick-to-it attitude other planets envy. They're not afraid to work hard. Since Taurus is ruled by Venus, it's not surprising to find that these people are sensual and luxury-loving, too. They love to be spoiled with the best—good food, fine wine, or even a Renoir painting. They need peace and quiet like no other, and don't like their schedules to be disrupted. However, they may need a reminder that comfortable habits can become ruts.

Gemini: Masculine, Mutable, Air

♊ This sign is famous for its duality and love of new experiences, as well as for its role as communicator. Gemini is mutable air, which translates into changing your mind, so expect your Gemini planet to be entertaining and versatile. This sign knows a little bit about everything. Gemini planets usually display at least two distinct sides to their personalities, are changeable and even fickle at times, and are wonderfully curious. This sign is ruled by Mercury, so if what you're doing involves talking, writing, gesturing, or working with hand-eye coordination, your Gemini planet will love it. Mercury also rules short trips, so any planet in Gemini is an expert at how to make its way around the neighborhood in record time.

Cancer: Feminine, Cardinal, Water

♋ Cancer is cardinal water, so it's good at beginning things. It's also the most privacy-oriented sign. Cancer types are emotionally vulnerable, sensitive, and easily hurt. They need safe "nests" to return to when the world gets to be too much. Cancer types say "I love you" by tending to your need for food, warmth, or a place to sleep. The problem is that they can become needy, dependent, or unable to function unless they feel someone or something needs them. Cancer rules the home and family. It's also in charge of emotions, so expect a Cancer to operate from his or her gut most of the time.

Leo: Masculine, Fixed, Fire

♌ Leo is fixed fire, and above all else represents pride and ego. Sun-ruled Leo wants to shine and be noticed. Natural performers, people in this sign are into drama and attract attention even when they don't necessarily want it. Occasionally your Leo friends may be touchy and high maintenance. Still, they are generous to a fault. Leo appreciates attention and praise with lavish compliments, lovely gifts, and creative outings designed to amaze and delight. Leo's specialties are having fun, entertaining, and making big entrances and exits.

Virgo: Feminine, Mutable, Earth

♍ Virgo may seem picky and critical, but that may be too simplistic. As a mutable earth sign, your Virgo planet delights in helping, and it's willing to adapt to any task. Having a keen eye for details may be another way to interpret a Virgo planet's automatic fault-finding ability. When Virgo's eye for detail combines with the ability to fix almost anything, you have a troubleshooter extraordinaire. This sign practices discrimination—analyzing, critiquing, and suggesting remedies to potential problems. This sign is also wonderful at making lists, agendas, and schedules. Keep your Virgo planet happy by keeping it busy.

Libra: Masculine, Cardinal, Air

♎ Libra adores balance, harmony, and equal give and take—no easy task. A more charming sign would be difficult to find, though. Libra's cardinal airy nature wants to begin things, and entertaining and socializing are high priorities. These expert people-pleasing Venus-ruled planets specialize in manners, courtesy, and small talk. Alone time may be shunned, and because they're gifted with the ability to pacify, they may sell out their own needs, or the truth, to buy peace and companionship. Seeing both sides of a situation, weighing the options, and keeping their inner balance by remaining honest may be Libra's hardest tasks.

Scorpio: Feminine, Fixed, Water

♏ Planets in this sign are detectives, excelling at the art of strategy. Your Scorpio planets sift through every situation for subtle clues, which they analyze to determine what's really going on. They're also gifted at sending subtle signals back to the environment, and at imperceptibly altering a situation by manipulating it with the right word or movement. Scorpio planets are constantly searching for intimacy. They seek intensity and may be crisis-oriented. They can be relentless, obsessive, and jealous. Remember, this is fixed water. Scorpios feel things deeply and forever. Give your Scorpio planets the opportunity to fire-walk, to experience life-and-death situations.

Sagittarius: Masculine, Mutable, Fire

♐ The enthusiasm of this mutable fire sign, ruled by Jupiter, spreads like a brushfire. These planets tend to never feel satisfied or content, and to always wonder if there's something even more wonderful over the next mountain. Your Sagittarius planets are bored by routine; they're freedom-oriented, generous, and optimistic to a fault. They can be excessive and overindulgent. They adore outdoor activities and foreign places and foreign people. They learn by first having the big picture explained. They're only too happy to preach, advertise, and philosophize. Sagittarius planets can be quite prophetic, and they absolutely believe in the power of laughter, embarrassing themselves at times to make someone laugh.

Capricorn: Feminine, Cardinal, Earth

♑ Your Capricorn planets, ruled by Saturn, have a tendency to build things, such as erecting structures and creating a career for you. Saturn will start up an organization and turn it into the family business. These planets automatically know how to run it no matter what it is. They're authority figures. They exercise caution and discipline, set down rules, and live by them. Capricorn is the sign with the driest wit. Here's where your sense of propriety and tradition will be strong, where doing things the old-fashioned way and paying respect to elders will be the only way to go. They want a return for the time they invest, and don't mind proving how valuable they are.

Aquarius: Masculine, Fixed, Air

♒ Aquarian planets present some unexpected contradictions because they are fixed air and unpredictable. This sign's ruler, Uranus, gets the credit for Aquarius's tumultuous ways. Aquarian energy facilitates invention and humanitarian conquests, to the amazement of the masses, and planets in this sign are into personal freedom like no other. They create their own rules, fight city hall whenever possible, and deliberately break tradition. They adore change. Abrupt reversals are their specialty, so others often perceive them as erratic, unstable, or unreliable. But when Aquarius energy activates, commitment to a cause or an intellectual ideal has a steadfastness like no other sign possesses.

Pisces: Feminine, Mutable, Water

♓ Mutable Pisces can't separate itself emotionally from whatever it's exposed to. While this is the source of Pisces' well-deserved reputation for compassion, it's also the source of a desire to escape reality. Planets in this sign feel everything—for better or worse—so they need time alone to unload and reassemble themselves. Exposure to others, especially in crowds, is exhausting to your Pisces planets. Here is where you may have a tendency to take in stray people and animals and where you'll need to watch for the possibility of being victimized or taken advantage of in some way. Pisces planets see the best in people or situations, and they can be disappointed when reality sets in. These planets are the romantics of the zodiac. Let them dream in healthy ways.

Houses: The Third Building Block

Houses are represented by twelve pie-shaped wedges in a horoscope chart. (See blank chart on page 206.) They're like rooms in a house, and each reflects the circumstances we create and encounter in a specific area of life. One room, the Sixth House, relates to our daily routine and work, while the Eleventh House relates to groups we may be affiliated with, for example. The sign (Aries, Taurus, etc.) on the cusp of each house tells us something about the nature of the room behind the door. Someone with Leo on the Sixth House cusp will create different routines and work habits than a person with Capricorn on that cusp. The sign influences the type of behavior you'll exhibit when those life circumstances turn up. Since the time of day you were born determines the sign on each of the houses, an accurate birth time will result in more accurate information from your chart.

The Twelve Houses

The First House

The First House shows the sign that was ascending over the horizon at the moment you were born. Let's think again of your chart as one big house and of the houses as "rooms." The First House symbolizes your front door. The sign on this house cusp (also known as the Rising Sign or Ascendant) describes the way you dress, move, and adorn yourself, and the overall condition of your body. It relates to the first impression you make on people.

The Second House

This house shows how you handle the possessions you hold dear. That goes for money, objects, and the qualities you value in yourself and in others. This house also holds the side of you that takes care of what you have and what you buy for yourself, and the amount of money you earn. The Second House shows what you're willing to do for money, too, so it's also a description of your self-esteem.

The Third House

This house corresponds to your neighborhood, including the bank, the post office, and the gym where you work out. This is the side of you that performs routine tasks without much conscious thought. The Third House also refers to childhood and grammar school, and it shows your relationships with siblings, your communication style, and your attitude toward short trips.

The Fourth House

This house is the symbolic foundation brought from your childhood home, your family, and the parent who nurtured you. Here is where you'll find the part of you that decorates and maintains your nest. It decides what home in the adult world will be like and how much privacy you'll need. The Fourth House deals with matters of real estate. Most importantly, this house contains the emotional warehouse of memories you operate from subconsciously.

The Fifth House

Here's the side of you that's reserved for play, that only comes out when work is done and it's time to party and be entertained. This is the charming, creative, delightful side of you, where your hobbies, interests, and playmates are found. If it gives you joy, it's described here. Your Fifth House shines when you are creative, and it allows you to see a bit of yourself in those creations—anything from your child's smile to a piece of art. Traditionally this house also refers to speculation and gambling.

The Sixth House

This house is where you keep the side of you that decides how you like things to go along over the course of a day, the side of you that plans a schedule. Since it describes the duties you perform on a daily basis, it also refers to the nature of your work, your work environment, and how you take care of your health. It's how you function. Pets are also traditionally a Sixth House issue, since we tend to them daily and incorporate them into our routine.

The Seventh House

Although it's traditionally known as the house of marriage, partnerships, and open enemies, the Seventh House really holds the side of you that only comes out when you're in the company of just one other person. This is the side of you that handles relating on a one-to-one basis. Whenever you use the word "my" to describe your relationship with another, it's this side of you talking.

The Eighth House

Here's the crisis expert side of you that emerges when it's time to handle extreme circumstances. This is the side of you that deals with agony and ecstasy, with sex, death, and all manner of mergers, financial and otherwise. The Eighth House also holds information on surgeries, psychotherapy, and the way we regenerate and rejuvenate after a loss.

The Ninth House

This house holds the side of you that handles new experiences, foreign places, long-distance travel, and legal matters. Higher education, publishing, advertising, and forming opinions are handled here, as are issues involving the big picture, including politics, religion, and philosophy.

The Tenth House

This spot in your chart describes what the public knows about you. Your career, reputation, and social status are found here. This is the side of you that takes time to learn and become accomplished. It describes the behavior you'll exhibit when you're in charge, and also the way you'll act in the presence of an authority figure. Most importantly, the Tenth House describes your vocation or life's work—whatever you consider your "calling."

The Eleventh House

Here's the team player in you, the side of you that helps you find your peer groups. The Eleventh House shows the types of organizations you're drawn to join, the kind of folks you consider kindred spirits, and how you'll act in group situations. It also shows the causes and social activities you hold near and dear.

The Twelfth House

This is the side of you that only comes out when you're alone, or in the mood to retreat and regroup. Here's where the secret side of you lives, where secret affairs and dealings take place. Here, too, is where matters like hospital stays are handled. Most importantly, the Twelfth House is the room where you keep all the traits and behaviors that you were taught early on to stifle, avoid, or deny—especially in public. This side of you is very fond of fantasy, illusion, and pretend play.

Aspects and Transits: The Fourth Building Block

Planets form angles to one another as they move through the heavens. If two planets are 90 degrees apart, they form a square. If they're 180 degrees apart, they're in opposition. Planets in aspect have twenty-four-hour communication going on. The particular angle that separates any two planets describes the nature of their conversation. Astrologers use six angles most often, each of which produces a different type of relationship or "conversation" between the planets they join. Let's go over the meaning of each of the aspects.

Ptolemic Aspects

The Conjunction (0–8 degrees)

♂ When you hear that two things are operating "in conjunction," it means they're operating together. This holds true with planets as well. Two (or more) planets conjoined are a team, but some planets pair up more easily than others. Venus and the Moon work well together because both are feminine and receptive, but the Sun and Mars are both pretty feisty by nature, and may cause conflict. Planets in conjunction are usually sharing a house in your chart.

The Sextile (60 degrees)

⚹ The sextile links planets in compatible elements. That is, planets in sextile are either in fire and air signs or earth and water signs. Since these pairs of elements get along well, the sextile encourages an active exchange between the two planets involved, so these two parts of you will be eager to work together.

The Square (90 degrees)

□ A square aspect puts planets at cross-purposes. Friction develops between them and one will constantly challenge the other. You can see squares operating in someone who's fidgety or constantly restless. Although they're uncomfortable and even aggravating at times, your squares point to places where tremendous growth is possible.

The Trine (120 degrees)

△ Trines are usually formed between planets of the same element, so they understand each other. They show an ease of communication not found in any of the other aspects, and they're traditionally thought of as "favorable." Of course, there is a downside to trines. Planets in this relationship are so comfortable that they can often get lazy and spoiled. (Sometimes they get so comfy they're boring.) Planets in trine show urges or needs that automatically support each other. The catch is that you've got to get them operating.

The Quincunx (150 degrees)

⚻ This aspect joins two signs that don't share a quality, element, or gender, which makes it difficult for them to communicate with each other. It's frustrating. For that reason, this aspect has always been considered to require an adjustment in the way the two planets are used. Planets in quincunx often feel pushed, forced, or obligated to perform. They seem to correspond to health issues.

The Opposition (180 degrees)

☍ When two planets are opposed, they work against each other. For example, you may want to do something, and if you have two opposing planets you may struggle with two very different approaches to getting the job done. If Mars and Neptune are opposing, you may struggle between getting a job done the quick, easy way or daydreaming about all the creative possibilities open to you. It's as if the two are standing across from one another with their arms folded, involved in a debate, neither willing to concede an inch. They can break out of their standoff only by first becoming aware of one another and then compromising. This aspect is the least difficult of the traditionally known "hard" aspects because planets "at odds" with one another can come to some sort of compromise.

Transits

While your horoscope (natal chart) reflects the exact position of planets at the time of your birth, the planets, as you know, move on. They are said to be "transiting." We interpret a transit as a planet in its "today" position making an aspect to a planet in your natal chart. Transiting planets represent incoming influences and events that your natal planets will be asked to handle. The nature of the transiting planet describes the types of situations that will arise, and the nature of your natal planet tells which "piece" of you you're working on at the moment. When a planet transits through a house or aspects a planet in your chart, you will have opportunities for personal growth and change. Every transit you experience adds knowledge to your personality.

Sun Transit

A Sun transit points to the places in your chart where you'll want special attention, pats on the back, and appreciation. Here's where you want to shine. These are often times of public acclaim, when we're recognized, congratulated, or applauded for what we've done. Of course, the ultimate Sun transit is our birthday, the day when we're all secretly sure that we should be treated like royalty.

Moon Transit

When the Moon touches one of the planets in our natal chart, we react from an emotional point of view. A Moon transit often corresponds to the highs and lows we feel that last only a day or two. Our instincts are on high during a Moon transit and we're more liable to sense what's going on around us than to consciously know something.

Mercury Transit

Transiting Mercury creates activity in whatever area of life it visits. The subject is communication of all kinds, so conversation, letters, and quick errands take up our time now. Because of Mercury's love of duality, events will often occur in twos—as if Hermes the trickster were having some fun with us—and we're put in the position of having to do at least two things at once.

Venus Transit

Transiting Venus brings times when the universe gives us a small token of warmth or affection or a well-deserved break. These are often sociable, friendly periods when we do more than our usual share of mingling and are more interested in good food and cushy conditions than anything resembling work. A Venus transit also shows a time when others will give us gifts. Since Venus rules money, this transit can show when we'll receive financial rewards.

Mars Transit

Mars transiting a house can indicate high-energy times. You're stronger and restless, or perhaps cranky, angry, accident-prone, or violent. When Mars happens along, it's best to work or exercise hard to use up this considerable energy. Make yourself "too tired to be mad." These are ideal times to initiate projects that require a hard push of energy to begin.

Jupiter Transit

Under this transit you're in the mood to travel, take a class, or learn something new about the concerns of any house or planet Jupiter visits. You ponder the big questions. You grow under a Jupiter transit, sometimes even physically. Now is the time to take chances or risk a shot at the title. During a Jupiter transit you're luckier, bolder, and a lot more likely to succeed. This transit provides opportunities. Be sure to take advantage of them.

Saturn Transit

When Saturn comes along, we see things as they truly are. These are not traditionally great times, but they are often times when your greatest rewards appear. When Saturn transits a house or planet, he checks to see if the structure is steady and will hold up. You are then tested, and if you pass, you receive a symbolic certificate of some kind—and sometimes a real one, like a diploma. We will always be tested, but if we fail, life can feel very difficult. Firming up our lives is Saturn's mission. This is a great time to tap into Saturn's willpower and self-discipline to stop doing something. It is not traditionally a good time to begin new ventures, though.

Uranus Transit

The last thing in the world you'd ever expect to happen is exactly what you can expect under a Uranus transit. This is the planet of last-minute plan changes, reversals, and shock effects. So if you're feeling stuck in your present circumstances, when a Uranus transit happens along you won't be stuck for long. "Temporary people" often enter your life at these times, folks whose only purpose is to jolt you out of your present circumstances by appearing to provide exactly what you were sorely missing. That done, they disappear, leaving you with your life in a shambles. When these people arrive, enjoy them and allow them to break you out of your rut—just don't get comfortable.

Neptune Transit

A Neptune transit is a time when the universe asks only that you dream and nothing more. Your sensitivity heightens to the point that harsh sounds can actually make you wince. Compassion deepens, and psychic moments are common. A Neptune transit inspires divine discontent. You sigh, wish, feel nostalgic, and don't see things clearly at all. At the end of the transit, you realize that everything about you is different, that the reality you were living at the beginning of the transit has been gradually eroded or erased right from under your feet, while you stood right there upon it.

Pluto Transit

A Pluto transit is often associated with obsession, regeneration, and inevitable change. Whatever has gone past the point of no return, whatever is broken beyond repair, will pass from your life now. As with a Saturn transit, this time is not known to be wonderful, but when circumstances peel away everything from us and we're forced to see ourselves as we truly are, we do learn just how strong we are. Power struggles often accompany Pluto's visit, but being empowered is the end result of a positive Pluto transit. The secret is to let go, accept the losses or changes, and make plans for the future.

Retrograde Planets

Retrograde literally means "backward." Although none of the planets ever really throw their engines in reverse and move backward, all of them, except the Sun and Moon, appear to do so periodically from our perspective here on Earth. What's happening is that we're moving either faster or slower than the planet that's retrograde, and since we have to look over our shoulder to see it, we refer to it as retrograde.

Mercury Retrograde: A Communication Breakdown

The way retrograde planets seem to affect our affairs varies from planet to planet. In Mercury's case, it means often looking back at Mercury-ruled things—communications, contracts, and so on. Keep in mind that Mercury correlates with Hermes, the original trickster, and you'll understand how cleverly disguised some of these errors can be. Communications become confused or are delayed. Letters are lost or sent to Auckland instead of Oakland, or they end up under the car seat for three weeks. We sign a contract or agreement and find out later that we didn't have all the correct information and what we signed was misleading in some way. We try repeatedly to reach someone on the telephone but can never catch them, or our communications devices themselves break down or garble information in some way. We feel as if our timing is off, so short trips often become more difficult. We leave the directions at home or write them down incorrectly. We're late for appointments due to circumstances beyond our control, or we completely forget about them.

Is there a constructive use for this time period? Yes. Astrologer Erin Sullivan has noted that the ratio of time Mercury spends moving retrograde (backward) and direct (forward) corresponds beautifully with the amount of time we humans spend awake and asleep—about a third of our lives. So this period seems to be a time to take stock of what's happened over the past three months and assimilate our experiences.

A good rule of thumb with Mercury retrograde is to try to confine activities to those that have "re" attached to the beginning of a word, such as reschedule, repair, return, rewrite, redecorate, restore, replace, renovate, or renew.

Retrogrades of the Other Planets

With Venus retrograde every eighteen months for six weeks, relationships and money matters are delayed or muddled.

With Mars retrograde for eleven weeks and then direct for twenty-two months, actions initiated are often rooted in confusion or end up at cross-purposes to our original intentions. Typically under a Mars retrograde, the aggressor or initiator of a battle is defeated.

Jupiter retrogrades for four months and is direct for nine months. Saturn retrogrades for about the same amount of time. Each of the outer planets—Uranus, Neptune, and Pluto—stays retrograde for about six or seven months of every year. In general, remember that actions ruled by a particular planet quite often need to be repeated or done over when that planet is retrograde. Just make sure that whatever you're planning is something you don't mind doing twice.

Moon Void-of-Course

The Moon orbits Earth in about twenty-eight days, moving through each of the signs in about two days. As she passes through the thirty degrees of each sign, she visits with the planets in order by forming angles, or aspects, with them. Because she moves one degree in just two to two and a half hours, her influence on each planet lasts only a few hours. As she approaches the late degrees of the sign she's passing through, she eventually forms what will be her final aspect to another planet before leaving the sign. From this point until she actually enters the new sign, she is referred to as being "void-of-course" (v/c).

The Moon symbolizes the emotional tone of the day, carrying feelings of the sign she's "wearing" at the moment. She rules instincts. After she has contacted each of the planets, she symbolically "rests" before changing her costume, so her instincts are temporarily on hold. It's during this time that many people feel fuzzy, vague, or scattered. Plans or decisions do not pan out. Without the instinctual knowing the Moon provides as she touches each planet, we tend to be unrealistic or exercise poor judgment. The traditional definition of the void-of-course Moon is that "nothing will come of this," and it seems to be true. Actions initiated under a void-of-course Moon are often wasted, irrelevant, or incorrect—usually because information needed to make a sound decision is hidden or missing or has been overlooked.

Now, although it's not a good time to initiate plans when the Moon is void, routine tasks seem to go along just fine. However, this period is really ideal for what the Moon does best: reflection. It's at this time that we can assimilate what has occurred over the past few days. Use this time to meditate, ponder, and imagine. Let your conscious mind rest and allow yourself to feel.

On the lighter side, remember that there are other good uses for the void-of-course Moon. This is the time period when the universe seems to be most open to loopholes. It's a great time to make plans you don't want to fulfill or schedule things you don't want to do. In other words, like the saying goes, "To everything, there is a season." Even void-of-course Moons.

The Moon's Influence

As the Moon goes along her way, she magically appears and disappears, waxing to full from the barest sliver of a crescent just after she's new, then waning back to her invisible new phase again. The four quarters—the New Moon, the second quarter, the Full Moon, and the fourth quarter—correspond to the growth cycle of every living thing.

The Quarters

First Quarter

This phase begins when the Moon and the Sun are conjunct one another in the sky. At the beginning of the phase, the Moon is invisible, hidden by the brightness of the Sun as they travel together. The Moon is often said to be in her "dark phase" when she is just new. The New Moon can't actually be seen until 5½ to 12 hours after its birth. Toward the end of the first-quarter phase, as the Moon pulls farther away from the Sun and begins to wax toward the second quarter stage, a delicate silver crescent appears. This time corresponds to all new beginnings; this is the best time to begin a project.

Second Quarter

The second quarter begins when the Moon has moved 90 degrees away from the Sun. At this point the waxing Moon rises at about noon and sets at about midnight. It's at this time that she can be seen in the western sky during the early evening hours, growing in size from a crescent to her full beauty. This period corresponds to the development and growth of life, and with projects that are coming close to fruition.

Third Quarter

This phase begins with the Full Moon, when the Sun and Moon are opposite each other in the sky. It's now that the Moon can be seen rising in the east at sunset, a bit later each night as this phase progresses. This time corresponds to the culmination of plans and to maturity.

Fourth Quarter

This phase occurs when the Moon has moved 90 degrees past the full phase. She is decreasing in light, rises at midnight, and can be seen now in the eastern sky during the late evening hours. She doesn't reach the highest point in the sky until very early in the morning. This period corresponds to "disintegration"—a symbolic "drawing back" to reflect on what's been accomplished. It's now time to reorganize, clear the boards, and plan for the next New Moon stage.

The Moon Through the Signs

The signs indicate how we'll do things. Since the Moon rules the emotional tone of the day, it's good to know what type of mood she's in at any given moment. Here's a thumbnail sketch to help you navigate every day by cooperating with the Moon no matter what sign she's in.

Aries

The Moon in Aries is bold, impulsive, and energetic. It's a period when we feel feisty and maybe a little argumentative. This is when even the meekest aren't afraid to take a stand to protect personal feelings. Since Aries is the first sign of the zodiac, it's a natural starting point for all kinds of projects, and a wonderful time to channel all that "me first" energy to initiate change and new beginnings. Just watch out for a tendency to be too impulsive and stress-oriented.

Taurus

☽ ♉ The Moon in Taurus is the Lady at her most solid and sensual, feeling secure and well rooted. There's no need to stress or hurry—and definitely no need to change anything. We tend to resist change when the Moon is in this sign, especially change that's not of our own making. We'd rather sit still, have a wonderful dinner, and listen to good music. Appreciating the beauty of the earth, watching a sunset, viewing some lovely art, or taking care of money and other resources are Taurus Moon activities.

Gemini

☽ ♊ This mutable air sign moves around so quickly that when the Moon is here we're a bit more restless than usual, and may find that we're suddenly in the mood for conversation, puzzles, riddles, and word games. We want two—at least two—of everything. Now is a great time for letter writing, phone calls, or short trips. It's when you'll find the best shortcuts, and when you'll need to take them, too. Watch for a tendency to become a bit scattered under this fun, fickle Moon.

Cancer

☽ ♋ The Moon in this cardinal water sign is at her most nurturing. Here the Moon's concerns turn to home, family, children, and mothers, and we respond by becoming more likely to express our emotions and to be sympathetic and understanding toward others. We often find ourselves in the mood to take care of someone, to cook for or cuddle our dear ones. During this time, feelings run high, so it's important to watch out for becoming overly sensitive, dependent, or needy. Now is a great time to putter around the house, have family over, and tend to domestic concerns.

Leo

♌ ♌ The Leo Moon loves drama with a capital *D*. This theatrical sign has long been known for its big entrances, love of display, and need for attention. When the Moon is in this sign, we're all feeling a need to be recognized, applauded, and appreciated. Now, all that excitement, pride, and emotion can turn into melodrama in the blink of an eye, so it's best to be careful of overreacting or being excessively vain during this period. It's a great time to take in a show (or star in one), be romantic, or express your feelings for someone in regal style.

Virgo

♍ ♍ The Moon is at her most discriminating and detail-oriented in Virgo, the sign most concerned with fixing and fussing. This Moon sign puts us in the mood to clean, scour, sort, troubleshoot, and help. Virgo, the most helpful of all the signs, is also more health conscious, work-oriented, and duty bound. Use this period to pay attention to your diet, hygiene, and daily schedules.

Libra

♎ ♎ The Libra Moon is most oriented toward relationships and partnerships. Since Libra's job is to restore balance, however, you may find yourself in situations of emotional imbalance that require a delicate tap of the scales to set them right. In general, this is a social, polite, and friendly time, when others will be cooperative and agree more easily to compromise. A Libra Moon prompts us to make our surroundings beautiful, or to put ourselves in situations where beauty is all around us. This is a great time to decorate, shop for the home, or visit places of elegant beauty.

Scorpio

♏ ♏ Scorpio is the most intense sign, and when the Moon is here, she feels everything to the nth degree—and needless to say, we do, too. Passion, joy, jealousy, betrayal, love, and desire can take center stage in our lives now, as our emotions deepen to the point of possible obsession. Be careful of a tendency to become secretive or suspicious, or to brood over an offense that was not intended.

Now is a great time to investigate a mystery, do research, "dig"—both figuratively and literally—and allow ourselves to become intimate with someone.

Sagittarius

☽ ♐ The Moon is at her most optimistic and willing to let go of things in Sagittarius. Jupiter, the planet of long-distance travel and education of the higher mind, makes this a great time to take off for adventure or attend a seminar on a topic you've always been interested in—say, philosophy or religion. This is the sign with the gift of prophecy and wisdom. When the Moon is in this sign, spend time outdoors, be spontaneous, and laugh much too loudly; just watch for a tendency toward excess, waste, and overdoing.

Capricorn

☽ ♑ The Moon is at her most organized, practical, and business-like in Capricorn. She brings out the dutiful, cautious, and pessimistic side of us. Our goals for the future become all-important. Now is the time to tend to the family business, act responsibly, take charge of something, organize any part of our lives that has become scattered or disrupted, set down rules and guidelines, or patiently listen and learn. Watch for the possibility of acting too businesslike at the expense of others' emotions.

Aquarius

☽ ♒ The Aquarius Moon brings out the rebel in us. This is a great time to break out of a rut, try something different, and make sure everyone sees us for the unique individuals we are. This sign is ruled by Uranus, so personal freedom and individuality are more important than anything now. Our schedules become topsy-turvy, and our causes become urgent. Watch for a tendency to become fanatical, act deliberately rebellious without a reason, or break tradition just for the sake of breaking it.

Pisces

☽ ♓ When the Moon slips into this sign, sleep, meditation, prayer, drugs, or alcohol is often what we crave to induce a trancelike state that will allow us to escape from the harshness of reality. Now is when we're most susceptible to emotional assaults of any kind, when we're feeling dreamy, nostalgic, wistful, or impressionable. It's also when we're at our most spiritual, when our boundaries are at their lowest, when we're compassionate, intuitive, and sensitive to those less fortunate. This is the time to attend a spiritual group or religious gathering.

2021 Eclipse Dates

May 26

Lunar Eclipse at 5° ♐ 26'

June 10

Solar Eclipse at 19° ♊ 47'

November 19

Lunar Eclipse at 27° ♉ 14'

December 4

Solar Eclipse at 12° ♐ 22'

2021 Retrograde Planets

Planet	Begin	Eastern	Pacific	End	Eastern	Pacific
Uranus	8/15/20	10:25 am	**7:25 am**	1/14/21	3:36 am	**12:36 am**
Mercury	1/30/21	10:52 am	**7:52 am**	2/20/21	7:52 pm	**4:52 pm**
Pluto	4/27/21	4:04 pm	**1:04 pm**	10/6/21	2:29 pm	**11:29 am**
Saturn	5/23/21	5:21 am	**2:21 am**	10/10/21	10:17 pm	**7:17 pm**
Mercury	5/29/21	6:34 pm	**3:34 pm**	6/22/21	6:00 pm	**3:00 pm**
Jupiter	6/20/21	11:06 am	**8:06 am**	10/17/21		**10:30 pm**
				10/18/21	1:30 am	
Neptune	6/25/21	3:21 pm	**12:21 pm**	12/1/21	8:22 am	**5:22 am**
Uranus	8/19/21	9:40 pm	**6:40 pm**	1/18/22	10:27 am	**7:27 am**
Mercury	9/26/21		**10:10 pm**	10/18/21	11:17 am	**8:17 am**
	9/27/21	1:10 am				
Venus	12/19/21	5:36 am	**2:36 am**	1/29/22	3:46 am	**12:46 am**

	Dec 2020	Jan 2021	Feb	Mar	Apr	May	Jun	Jul	Aug	Sep	Oct	Nov	Dec 2021	Jan 2022
☿			▓				▓				▓			
♀														▓
♃								▓	▓	▓	▓			
♄							▓	▓	▓	▓	▓			
♅	▓								▓	▓	▓	▓	▓	▓
♆								▓	▓	▓	▓	▓		
♇					▓	▓	▓	▓	▓	▓	▓			

2021 New and Full Moons

● New Moon, 23 ♑ 13, January 13, 12:00 a.m. EST

○ Full Moon, 9 ♌ 06, January 28, 2:16 p.m. EST

● New Moon, 23 ♒ 17, February 11, 2:06 p.m. EST

○ Full Moon, 8 ♍ 57, February 27, 3:17 a.m. EST

● New Moon, 23 ♓ 04, March 13, 5:21 a.m. EST

○ Full Moon, 8 ♎ 18, March 28, 2:48 p.m. EDT

● New Moon, 22 ♈ 25, April 11, 10:31 p.m. EDT

○ Full Moon, 7 ♏ 06, April 26, 11:32 p.m. EDT

● New Moon, 21 ♉ 18, May 11, 3:00 p.m. EDT

○ Full Moon/Lunar Eclipse, 5 ♐ 26, May 26, 7:14 a.m. EDT

● New Moon/Solar Eclipse, 19 ♊ 47, June 10, 6:53 a.m. EDT

○ Full Moon, 3 ♑ 28, June 24, 2:40 p.m. EDT

● New Moon, 18 ♋ 02, July 9, 9:17 p.m. EDT

○ Full Moon, 1 ♒ 26, July 23, 10:37 p.m. EDT

● New Moon, 16 ♌ 14, August 8, 9:50 a.m. EDT

○ Full Moon, 29 ♒ 37, August 22, 8:02 a.m. EDT

● New Moon, 14 ♍ 38, September 6, 8:52 p.m. EDT

○ Full Moon, 28 ♓ 14, September 20, 7:55 p.m. EDT

● New Moon, 13 ♎ 25, October 6, 7:05 a.m. EDT

○ Full Moon, 27 ♈ 26, October 20, 10:57 a.m. EDT

● New Moon, 12 ♏ 40, November 4, 5:15 p.m. EDT

○ Full Moon/Lunar Eclipse, 27 ♉ 14, November 19, 3:57 a.m. EST

● New Moon/Solar Eclipse, 12 ♐ 22, December 4, 2:43 a.m. EST

○ Full Moon, 27 ♊ 29, December 18, 11:36 p.m. EST

2021 Planetary Phenomena

Information on Uranus and Neptune assumes the use of a telescope. Resource: *Astronomical Phenomena for the Year 2021,* prepared jointly with Her Majesty's Nautical Almanac Office of the United Kingdom Hydrographic Office and the United States Naval Observatory's Nautical Almanac Office. The dates are expressed in Universal Time and must be converted to your Local Mean Time. (See the World Map of Time Zones on page 191.)

Planets Visible in Morning and Evening

Planet	Morning	Evening
Mercury	Feb. 15 – April 10 June 20 – July 25 Oct. 16 – Nov. 13	Jan. 5 – Feb. 2 April 27 – June 1 Aug. 10 – Oct. 3 Dec. 16 – Dec. 31
Venus	Jan. 1 – Feb. 14	May 5 – Dec. 31
Mars	Nov. 23 – Dec. 31	Jan. 1 – Aug. 23
Jupiter	Feb. 11 – Aug. 20	Jan. 1 – Jan. 16 Aug. 20 – Dec. 31
Saturn	Feb. 10 – Aug. 2	Jan. 1 – Jan. 7 Aug. 2 – Dec. 31

Mercury

Mercury can only be seen low in the east before sunrise or low in the west after sunset.

Venus

Venus is a brilliant object in the morning sky from the beginning of the year until mid-February, when it becomes too close to the Sun for observation. In early May it reappears in the evening sky, where it stays until the end of the year.

Mars

Mars is visible as a reddish object in the evening sky until late August, when it becomes too close to the Sun for observation. It reappears in the morning sky in late November.

Jupiter

Jupiter can be seen in the evening sky until mid-January, when it becomes too close to the Sun for observation. It reappears in the morning sky in the second week of February. From mid-November it be seen only in the evening sky.

Saturn

Saturn can be seen in the evening sky for the first week of January, until it becomes too close to the Sun for observation. It reappears in the morning sky in the second week of February. From late October it be seen only in the evening sky.

Uranus

Uranus can be seen can be seen only in the evening sky from late January until the second week of April, when it becomes too close to the Sun for observation. It reappears in the morning sky in late May.

Neptune

Neptune is visible in the evening sky at the beginning of the year. In mid-February it becomes too close to the Sun for observation and reappears in late March in the morning sky. From mid-December it can be seen only in the evening sky.

DO NOT CONFUSE (1) Jupiter with Saturn in early January and with Mercury in mid-January and mid-February to mid-March—on all occasions Jupiter is the brighter object; (2) Venus with Saturn in the second week of February, with Jupiter in mid-February, with Mercury in late May and in late December, and with Mars in July—on all occasions Venus is the brighter object; (3) Mercury with Saturn in late February and with Mars in mid-August—on both occasions Mercury is the brighter object.

2021 Weekly Forecasts

by Michelle Perrin, aka Astrology Detective

Overview of 2021

Focus on the Fixed Signs

After being relatively off the grid for quite a while, the focus returns to the fixed-sign axis in 2021. Both Saturn and Jupiter entered Aquarius in mid-December 2020, joining Uranus in the fellow fixed sign of Taurus. Uranus and Saturn will be in a close dance for much of 2021, staying in a relatively tight orb that will get triggered over and over by lunar transits throughout each month, creating a T-square whenever the Moon passes through Leo or Scorpio. This emphasis will be amplified whenever the fast-moving planets make their yearly passes through a fixed sign. Mars joins in by transiting Taurus, Leo, and Scorpio this year.

The world will be locked into an incessantly repeating, stubborn energy, which seems impossible to shake off. We will see clashes between the collective, the cultlike leader, and the individual, with all scrambling to find their place in the newly formed power structure. The old twentieth-century paradigm that puts pride of place on the individual is being torn down, as will become evident any time the Moon or any other planet transits independent Leo. The question is what will replace it? More on that in the next section.

As we shift into this new state of being, it will be difficult to give up on the comfortable, old ways of doing things. These growing pains will be played out again and again over the course of the year. Individualists may need to choose to be part of a utopian collective or to follow a charismatic leader, as it may get really rough when going it on your own. The era of the individual voice standing up to the Man, where everyone got along and respected each other for their own uniqueness, may be coming to an end.

On a more personal level, the energy will be shifting from a slightly manipulative one to a clear, open fight for dominance. Control freaks will be coming out of the woodwork, with their demands coming at a steady pace like an unrelenting hammer. This is a year for conditioning and grooming the outspoken and bold so that they cease to put up a fight. It will all just get too tiring. Look for people to check out instead of engage.

The Series of Saturn–Uranus Squares

February 17, 2021
June 14, 2021
December 24, 2021

Eras come and go. The Neoclassical era led to the Romantic, which in turn was replaced by the Victorian age, after which came the time we have been living in, at least until very recently. However, this as-yet-unnamed era is increasingly starting to look like a quaint relic of the past. We are turning a corner into a new age without really realizing we have already left the old one behind, creating a time where old paradigms are no longer relevant but a new social order has yet to congeal into anything solid.

Enter this year's series of three squares between Saturn in Aquarius and Uranus in Taurus. This is a relatively rare aspect, with the next one not occurring until 2043. The last time these squares happened was in 1999–2000, when the roles were reversed, with Saturn in Taurus and Uranus in Aquarius. This was the peak period of the dot-com bubble, which massively spiked during those two years. During this time, technology squared off against the brick-and-mortar world in a serious way. Even with the bust that followed, a corner was turned, prepping us for an existence where the digital realm became more relevant than "real" life.

Likewise, the Saturn-Uranus square prior to that one occurred between late 1975 and early 1977 in individualistic, fashionable Leo and destructive, edgy Scorpio. This period coincided almost exactly with the punk phenomenon. This gloriously creative, rebellious period emerged like a rocket from nowhere before burning out just as quickly. Yet during that short time, the movement swept away the bloated, tired, prog-rock, lentil-soaked remnants of listless hippiedom, paving the way for the on-the-go, booming, dynamic, hyper fashionable and individualistic 1980s.

As can be seen from the two previous periods, things change rapidly during these squares. Outmoded structures are swept away to make room for something new. These squares may also have a Lord of the Flies feel to them—a kind of giddy anarchy can take hold, where old systems are razed to the ground by those who are seeking a power grab, as well as by those who just enjoy seeing things burn. However, sometimes these cleansings by fire are necessary in order to move into the future free of old baggage.

This series of squares can also be looked at as the little sibling of the Uranus-Pluto squares of 2012–2015 in Aries and Capricorn. These squares also saw the Establishment being pitted against the New World Order and technology. The last time Uranus squared Pluto prior to this was in the early 1930s, ushering in a period that saw the rise of fascism and nationalism, two things that have also made a remarkable return in the past five years. With the recent turn away from globalism, along with 2020's Brexit, we may see other EU nations deciding to break away during the Saturn-Uranus squares of 2021, with the entire EU and its massive bureaucracy unraveling quickly and perhaps morphing into something totally different.

The last five years have also seen a total transformation in regard to the power of Big Tech. Silicon Valley has gone from being a magnet for utopian programmers who wanted to fight the power to actually being the power. It can even be argued that tech powerhouses now wield more influence and international control than the mainstream media or governments. For a large part of 2021, visionary Jupiter will be playing backup for Saturn in quixotic Aquarius, assisting it in its battle against a profits-minded, data-collecting, techy Uranus in Taurus. We may see a return to the ideals of the old "free and open" internet. Already, a number of grassroots alt-tech companies have emerged who don't need to rely on the financial backing of big investors, due to using blockchain technology to offer services that compete against the social media giants like Twitter, Facebook, and YouTube. We may see more viable alternatives to the existing establishment platforms and websites, taking us back to the days when being online was actually fun and exciting. As Old Tech has become increasingly entrenched, its products have become sanitized, stale, and boring. While they may not be going away, viable alt-tech alternatives may emerge, with some surprising new directions and powers arising in the online world.

Moreover, Saturn is in its ruling sign of Aquarius, giving it extra force when pitted against the heavy-hitter Uranus. Aquarius represents the utopian commune, the group collective, while Taurus has a top-down, submit-to-the-leader-in-order-to-belong vibe. More and more over the past few years, the public consciousness has grown less individualistic and more collective. The twentieth-century "I am" has morphed into the twenty-first-century "I identify as." Will the new era be one of group freedom or culty authoritarianism? The answer to this question may be played out in this series of squares.

No matter what happens, though, we will be able to move from this period of bloated stagnation to something fresh, new, and dynamic. Most importantly, the memes are sure to be extremely dank.

Three Outer Planets in Their Ruling Signs

This year sees three of the five heavy-hitting outer planets in their ruling signs. Neptune has been in Pisces since 2011, while Saturn moved from one of its ruling signs, Capricorn, into the other, Aquarius, in mid-December 2020. Jupiter joins the mix when it enters Pisces in mid-May. It then retrogrades back into Aquarius in late July before returning to Pisces for good in the closing days of 2021.

Jupiter is the traditional ruler of Pisces, while Neptune is its modern ruler, much as Uranus is the modern ruler of Aquarius, which is traditionally ruled by Saturn. When a planet is in its ruling sign, it is astrologically "at home." Its energy will flow in its purest, most unbridled form.

Saturn in Capricorn is all about big business, the Establishment, and moving up the hierarchy to worldly success, while Aquarius takes the Saturnian drive and harnesses it to make the entire world a better place for all. The last time Saturn was in techy, utopian Aquarius was in 1991, the same year a web browser was released to the general public, enabling all of society to access the internet, instead of just the government and academia. In addition to this year's series of tech-oriented Saturn-Uranus squares, the publicly accessed internet will be having its first Saturn Return! So look for a lot of happenings in the digital realm.

Neptune was discovered in 1846, when it was transiting Pisces. From 1855 to 1856, it was joined by its co-ruler, Jupiter. This year, 2021, marks only the second time since Neptune was located that the two co-rulers have both been in Pisces at the same time.

Neptune's entry into Pisces in 2011 marked the beginning of the "woke" era of social justice, which can sometimes take what starts out as an excellent idea and dilute it to the extremes, getting lost in the weeds to the point that basic facts of science are denied and the average person no longer understands what's going on. At the same time, there has been a hyper focus on feelings and not wanting to hurt them at all costs. An example of these trends is when a leading British Member of Parliament, Dawn Butler, stated in 2020 that assigning a baby a sex of male or female at birth is "dog-whistle transphobia."

Likewise, Jupiter in Pisces will bring an almost religious zeal to right-fighting. Both Jupiter and Pisces can have a judgmental vibe. With the Gas Giant operating at full force, there is a risk that if you don't fall in line with the official virtuous narrative, you could be accused of wrongthink and shunned in an Orwellian manner straight out of *1984*. On the positive side, Jupiter's straightforward optimism will go a long way toward diluting the murkier, more manipulative sides of Neptune.

January 1–3

A Truly Happy New Year

The first hours of the new year start with a party-hearty Moon in Leo squaring off against boundary-pushing Uranus in the gourmand sign of Taurus. There could be a tendency to overindulge in the festive spirit, which could lead to hangovers, regretful hookups, or even accidents. Make sure to have a designated driver and watchful friend on hand to keep things in line. Later the same day, a sextile between Mercury and Neptune in industrious Capricorn and dreamy Pisces will kick off the new year with positive mental energy, which is overflowing with constructive plans for the future. This is followed by two super-positive Lunar Grand Trines on the 2nd and 3rd. The first is a robust meeting of a Leo Moon, Venus in Sagittarius, and Mars in its ruling sign of Aries, promising that the first weekend of 2021 will be brimming with enthusiasm, fun, and excitement. Things get back to business on Sunday with a loose Grand Trine between a Virgo Moon, Capricorn Sun, and Uranus in Taurus. This is an ideal day for brainstorming an action plan for the next twelve months; out-of-the-box thinking and innovative solutions are the keys to increased stability and security.

January 4–10

Shifting Gears

While the mind is willing, it may be hard to roll up one's sleeves and settle into the nitty-gritty by doing the heavy lifting required of hard labor. The transition from holiday merry-making to wintertime industriousness could be more painful than usual. The week starts off with a conjunction between Mercury and Pluto in industrious Capricorn, strengthened by a trine with the Virgo Moon. Unfortunately, the Moon is also opposing daydreaming Neptune in Pisces and squaring goof-off Venus in Sagittarius, considerably weakening the conjunction's deep mental focus. Mars's entry into hardworking Taurus on Wednesday is greeted by Thursday's Lunar T-square, which drags in a huge number of planets, including the Scorpio Moon; Mars and Uranus in Taurus; Saturn and Jupiter in Aquarius; and Mercury in the final degrees of Capricorn. Noble, visionary plans can prove overwhelming, causing blocks of energy and anxiety when attempting to put them into practice, especially if deadlines are looming. This will leave everyone exhausted by the end of the week, with Friday evening's square of Mercury and Mars. Luckily, the weekend promises great fun and a boost in energy, thanks to a trine between playful Venus and Mars.

January 11–17

Everyone Wants to Be a Winner

It's the beginning of the new year, so it's no surprise that everyone is jostling for position, hoping to make their own resolutions come true, even if it means stepping on the toes of everyone around them. There is a slight bullying energy to Wednesday's Capricorn New Moon, which brushes up against a domineering, extremely driven Pluto. This is the ideal time to make an action plan for the upcoming year, plotting out the perfect road map for increased success and social standing—but you may need to play down-and-dirty to make your goals come true, as everyone will be elbowing their way to carve out an advantage. This week also sees a clash between the innovative visionary and the established status quo. Mercury, Saturn, and Jupiter in lofty Aquarius are squaring off against Mars and Uranus in bossy Taurus in an epic showdown worthy of David and Goliath. The shrewd, calculating, energetic force of the upstart renegade could cause traditional authority figures to lose their cool and make mistakes, thereby losing the upper hand. This can take place in the private realm, where right-fighters will stand up to local tyrants, or in the public space. The year could start off with skirmishes, protests, or even bouts of street fighting. The secret to getting through this challenging energy is to keep your cool and use your wits to outsmart your opponents.

January 18–24

Burn It All Down

The three planets of unrest, rebellion, and upheaval are meeting up this week, creating a spirit of gleeful, frenzied anarchy. Warrior Mars conjuncts radical Uranus in Taurus on Wednesday, followed by a square between Mars and ideological Jupiter on Saturday. This energy is compounded by the Taurus Moon, which is mimicking Mars's every move midweek. While Taurus is seen as a sign of stability, it also has a radical edge; after all, some of the most secure environments have been created by iron-fisted despots. From Pol Pot and Adolf Hitler to Jim Jones and Marshall Applewhite, Taurus has had its fair share of authoritarian tyrants and controlling cult leaders whose promise of paradise requires razing it all to the ground and starting over from Year Zero. Aquarius, however, fights for the freedom of the little guy, with Jupiter being a planet that exalts blinded zealotry. The forces of woke righteousness could bash against the perceived fascistic threats of the powers-that-be. Seeing how this all plays out during the week of the US presidential inauguration on January 20, we could expect to see clashes, riots, and street violence. As both sides are extremist and aggressive in their own way, it may be hard to determine which truly represents the side of good. A punch-drunk return to sobriety occurs on Saturday night, when the Sun conjuncts rational Saturn.

January 25–31

Smoldering Embers

The Sun keeps shining its light on issues dredged up by last week's skirmishes by hitting the same points previously scorched by Mars, only this time from the more emotionally detached sign of Aquarius. It squares off against Uranus before conjuncting Jupiter on Thursday. The Full Moon in Leo on the same day just wants to have fun, however, and is fighting for its right to party by standing up to all the dreary drama going down in Taurus and Aquarius—creating a T-square with Uranus and Mars, as well as Saturn, the Sun, and Jupiter. Meanwhile, the conjunction of Venus and Pluto serves as a kind of planetary League of Nations, striving to regain a semblance of order through institutional leadership and diplomacy. Peace is restored at the weekend when the Moon enters the sign of no-nonsense nursemaid Virgo, sending out restorative trines to Mars, Uranus, and Pluto, while Mercury's retrograde motion on Saturday is taking a time-out to review and reflect on the tensions of the past few weeks.

February 1–7

Outrage Mobs versus Even-Keeled Moderates

The week kicks off with an outraged Mars in domineering Taurus squaring off against a just-want-to-express-myself Sun in freewheeling Aquarius. Luckily, attempts at cancel culture will get nipped in the bud, with the Moon in nursemaid Virgo sending calming vibes to Venus, Saturn, and Jupiter. Peace is short-lived, however, as Monday's contentious energy is stirred up later in the week by a stubborn lunar T-square in the fixed signs of Scorpio, Taurus, and Aquarius on Wednesday and Thursday, when everyone will think they are in the right and no one will want to give in. A return to harmony comes in time for the weekend, when diplomatic Venus conjuncts no-nonsense Saturn in Aquarius, the sign of universal love. Yet tempers will flair once again on Saturday night, with the square of Venus and rabble-rousing Uranus. Group outings could be rife with drama, squabbles, and even an unforeseen fistfight or two. Luckily, a collective sleep-in on a lazy Sunday will reduce the tension dramatically.

February 8–14

A Loving Start to the Lunar New Year
After a drama-filled start to 2021, wouldn't it be nice if we could do a reset and start again? The Lunar New Year on Friday gives us the chance to do just that. The week starts off on a highly productive note with the Sun's conjunction to mental Mercury in out-of-the-box Aquarius, making it an excellent day for brainstorming, while the Moon's trines to Uranus and get-it-done Mars in the industrious earth signs of Capricorn and Taurus will make sure all those great ideas are actually put into practice. Wednesday is a moment of reckoning, however, with Mercury reaching a defining moment in its current retrograde cycle. It is squaring off against Mars at the same time that the Moon is conjunct Saturn, Jupiter, and Venus and is squaring Uranus. This will be a Judgment Day of sorts, when past slights and resentments are dredged up and stewed over in our minds, thereby allowing us to take the actions necessary to regain emotional balance. Use this time to sort the wheat from the chaff by standing up to bullies and irresponsible flakes, as well as cutting off abusive relationships and making peace with those who merit it.

This will lead to a new outlook at Thursday's loner New Moon in Aquarius, which is not making any truly close aspects; this is a perfect time to carve out an individual space within the overall collective. Meeting up on the same day and in the same sign, Venus and Jupiter are bursting with love, peace, and harmony, just in time to ring in the Year of the Ox. The weekend is also filled with upbeat, get-along vibes due to the conjunction of Mercury and Venus. Saturday is a great day to immerse yourself in art, thanks to the sextile between Mars and dreamy Neptune, while Sunday promotes intellectual pursuits, with

Mercury's conjunction to Jupiter. There will be nothing more romantic this Valentine's Day than vibrant communication while bonding with your sweetie.

February 15–21

New World Order

This week is bookended by two charming, soft, dreamy days surrounding one of the most hard-core astrological aspects of the decade, making the week a bit like a nuclear bomb delivered in beautiful packaging and topped off with a bright, shiny bow. Monday sees a poetic Pisces Moon sending out loving vibes to a stellium of planets in idealistic Aquarius, including Saturn, Jupiter, Mercury, and Venus, making it an ideal time for art, daydreaming, and whispering sweet nothings. Gather ye rosebuds while ye may, because things blow out of bounds on Wednesday at the first of the year's three meetings between the powerhouse planets of Saturn and Uranus in Aquarius and Taurus. This square is given additional emotional power by the Moon's exact conjunction to Uranus. This is a period when the revolutionary power of the controlling bully is released in full force, running roughshod over the existing establishment. Cool-headed, well-intentioned players will be at a disadvantage when confronted by righteous, power-hungry zealots.

Choose your side—or escape the Maya all together by opting to stay out of the fray, because the Moon's presence promises that there will be nothing but pain in getting involved. When diplomatic Venus tries to make peace with angry, out-of-control Mars on Friday, remember that there is no such thing as negotiating with crazy. Instead of hitting your head endlessly against a manipulative brick wall, wait for the weekend, when Mercury turns direct, bringing greater mental clarity, and a couldn't-give-AF Gemini Moon sends out harmonious vibes to Saturn, Mercury, and Jupiter. The old adage will once again ring true: Living well is the best revenge.

February 22–28

Consolidation of Power

The outcomes of last week's power struggles take further root this week as a new order sets about establishing and strengthening itself. At the same time, there will be a sense of relief that the main battle is over for now and life can get back to normal. After a low-key start to the week, Mars trines Pluto in the hierarchy-loving signs of Taurus and Capricorn on Wednesday. This is a relatively strong aspect that embraces the positive sides of transformative change by creating the promise of a hopeful, stable future ruled by competent forces—at least for those who fall in line and play the game. This is not a great week for those who go their own way, however. From Wednesday to Friday, the Leo Moon creates a T-square between a pileup of planets in Taurus and Aquarius, creating a divide between the group, the leader, and the individual. Those who stand out too much may feel like the tall poppy singled out to be cut down. It may be better to keep a low profile and work temporarily behind the scenes until plans are better crafted. A sense of cozy comfort takes hold at the Grand Earth Trine on Sunday, between a Virgo Moon, Pluto in Capricorn, and Mars in Taurus. This is the perfect time to work on home-improvement projects or have an old-fashioned Sunday roasted meal with the entire extended family gathered round.

March 1–7

Truth and Lies

A lunar T-square on Wednesday draws in the usual suspects from the fixed signs, including a surreptitious Scorpio Moon, along with straightforward Saturn, Jupiter, and Mercury in Aquarius and an on-edge Uranus in Taurus. Luckily, dynamic Mars bursts into party-hearty Gemini on the same day, saying enough to all the power games and manipulation tactics—it's time to have some fun! Venus assists in turning the beat around through its sextile of Uranus, bringing sudden diplomatic solutions to volatile situations. When Mercury conjuncts truth-seeking Jupiter on Thursday, long-buried secrets may be blurted out and laid out to the judgment of all, with overdue consequences finally being faced. Despite the bright, early spring weather, there will be a lot of shadiness on Friday and Saturday, when a goodhearted Moon in Sagittarius gets walked all over by squares to the Sun, Venus, and Neptune in oblique Pisces. There will be a lot of deviousness masquerading as victimhood, so thoroughly vet those who claim to need your help in order to avoid being taken advantage of.

March 8–14

Feeling Groovy

The Moon makes a quick succession of conjunctions throughout the week, zooming over Pluto, Saturn, Jupiter, Mercury, Venus, Neptune, and the Sun, leading to feelings of emotional well-being and grounding. The Sun and Venus meet up with Neptune on Wednesday and Saturday, respectively, adding an artistic vibe to the mix. Saturday's Pisces New Moon is especially harmonious and poetic, as it is quite close to the esthetic and imaginative planets of Neptune and Venus. This is an excellent day to dust off old creative projects and make a vow to complete them over the next year. Overall the entire period is an auspicious time for teamwork, connections, and communications. The only minor glitch is on Thursday, when the only aspect is a lunar square of Mars in Gemini, which could lead to a depletion of energy as well as needless rumination on perceived emotional slights. But overall it is a mellow, comforting week. So slow down in order to take full advantage of this ethereal, daydreamy energy.

March 15–21

Spring Has Sprung

This week doesn't really get going until the weekend, when the spring equinox is greeted with a burst of enthusiasm. The Sun in fanciful Pisces sextiles Pluto in productive Capricorn on Tuesday, making this an excellent day to schedule development meetings where out-of-the-box, easy-to-implement solutions are required. With the Moon conjunct Uranus in Taurus on the same day, a spirit of ingenuity, innovation, and pragmatism will abound. This energy is reinforced by a sextile between Venus and Pluto on the 18th, when everyone will be able to come together as a team to work toward a higher goal. On Friday, the Moon conjuncts Mars in Gemini while trining Saturn in Aquarius, making this a work-hard, play-hard kind of a day, so make sure to schedule a TGIF happy hour to blow off some steam. When the Sun enters Aries on Saturday a whole new astrological cycle is upon us, which is greeted by a bold, determined trine between Mars and Saturn on Sunday. This highly industrious, extremely exuberant energy has a visionary edge due to Mercury's sextile of Uranus on the same day, which will provide all the ideas and creativity needed to do something completely new and one-of-a-kind. Greet the new season by dreaming big and daring to push past the present confining boundaries to construct a sturdier base for the future. Sometimes it is possible to dig yourself out of a hole.

March 22–28

Intrigue and Alliances

A series of challenging transits emanating from the Mercury-ruled signs of Virgo and Gemini make this a week of paranoia and plotting. A square between Mercury in Pisces and Mars in Gemini on Tuesday will see shadowy, out-of-sight forces constructing secretive machinations against transparent, cards-on-the-table right-fighters. All of this scheming will make things very hard for those who are not aligned with a group, as shown by Wednesday's T-square of an independent Leo Moon struggling to stay afoot against groupthink Saturn in collectivist Aquarius and Uranus in follow-the-leader Taurus. Luckily, the Sun's conjunction of Venus in the brave, mercenary sign of Aries on Friday will help forge coalitions and rally the troops, which will be needed later in the day when a Virgo Moon guilefully pushes the emotional buttons of Mars. Manipulative, cool-headed forces will trigger others into angry outbursts in order to gain the upper hand, so try to maintain control of your emotions. Deception and lies can also abound on Saturday, when the Virgo Moon is beguiled by oppositions to cunning Mercury and seductive Neptune. All of this energy comes to a head when the Libra Full Moon on Sunday says enough is enough to a stellium of the Sun, Venus, and Chiron colluding together. A little diplomacy and friendly sympathy could lead to a détente and decline in tensions.

March 29–April 4

Idealistic and Humanitarian

Set about getting in touch with your utopian dreams on Monday, when Mercury meets Neptune in Pisces, setting the tone for a rather chill week where the focus is on envisioning how to make improvements that benefit the greater good. On Tuesday, Wednesday, and Thursday, Venus, the Sun, and the Moon consecutively send a sextile each to constructive Saturn in hippie, collectivist Aquarius. These are good days for working together with people in your community to make small improvements that make a big difference. Organize a neighborhood trash cleanup or beautify untidy public spaces with some guerilla gardening; sometimes the most effective changes for the many can be made by the efforts of the few. Friday is also an excellent day for brainstorming transformative projects, thanks to Mercury's sextile of Pluto. For those who observe Easter, petty skirmishes could arise over who does what duty, as everyone wants to be the center of attention. Remember that this holiday has a sacred underpinning signifying rebirth and renewal and is not about whose ham gets the most likes on Instagram.

April 5–11

Low-Key and Lazy

Friday's energy-dissipating square between Mars and Neptune is like a vortex sucking in all of this week's previous, fairly minor aspects, making it a rather lackadaisical period where it is hard to get anything done. Fortunately, the aspects present from Monday through Thursday are quite toned down and upbeat. A general air of emotional balance is granted from the Moon's conjunction of Pluto, Saturn, and Jupiter, while it also sextiles Mercury, the Sun, Venus, and Uranus. Tuesday is an especially feel-good day, due to a sextile between Venus and Mars promoting human connection and cooperation. Friday's Mars-Neptune square is strengthened by the Moon's conjunction of Neptune; any demands for effort or labor will be greeted by grumpy groans. Saturday is an excellent day for dating, romance, and intellectual discovery, thanks to Venus and Mercury in adventurous Aries sending amicable sextiles to Saturn and Jupiter in open-minded Aquarius. The week ends with Sunday's New Moon in Aries, which is lovingly sandwiched between Mercury and Venus while sending out loose sextiles to Mars and Jupiter. This is a great day to make an action plan so you can start checking things off your bucket list while you can still fully enjoy them. Otherwise it's a rather lazy day, due to a square between Venus and Pluto, so put off practical chores and errands, and instead, bask in the luxury of doing nothing.

April 12–18

Stand Up for Your Rights

This will be a week when it's easy to stand up to the powers-that-be and take back control of your own life. The Moon will be squaring off against the forces of the establishment, Pluto and Saturn, on Monday and Tuesday, with the Sun and Mercury joining in by squaring Pluto on Friday and Saturday, respectively. Both of these light-giving orbs will be receiving a lot of boosting, supportive rays that will help flip the script and overcome oppression. Monday's lunar conjunction of Venus, while sextiling Mars and righteous Jupiter, will bring a combination of group effort, diplomacy, pluck, and fury that will set wrongs right. Tuesday favors the rebellious upstart due to the Moon's conjunction of Uranus, strengthened by the Sun's sextile with renegade Mars. Saturday is a bounteous day, positively jam-packed with uplifting, rallying vibes, including a superpowerful trine between a bellicose Mars in Gemini and Jupiter in fight-for-the-little-guy Aquarius. Mercury's sextile of both of these planets will lend an intellectual edge to their brawn and élan. The Moon also joins in by conjuncting Mars and sextiling Venus, which has just moved into its ruler, Taurus, adding a spirit of cooperation and emotional unity. A cheerful outlook is guaranteed on Sunday, due to the conjunction of the Sun and Mercury.

April 19–25

The Cult of Collectivity

The Sun and Mercury join Venus and Uranus in Taurus on Monday, leading to a cultish, kumbaya blindness. Tuesday's independent Leo Moon is not happy being bullied by a highly organized dog pile of planets in Taurus, while aloof Saturn in Aquarius refuses to lend support for fear of group shunning during the lunar opposition on Wednesday. Judgy Jupiter jumps into the fray on Thursday by facing off against the Moon hours before a gleefully zealous conjunction of Venus and Uranus, which just wants to tear it all down out of a sense of compassion and love. After its move into the people-pleasing sign of Virgo, the Moon is ready to play ball on Friday by sending fawning vibes to Uranus and Venus, a self-serving, delusionary tactic that is reinforced by the Moon's opposition to Neptune later in the day. Mars loses some of its fighting spirit when it moves into Cancer on Friday, preferring to turn its attention to domestic matters and lazing around the house. A sense of order and stability resumes on Sunday, when Saturn finally takes on its leadership role, squashing the upstarts Mercury and Venus through energy-zapping squares.

April 26–May 2

Escape the Matrix

A breakaway Full Moon in lone-wolf Scorpio on Monday makes this an excellent day to secretly detach from domineering people and go your own way. This energy is reinforced on Tuesday as the Moon creates a T-square, loosely pulling in Uranus, Mercury, and Venus in Taurus, along with Saturn in Aquarius. This fixed-sign energy makes this an extremely stubborn day when no one will give an inch. Do all you can to stay out of the fray by putting off decisions and meetings to another day. Continue to operate on the down low on Thursday, when strategic Mercury sextiles Neptune and the Moon squares Neptune, helping keep plans and options a closely guarded secret. Freedom reigns supreme on Friday, when the Sun conjuncts Uranus, an aspect that is supported by a harmonious lunar trine the next day. Sunday is an extremely empowering day due to the Moon's conjunction of

Pluto in exact trine to Mercury. This is a positive, can-do day when anything can be tackled. With Venus also sextiling Neptune, it is a wonderful period for art and romance as well as relaxing with friends and loved ones.

May 3–9

Days of Deprogramming

The battle of the fixed signs continues as the Sun, Mercury, Venus, and Uranus in Taurus square off against the Moon, Saturn, and Jupiter in Aquarius. Both of these signs are stubborn in their own right, with Aquarius operating through cool detachment and Taurus exerting visceral attempts at total control. The dispassionate objectivity of the Aquarian influences will be able to mitigate and unravel the Taurean cult of personality, which is being reinforced by the Sun's transit of Taurus this month. The week's best weapons are a combination of aloof indifference and icy judgment on Monday, Tuesday, Wednesday, and Friday. Thursday is the best day of the week by far, so try to arrange all important meetings and social outings at this time. A trine between Venus and Pluto will crush feelings of petty competitiveness, allowing harmonious team efforts to thrive at work, while the Moon's conjunction of Neptune and sextile of the Sun makes it an excellent moment for dating and after-hours romance. Venus moves from Taurus into Gemini late Saturday, creating a harmonious flow of communication in the coming weeks.

May 10–16

Spiritual Boost

This week's big news is Jupiter's entry into Pisces on Thursday, where it is lovingly welcomed by Neptune; the sign's ancient and modern rulers are both enjoying a stay at home at the same time, something that hasn't happened since the mid-1800s. This is doubly fortunate, as it takes some of the edge off the fixed-sign axis that has been operating at full throttle since the beginning of the year. With Jupiter moving into harmonious aspect with Uranus and Pluto in the earth signs, four out of the five heavy-hitting outer planets will now be working together instead of being at odds. Jupiter in Pisces is compassionate, openhearted, and emotionally just, giving this week a much-needed boost of spiritual enlightenment. Moreover, this week sees Jupiter, Neptune, Saturn, Mercury, and the Moon all in their ruling signs. It is relatively rare to have so many planets at home at the same time, giving this period a feeling of puzzle pieces snapping into place. In other news, there is a lovely Taurus New Moon on Tuesday sextiling Neptune, making sure things are harmonious and shipshape for Jupiter's shift on Thursday, when the Sun also sends positive vibes to Neptune. Mars's sextile to Uranus on Tuesday adds a jolt of energy and excitement to the New Moon. Changes are afoot!

May 17–23

What's Going On?

This week's mix of nonstop, simultaneous harmonious and challenging aspects creates an aura of confusion combined with hope. With Jupiter's recent sign shift, there is a lingering anxious-yet-giddy feeling that comes when we turn a corner without knowing what lies beyond it. This week gets off to a lazy start. Mars in Cancer just wants to laze in bed; unfortunately, it is opposed by boss-from-hell Pluto in Capricorn. Luckily, a Taurus Sun quickly comes to the rescue, adding a large dose of motivation and energy to get the job done. A lunar T-square with Uranus and Saturn on Tuesday creates tension between those who want to embrace the new and those who want the status quo to remain unchanged forever. Luckily the Moon's sextiles of Venus and Mercury add a spirit of cooperation and understanding that loosens up the standoff.

Another T-square quickly follows on Wednesday—this time on the mutable axis—between the Virgo Moon, Taurus Sun, and recent Piscean transplant Jupiter. There may be suspicion and paranoia of bold new ideas that could shake up the established order, leading to petty attempts at control and passive aggression. Later that day, Venus's trine of Saturn in the more rational air signs reestablishes a sense of stability and self-esteem. Friday is yet another new day with yet another new mutable T-square, this time between the Moon, Neptune, and Mercury, which is joined by the Sun's square of Jupiter, once again dredging up feelings of distrust against this newly arrived upstart. Fortunately, a lunar trine uniting the earth and air signs fights back with confidence and force. The weekend has an equally mixed energy, with Mercury's square of Neptune being offset by the Moon's trine of Saturn on Saturday, while Sunday's lazy lunar squares of Mars and Pluto are given a softer edge by the Moon's trines of Venus and Mercury in energetic Gemini, making this an excellent day for chatting and hanging out with friends.

May 24–30

Not for the Kind of Heart

This week the year's first eclipse officially takes place—a Lunar Eclipse in Sagittarius on Wednesday. The calm before the storm comes in the form of Tuesday's uplifting Grand Water Trine, including a Scorpio Moon, Mars in Cancer, and Neptune in Pisces. This is followed by the lunar T-square eclipse on Wednesday, with the Moon opposing the Sun in Gemini and squaring Jupiter in Pisces. Sagittarius is Jupiter's other ruling sign, which will give this challenging aspect the judgmental edge of a religious zealot. Get ready for outrage mobs to go on cancel-culture rampages. It may be best to stay off social media today and think twice before posting a controversial opinion or something with edgy humor. Luckily, the Moon is sextile to Saturn, which offers stability if you opt to stay out of the fray. Things don't get any better on Thursday, due to the T-square between Venus, Neptune, and the Moon. To say people are susceptible to easily hurt feelings today is a massive understatement. Misunderstandings abound, with everyone projecting and reading into things, so put off heavy conversations of an emotional nature to another day. While Saturday's conjunction of Mercury and peace-loving Venus seems to put things on the mend, confusion returns when Mercury turns retrograde later in the day.

May 31–June 6

Mesmerized by False Prophets

Memorial Day Monday features an escapist Mars trine of Neptune, making this a perfect day to kick back and enjoy life. This aspect also has a slightly transcendental edge that could awaken spiritual enlightenment but could just as easily lead to getting swept up in snake-oil self-help movements that offer painless solutions to complex problems. This could be compounded on Thursday, when the Moon conjuncts Neptune in spiritual Pisces, leaving a squared Mercury retrograde confused and confounded in its ruling sign of Gemini. Luckily, the Sun's trine of Saturn later in the day will bring a dose of rationality, while Venus's trine of Jupiter brings a bounty of love and compassion, making it an excellent date night. An ornery Saturday awaits due to the exact opposition of Mars and Pluto, which is drawn into a T-square with the Moon at the same time that Mercury squares Neptune. It may be easy to get drawn into seductively utopian causes and schemes that fight against the status quo, but is their real ideal justice or the establishment of a new power order?

June 7–13

Snap Out of It

The week gets off to a jaunty start due to a lunar conjunction of electrifying Uranus, which quickly rebounds the Monday morning stagnation that was caused by a stultifying square of Saturn. The big news, however, comes at the year's first Solar Eclipse on Thursday in the no-bullshit sign of Gemini. This eclipse will be conjunct Mercury retrograde while squaring Neptune, urging all of us to snap out of our collective stupor. If you have been running away from problems, seeking enlightenment from false gurus, or self-medicating through addiction, the Wizard of Oz–like curtain will be pulled back to show the stark, grinding mechanism propagating it all, leaving confusion and denial in its wake. There may be a deep desire to continue burying one's head in the sand, but with the Moon's trine of Jupiter on Friday and its conjunction of Venus, a healthier emotional outlook will prevail, based on optimism and collaboration. Mars's entry into glamorous Leo will also bring a much-needed boost of fun and excitement, pushing us to direct our energies into more uplifting, pleasurable pursuits and stop any incessant pity parties or navel gazing. The Sun's square of manipulative, deceptive Neptune on Sunday occurs just after the conjunction of the Moon and Mars in Leo; everyone is tired of the game-playing, preferring instead to show an open, honest hand.

June 14–20

Fight the Power

On Monday, a rare square between the heavy-hitting planets of rebellious Uranus and establishment-loving Saturn is transformed into a fixed-sign T-square with the Leo Moon, making the day fraught with tension, fights, and a punk-rock attitude. Forces of innovation may brush up against the old ways of doing things, leading to frustration and roadblocks. This is the second in a series of these squares. The first was in mid-February, so look for a replay of issues that erupted at that time. This all leads to an aura of suspicion and paranoia on Thursday, when a touchy Virgo Moon forms a T-square with Neptune, Mercury retrograde, and the Sun. Luckily, by Saturday's Lunar Grand Trine in the air signs, which draws in Mercury and Saturn, a return to realistic thinking will prevail—even if it means ruffling some feathers by setting emotional boundaries when the Moon squares Venus later in the day. Father's Day sees a return to tensions when an archetypally female Moon squares off against Pluto.

June 21–27

Sensitive and Bighearted

This week is defined by a bountiful, generous, radiant energy, which could run roughshod over the more meek of heart who may have a hard time getting their voices heard over the world's confident extroverts. The Grand Water Trine on Monday between a Scorpio Moon and the exact trine of Venus and Neptune starts the week off with a healing, loving vibe that is filled with emotional closeness, making this a good day for strengthening bonds and working out issues. When Mercury turns direct on Tuesday, all the cloudy, distrustful thinking of the past few weeks will dissipate, bringing back clarity and discernment. The Sun's trine to Jupiter on Wednesday provides a boost of optimism, joy, generosity, and bounteous self-esteem. When a sensitive, low-key Venus in Cancer opposes dominant, peacocking Pluto on Wednesday, quiet souls could feel overwhelmed by the go-for-it actions of the self-assured. Make an effort to validate the feelings and contributions of the introverts in your life. Thursday's Full Moon in Capricorn is quite productive, as it squashes out ego drives so that team members will happily help each other to reach common objectives. The weekend becomes more tense, when Saturday's lunar conjunction of Pluto and opposition of Venus drags up the emotionally sensitive vibes from earlier in the week. An icy, repressed rage could detonate at any moment on Sunday, due to a T-square between the Moon conjunct Saturn against a Leo Mars and Uranus in Taurus.

June 28–July 4

Walking on Eggshells

The week's early buoyant, dreamy energy is defined by the Moon's conjunctions of Jupiter and Neptune on Monday and Wednesday, respectively, along with its trine of the Sun on Tuesday. Things soon take a more aggressive tone, due to Mars's opposition of Saturn on Thursday and its square of Uranus on Saturday, which is reinforced by Sunday's lunar T-square conjunct Uranus, which drags in Saturn, Mars, and Venus, making the latter half the week a period of rinse-and-repeat squabbles and emotional eruptions. While a frustrating standoff between robust dynamism and slow-moving, change-resistant powers slows things down on Thursday, Saturday's energy is much more volatile, being prone to nervous anxiety and sudden outbursts. With Venus thrown into the mix on Sunday, feelings could be hurt, leaving everyone emotionally exhausted.

July 5–11

Paranoia and Projection

This is a week marked by easily hurt feelings, often based on preconceived notions instead of anything rooted in actual reality. The persecution complex kicks off on Tuesday, when an inquiring Mercury squares nebulous Neptune hours before an overly sensitive Venus opposes stern Saturn. The Moon joins in by squaring Neptune on Wednesday before its conjunction of Mercury on Thursday, when clear thinking could be clouded by emotional responses. Thursday is also a day when inflated egos could fly off the handle in a narcissistic rage at any perceived slights, due to the square of Venus in Leo and Uranus. The loner New Moon in Cancer on Friday creates a kind of cosmic quarantine, where people may just isolate themselves at home or in their room in order to prevent the further spread of infection by emotional contagion. The weekend has a rebellious tinge to it due to the Moon's opposition of domineering Pluto on Saturday, followed by Sunday's T-square between the Moon, Uranus, and Saturn, with the Moon close to touchy Venus and quick-tempered Mars. Attempts at rational reasoning are sure to fail, only leading to greater squabbles and petty responses. Better to go off the grid.

July 12–18

Get the Party Started

Finally a summertime mood prevails, filled with high spirits and a carefree attitude. Buoyant energy opens the week, with the Moon conjuncting both Venus and Mars in just-wants-to-have-fun Leo. On the same day, Mercury's trine of Jupiter exudes an intellectual, open-minded vibe, bringing a bit of substance to the frivolous good times. Tuesday is nonstop glamour-a-go-go thanks to the meeting of Mars and Venus in Leo, making this an excellent day for shopping, changing your look, and unleashing your inner vamp. The auspicious vibrations continue on Wednesday and Thursday as the Virgo Moon trines Uranus and Pluto, adding a splash of spontaneity and confidence. The

Sun joins in on Thursday with a cheerful trine of otherworldly Neptune. No one will feel like working or obeying orders at the weekend, thanks to the Sun's opposition of Pluto in a T-square with the Moon on Saturday, compounded by a lunar T-square with Saturn and Uranus on Sunday. Forget about duties or obligations. Unplug and enjoy life.

July 19–25

It All Comes Out in the Wash

This week features an overdose of rather minor aspects of both a harmonious and a challenging nature. The period's prevailing energy is a bit all over the place, without any real theme emerging, so it all evens out in the end. Monday starts out with a dreamy Grand Water Trine between the Moon, Sun, and Neptune, which is mitigated by a combative fixed-sign lunar T-square dragging in the Moon, Mars, Venus, and Jupiter. The Moon in the purposeful sign of Scorpio may be tired of the superficial antics of Mars and Venus in Leo and come down hard in righteous indignation. Luckily, the good-natured Grand Trine will quickly soothe and diffuse tensions.

On Wednesday, there is one final, bighearted trine between the Moon and Venus, just before the planet of beauty bids farewell to bling-bling Leo and enters the more toned-down, decorous sign of Virgo. On Thursday, Venus will bite off more than it can chew in its opposition of Jupiter; if you offer to lend a hand, people may demand your entire arm. Friday's Full Moon in Aquarius pits the Sun and Mercury against the Moon, Pluto, and Saturn, giving it a Davey-and-Goliath edge, where innovative ideas and sheer pluck could bring down the powers-that-be. Saturday is an excellent time for artistic pursuits thanks to Mercury's trine of Neptune, while activists may be butting heads with the establishment when Mercury opposes Pluto on Sunday. Think twice before going to a protest that day; the Moon's conjunction of Jupiter opposes Mars, and ideological differences could soon morph into physical violence.

July 26–August 1

A Blast from the Past

Sometimes workers at European construction sites will accidentally dig up a live, unexploded German bomb from World War II. Likewise, this rather harmonious week gets distracted when live-wire Jupiter retrogrades back into Aquarius on Wednesday and almost immediately opposes Mars in Leo, unearthing long-forgotten, volatile, and dangerous energies. Jupiter has been peacefully inhabiting its ruling sign of Pisces since mid-May, and its reentry into Aquarius will once again focus the spotlight on the fixed-sign axis, dredging up the stubborn, rebellious vibes from the first half of the year.

When Jupiter opposes Mars in blazing Leo on Thursday, a powder keg of rage and indignation could explode at any moment. Jupiter brings a slightly righteous edge, so expect a spectacular storm of fire and brimstone to rain down from the heavens. The dust settles with Mars's entry into Virgo that same evening. The aftermath of this destruction will be reckoned with at the censorious T-square on Saturday between an upstart Moon conjunct Uranus, which pulls in the Sun and Mercury in Leo, along with Saturn in Aquarius. This energy will express itself through a jittery anxiety that comes when our natural expression is being repressed by outside forces. The individualistic, confident Sun conjuncts Mercury on Sunday, giving Mercury the boost needed to plot to take back control from Saturn, which it opposes later in the day.

August 2–8

Mother's Little Helper

A number of challenging transits to agitated Uranus and perfectionist Saturn throughout the week will have everyone reaching for the collective Valium like a 1950s housewife being castigated by a father who knows best. An aura of suburban conformity kicks off the week, due to the Sun's opposition of Saturn, which is soon rebelled against by a T-square between the Moon on the cusp between Taurus and beatnik Gemini subverting Mars in people-pleasing Virgo and judgmental

Jupiter in Aquarius. A feeling of wheel-spinning anxiousness prevails at the square between Mercury and Uranus on Tuesday, which is mimicked by the Sun's square of Uranus on Friday. A sensitive, feminine Moon is dominated by oppositions to patriarchal Pluto and Saturn on Friday and Saturday, respectively, leading to Sunday's strung-out Leo New Moon in square to Uranus. Use this day to overcome fears by expressing your true individuality.

August 9–15

Seeking Something to Believe In

Even though the Moon gets a boost through its conjunction of Mercury and Mars on Monday, the week gets off to a lazy, sluggish start due to the Moon's opposition of overwhelming Jupiter. There is a tendency to take on too much work and get stopped in one's tracks, an attitude that is strengthened by Venus's lackadaisical opposition to Neptune that same day. Mercury opposes Jupiter on Tuesday and quickly starts wondering what is the point of it all as it searches for deeper underlying significance. When intellectual Mercury moves into its ruling sign of Virgo the next day, things click into place. This energy is strengthened by trines from the Moon and Venus to productive, transformative Pluto, bringing an aura of purposefulness to all endeavors. It may be better to lie low at the weekend to escape the general prevailing feeling of stubborn subterfuge on Saturday, when a secretive Scorpio Moon makes a T-square to Saturn and Uranus in the fixed signs. This intransigent energy continues with another fixed lunar T-square on Sunday between the Moon, Sun, and Jupiter. Slighted egos could spin out of control, so steer clear of any self-involved narcissists in your life.

August 16–22

Up By the Bootstraps

A spirit of cooperation, diplomacy, and romance returns on Monday, when Venus moves into its ruling sign of Libra. Until Sunday, the Sun, Mercury, Venus, Saturn, and Neptune will all be in their home signs, making this a can-do week filled with power and performance.

Tuesday is a great day for personal renewal thanks to the energetic Sagittarius Moon's trine of the Leo Sun and sextile of Jupiter. Wednesday is a great day to plan projects and work to get them done; the conjunction of Mercury and Mars will receive uplifting vibes from a productive Moon, bestowing a sense of motivation and enthusiasm to work projects. Friday is defined by lightning-quick thought that can easily find innovative solutions to any task at hand, while the Moon's trine of Venus promotes teamwork without feelings of petty competition getting in the way. When the Moon conjuncts Saturn in the early evening, everyone can feel satisfied from a job well done. On Sunday, the Leo Full Moon conjunct Jupiter bids a fond farewell to a joyful Sun in Leo, before the Sun begins its yearly sojourn through Virgo later the same day. This is a great moment to harmonize your own individual needs with the demands of the greater societal collective. Mars's trine of Uranus on Sunday finishes out this week's self-starting, highly fruitful energy. Clear out your to-do list by taking care of long-lingering chores and duties.

August 23–29

The Power of Negative Thinking

Even though the week starts off with a constructive, cooperative trine between Venus and Saturn in the rational air signs, an overly sensitive Moon kicks up suspicion and intrigue through its opposition to Mercury and Mars later in the day. Steer clear of gossips looking to stir up trouble. The spirit of delusion and covert mental manipulation continues on Tuesday, when Neptune conjuncts the Moon and opposes Mercury. If you insist on thinking the worst, these fanciful doubts and projections could become reality when the Moon opposes Venus on Wednesday, leading to hurt feelings and emotional distancing. When Mercury trines Pluto on Thursday, followed by the Moon's conjunction of Uranus and trine of Mars on Saturday, all the paranoia from earlier in the week will be shaken off, as if awakening from a bad dream. Sunday's Grand Earth Trine between the Moon, Mercury, and Pluto completes the week on a positive note by reestablishing positive thoughts whose transformative power can be put to work for the greater good.

August 30–September 5

The Long Hot Summer Just Passed You By

The end of summer conjures up a sweetly melancholic vibe as the last days of the sunny season are enjoyed and mourned in equal measure. A laid-back Moon is sending easygoing trines to Venus and Jupiter in the air signs on Tuesday. This mellow energy is mitigated, however, by an energy-depleting, doleful T-square between the Moon, Mars, and Neptune the same day. The sense of lingering despondency is carried on by the Moon's moody squares of Mercury and Venus on Wednesday and Thursday, respectively. The week's main focal point is Mars's opposition of Neptune, also occurring on Thursday, making it a moment of ruminating over lost opportunities and roads not traveled. Even though the summer has ended, it doesn't mean your dreams have to as well. Look to the future and plan big; if you do, the trine between Mercury and Saturn on Saturday will help you make your projects a reality. The week ends on a similarly glum note when Venus squares Pluto on Sunday evening; it may be best to turn in early to stay out of the path of control freaks demanding their own way.

September 6–12

Turning a Page

For readers in the United States, Monday's Labor Day festivities will be overflowing with expansive, goodhearted vibes. Rarely is a public holiday filled with such a large number of positive astrological transits, so enjoy the day by kicking back with friends and family or enjoying some me time by exploring your true passions. If you're outside the US, you too can enjoy these harmonious vibes, which mark a stark end to the previous week's somber energy. Labor Day is often considered the unofficial start of autumn, and this year it coincides with an exuberant, forward-looking New Moon in exact trine with pioneering Uranus. The powerful, transformative trine between Pluto and Mars on the same day makes this an excellent moment to plan for the times ahead, while another trine between Venus and Jupiter is absolutely bursting with harmony and compassion. This latter aspect is especially romantic, making this a perfect date night.

The rest of the week is filled with a similar, emotionally satisfying energy due to a series of lunar conjunctions to Mars, Mercury, and Venus on Tuesday, Wednesday, and Friday, respectively. Combine these with the Moon's trines of Pluto, Saturn, and Jupiter on Tuesday, Wednesday, and Thursday, and you're left with a stabilizing week when it's easy to get things done. Saturday is a stubborn and skittish day, due to the Scorpio Moon's opposition of Uranus and square of Jupiter in the fixed signs. With a lunar trine of Neptune on the same day, it's better to seek escapism over confrontation.

September 13–19

Testing the Waters

This week has a start-and-stop feel to it. Things that get off on a good foot may fail, leaving everyone to pick themselves up, dust themselves off, and start all over again. Don't be afraid to try new things and experiment with new approaches; only then can the way forward be found. Things get off to a confusing start on Monday and Tuesday when Neptune squares the Moon and opposes the Sun. The resulting mental fog could drain away energy and drive, as witnessed by the lunar square of Mars on Tuesday. The bewilderment continues during Wednesday's lunar square of Mercury, but a sense of purpose, determination, and confidence manifests on Thursday, when the Moon meets Pluto, with both sending out an uplifting trine to the Sun. The Moon also trines determined Mars on the same day, making this the most productive period of the workweek, so try to schedule as much as possible at this time. Things grind back down to a halt on Friday during the fixed-sign T-square between the Moon conjunct Saturn, drawing in Venus in Scorpio and Uranus in Taurus. Everyone is at odds over how to do things, leading to nothing getting done. Luckily, a jauntier outlook arrives at the weekend, when the Moon conjuncts bighearted Jupiter shortly after trining Mercury on Saturday and before its trine of compassionate Venus on Sunday. This is a great period for heart-to-heart talks and volunteer work.

September 20–26

Put the Cart before the Horse

A bit of strategic planning will go a long way in terms of getting things done efficiently and effectively this week. The early days are best for thinking and planning, because stagnant, resistant midweek energy will tend to throw a wrench in the works and stall things. The week starts off with an inspired Full Moon conjunct Neptune, making this an excellent day for creative visualization; its opposition of the Sun and Mars, however, has a hard time actually getting things done. Bosses may squash innovative ideas on Wednesday, leading to feelings of not being appreciated. Put off making any important pitches until another day. Thursday is a tricky day due to everyone being overly sensitive and quick to internalize requests for revisions, due to the opposition of Venus and Uranus.

An exhausted square of the Moon and Saturn grinds things to a standstill by Thursday night. Energy is restored on Friday when the Moon conjuncts a revved-up, devil-may-care Uranus and charges full steam ahead, not really caring about the feelings of others when it opposes Venus later in the afternoon. Luckily, an extremely productive energy returns for the weekend, when Mars trines Saturn on Saturday, and the best-laid plans can now be carried out to perfection. A zesty Grand Trine in the air signs between the Moon, Sun, Mars, and Saturn keeps things humming along on Sunday. Even though it's the weekend, this is an excellent day to work on projects and blast through any pileups of duties and chores.

September 27–October 3

Dream Big, Work Small

Enthusiastic, ambitious ideas will pop up early in the week, but exhaustion could set in beginning on Wednesday. Implementing enterprising plans may prove overwhelming, leading to stagnation and defeatism. Therefore, it's important to break innovative, large-scale tasks down into their smallest details and focus on taking one step at a time. Mercury turns retrograde on Monday, making it difficult to envisage the true feasibility of brainstormed proposals; try not to commit to plans or you may be biting off more than you can chew. The Moon's trines of Jupiter and Mercury on Monday and Tuesday, respectively, could lead to lofty goals, while its square of seductive Neptune on the first day of the week will keep us blinded to practicality. Even though the Sun is ready to work on Wednesday, thanks to a trine with get-it-done Saturn, the Moon's square of Mars could lead to easily dissipated energy. Venus trines Neptune the same day, promoting teamwork, but efforts could quickly devolve into socializing and chitchat. It may be better to work alone if you really want to see results on this day.

Thursday's Grand Trine of the Moon, Venus, and Neptune continues this energy, making it a good day for unstructured vision quests. Bosses and overseers may not be easily won over, however, due to a T-square between the Moon, Mercury, and Pluto, as well as a square between Venus and Jupiter; pie-in-the-sky ideas may seem ludicrously unrealistic when pitched. Friday continues in the same vein, as the Moon opposes Saturn and squares Uranus, along with Mercury squaring Pluto. Innovative ideas will be met with resistance. It's necessary to create action plans that show an easy route to implementation if you want your propositions to be taken seriously. Exhaustion sets in on Saturday with a T-square in the fixed signs between the Moon, lazy Venus, and burnt-out Jupiter. A sextile between Pluto and Venus that morning will do much to recharge our batteries via chilled-out socializing, leading to renewed mental energy at Sunday's trine between Mercury and Jupiter.

October 4–10

Go Your Own Way

If you seek validation from society or from those in power this week, you will be undermined every step of the way, but those brave souls who dare to forge their own path will be able to go the distance. Wednesday's exuberant New Moon is conjunct Mars, making this an excellent time to construct an action plan for the upcoming year. With the Moon also conjuncting Mercury retrograde while trining Jupiter later in the day, it's also a good time to make peace with estranged friends and family. If you became distant with former loved ones due to the ideological and political divides of the past few years, you can once again find common ground if you reach out now. Venus enters friendly Sagittarius on Thursday, bringing a sociable, benevolent tinge to personal relations. The Moon will be squaring Pluto and Saturn in succession the same day; bosses and control freaks will be out in full force, and nothing will be able to appease them, other than complete submission. It may be better to lie low and remove yourself from their line of fire. The Sun's conjunction of Mars the next day comes to the rescue, bringing bravery and determination to the individual. Saturday is an extremely auspicious day, overflowing with diplomatic Libran/Venusian energy, thanks to the Sun's conjunction of Mercury, Mercury's conjunction of Mars, and the Moon's conjunction of Venus while sextiling Pluto and Saturn. This is another excellent time to break free from groupthink and bury the hatchet with those who have fallen off your radar. You will be able to transform strained ties through love, warmth, and compassion.

October 11–17

Shake It Up

If you dare to rock the boat this week, it won't tip over but will propel you down your chosen path. For those taking part in Canadian Thanksgiving, the week starts off with a jovial, bighearted sextile between the Sagittarius Moon and feel-good Jupiter—no family dysfunction around the dinner table this year! Energies suddenly shift on Tuesday, when a lunar trine of rebellious Uranus makes waves, the ripples of which become evident later in the day when the Moon squares an angry and offended Mars and Sun. After this disruption, a new power structure begins to evolve on Wednesday, with the Moon conjunct transformative Pluto and Venus sextile authoritative Saturn. On Thursday, unconventional thinking will bring new grounding via the lunar conjunction of Saturn while trining Mercury retrograde and square Uranus. The Moon, Mars, Jupiter, and the Sun are all aligned in a robust trine on Friday, favoring the bold and courageous. This is an excellent day to try new things and face challenges. The Sun faces off against domineering Pluto on Sunday; if you dare to stand up to the bullies and control freaks in your life, you will be left with a deep sense of emotional satisfaction brought about the lunar conjunction of Neptune.

October 18–24

Hit the Brakes

With Mercury turning direct on Monday, energy will start to flow unhindered, leading to renewed feelings of dynamism and vigor. An extremely fervent trine between high-octane Mars and heady Jupiter will get the week off to a roaring start. Unfortunately, things may start moving so fast that you need to hit the breaks to regain a sense of control on Wednesday at the Full Moon, forming a T-square with the Sun, Mars, and Pluto. This same dichotomy between speed and caution is repeated on Thursday when the Moon squares Saturn and conjuncts Uranus. Things come to a head on Friday when a vibrant, free-spirited Mars in bohemian Libra squares a recalcitrant Pluto in orthodox Capricorn. The unbridled vibes of the bold will be squashed by stick-in-the-mud, traditionalist forces that don't appreciate renegade spirits. It's better to lie low than use up all your energy fighting those whose attitudes will never budge. An exhausted T-square between the Moon, Neptune, and Venus on Sunday makes this an excellent day to sleep late, lounge around, and engage in idle socializing.

October 25–31

Head in the Clouds

Get as much work done as you can on Monday, because after the day's invigorating trine in the air signs between the Gemini Moon, Mars, and Jupiter, which also pulls in the Scorpio Sun, the energy weakens considerably. It is an unrealistic period, with people acting in a dreamy fashion, without considering the consequences or feasibility of their actions. This shift is evident at Tuesday's pie-in-the-sky, super-lazy square of Venus and Neptune. This idle energy is underscored by Wednesday's lunar square of Mercury and opposition of Pluto while trining Neptune; overly optimistic thinking will be at odds with the pressures of reality. On Thursday, an extremely obstinate fixed-sign T-square between the Leo Moon, Scorpio Sun, and Jupiter is enabled by a sextile between Venus and Jupiter, which buries its head in the sand, pretending that everything is okeydokey instead of helping resolve conflicts. A sense of futility sets in Saturday with the Sun's square of Saturn. Instead of concentrating on chores, duties, and professional ambitions, it's better to shift your attention to fun and socializing, which is bolstered by the Moon's sextile of party-hearty Mars and trine of chitchatty Venus in boisterous Sagittarius. Mars moves into its ruling sign of Scorpio on Saturday, promising a hot and spicy end to the year. Plenty of tricks and treats are in store on this enjoyable Halloween, thanks to the Moon's sextile of the Sun in spooky Scorpio and trine to cheeky Uranus.

November 1–7

Duper's Delight

Watch out for a super-trusting trine between Mercury and Jupiter on Monday, as well as one by the Moon and Pluto. Gullibility abounds, which can be taken advantage of by a T-square between the Moon, Venus, and Neptune on the same day. It will be easy to fall for flattery and be groomed by the powers-that-be, who will come back to abuse you later in the week. It will be very hard to know who to trust this week. Others may be colluding with people at the top without you knowing during the square between Mercury and Pluto on Tuesday. Be careful of competitive colleagues who take to gossiping behind your back. They may even present your ideas as their own to bosses and management. If you feel suspicious about someone, your instincts are probably correct, so keep things to yourself this week.

Silver-tongued wolves in sheep's clothing abound on Wednesday, when the Moon conjuncts smooth-talking Mercury in Libra while trining Jupiter yet squaring Pluto. It will be easy for words to be used to undermine the success of others or exploit others to one's own ends. On Thursday, the Moon conjuncts social-climbing Mars and squares Saturn shortly before the New Moon opposes Uranus. There is an aura of ruthless ambition in the air, which could pull the rug out from under the feet of those who have grown complacent in their security.

A sense of cooperation returns on Saturday, with an amicable sextile between Mercury and Venus. Put up a sharp boundary between yourself and your working life this weekend, and enjoy a relaxing, uplifting time with friends or romantic partners.

November 8–14

Collective Bargaining

After last week's cutthroat energy, the stars are pushing us to forge alliances with like-minded individuals. After all, it's easier to put up a fight and defend yourself if you know that someone else has your back. Monday is an excellent day for networking and creating coalitions, with the Moon conjunct friendly Venus in pragmatic Capricorn forming a trine to spontaneous Uranus and strategic sextiles to Mercury and Mars. There will be a sense of renewed personal power at Tuesday's lunar conjunction of Pluto while sextiling the Sun.

The battle lines are drawn, culminating in an epic showdown on Wednesday during the fixed-sign T-square between street-smart Mercury conjunct scrappy Mars in formidable Scorpio, the Moon conjunct establishment Saturn in Aquarius, and light-the-fuse-and-see-what-happens Uranus in Taurus. Manipulative attempts of bosses and those in control will backfire, and people will refuse to be oppressed any longer. This is an extremely stubborn energy, where fights can flair easily, so put off sensitive negotiations to another day. A sense of peace and calm is restored on Friday, at least temporarily, by the Sun's trine of Neptune and the Moon's sextile of diplomatic Venus. People may jump to the wrong conclusions at Saturday's opposition between a deeply suspicious Mercury in Scorpio and Uranus. Luckily, things will quickly be smoothed out thanks to a chilled-out Moon conjunct Neptune while trining the Sun.

November 15–21

Expect the Unexpected

This is a week when deep, dark secrets could be outed by the powerful, shining rays of truth, and when people suddenly stand up to fight against stagnant, restrictive structures that no longer serve a purpose. There is a sense in the air that anything could happen, with the commingling mixture of excitement and trepidation that entails. Three squares to open-book Jupiter from the Sun, Moon, and Mercury in surreptitious Scorpio throughout the week could trigger the release of long-hidden information into the light, prodded by Friday's lone-wolf Lunar Eclipse in Taurus, which will put an end to any dishonest situations. With Venus trining Uranus on the same day, however, forgiveness and compassion are easy to come by, allowing for rifts to be mended quickly. Wednesday's volatile opposition of Mars to the Moon's conjunction of Uranus could cause tempers to flair at the slightest provocation. With Saturn being loosely drawn into this contentious mix, outmoded structures could be razed to the ground to make way for the new. Combined with the Lunar Eclipse on Friday, this is an excellent period to muster up the courage to leave a controlling, stagnant relationship. A T-square on Thursday between the Moon, Mercury, and Jupiter on the fixed-sign axis could lead to further revelations of lies and manipulations. Mercury's empowering sextile of Pluto on Sunday, however, will aid those who've been deceived to regain a sense of power and strength.

November 22–28

Best-Laid Plans

Readers from the United States will be happily looking forward to the Thanksgiving holiday, with a vibrant, energetic, and inspired Grand Trine between the Moon, Mars, and Neptune on Tuesday. These vibes will be so uplifting that the Moon in family-oriented Cancer will forget all past slights and pains caused by its oppositions to Venus and Pluto on Tuesday and Wednesday, respectively. Hump day's trines of the Moon to the Sun and Mercury will see everyone in an optimistic, chatty mood in anticipation of one the year's biggest holidays. On Thanksgiving Day, all that cheerful goodwill comes crashing down more quickly than energy levels after eating an extra-large portion of tryptophan-rich turkey when a dramatic, matriarchal Leo Moon opposes aloof, patriarchal Saturn in Aquarius, forming a fixed-sign T-square with Uranus. A further square between the Moon and Mars later in the day adds to this contentious, dysfunctional energy, leaving everyone up for a fight. It may be best to skip the pumpkin pie and flee from this tinderbox atmosphere—it will be better for your waistline and sanity. Everyone will be in a better frame of mind come Sunday evening, when the Sun conjuncts Mercury, knowing that the holiday is over and it's back to reality.

November 29–December 5

Achieving Is Believing

This is a dreamy week filled with a desire to get in touch with and focus on your biggest goals in life. An action plan can be put into place through brainstorming and creative visualization to make these deep desires manifest into reality. On Monday, a superproductive trine between visionary Neptune and Mars in its ruling sign of Scorpio makes this an excellent day for creativity, goal-setting, and inspiration. With the Moon trine workhorse Saturn while sextiling Mercury on the same day, it will be easy to set about implementing these plans so they can pan out and come to fruition. This combination of get-it-done productivity and imaginative reverie is reinforced on Tuesday by Mercury and the Sun's sextiles to Saturn, as well as artsy Venus's sextile of Neptune. The day closes out with the Moon basking in a boatload of inspiration, thanks to a trine from bountiful Jupiter. Friday is another great day to plot out your aims and shoot for the stars, due to the Moon's trine of Neptune while conjuncting Mars and sextiling Venus and Pluto. Saturday's Solar Eclipse in Sagittarius near Mercury has an up-by-the-bootstraps feel to it; if you believe in yourself, anything is possible. This all leads to a relaxing Sunday, when a satisfied Moon sextiles jovial Jupiter.

December 6–12

Ball of Confusion

It will be hard to know where to focus your energy due to the scattershot nature of this week's transits. Things get off to an incredibly buoyant start on Monday when the Moon conjuncts cooperative Venus and powerful Pluto in the productive sign of Capricorn. This energy is strengthened by dynamic Mars's motivating sextiles of Pluto and the

Moon the same day. However, a bleaker, more bewildered note takes hold on Tuesday, when precise Mercury and vague Neptune are at odds, along with a mood-dampening conjunction of the Moon and Saturn. Things spin out of control on Wednesday, when an angry Mars squares a morally righteous Jupiter, making it difficult to discern who is the oppressor and who is the oppressed in this age of cancel culture. This energy is once again triggered on Thursday when the Moon conjuncts Jupiter while squaring Mars, rubbing salt in yesterday's wounds. On Friday, the Moon's conjunction of Neptune while squaring the Sun and sextiling Uranus attempts to undermine the efforts of confident, talented people through manipulation and gaslighting. If someone in your sphere is targeted with strictly hearsay accusations, get all the facts before joining the dog pile. Empowerment returns in time for the weekend, when Venus conjuncts Pluto, Mercury sextiles Jupiter, and the Moon trine Mars on Saturday. This is an excellent time to relax and have fun by exploring intellectual pursuits and tending to the ones you love. This is also an extremely auspicious time to help out people in need so their holiday season will be a little bit brighter.

December 13–19

Ghosts of Christmas Past

These are the final days of the season prior to next week's winter solstice, and there is definitely a feeling of shifting energies, imminent endings, and reflections on times past. It all starts with two planets changing signs on Monday. Fiery Mars moves into robust Sagittarius, followed by Mercury's entry into business-minded Capricorn, which will help us all stick to a budget during the festive season. While there is a lot of good cheer on Thursday, with the Moon trining Pluto and Venus, there is also the potential for a bit too much merrymaking, leading to feelings of physical and spiritual exhaustion, due to a T-square between the Moon, Mars, and Jupiter. Saturday's Full Moon in Gemini sends out a loose T-square to Neptune in Pisces. The feeling of end-of-year melancholy intensifies when Venus goes retrograde on Sunday, leading to Scrooge-like ruminations on missed opportunities and paths not taken in proverbial forks in the road.

December 20–26

Not the Gift You Wanted

Festive cheer is in the air on Monday due to Mercury's zesty trine of invigorating Uranus. Things take a decidedly more "bah, humbug" tone on Tuesday, when an overly sensitive Cancer Moon gets walked all over in its oppositions to Pluto and Venus in Capricorn, leading to slights and easily hurt feelings. With the Moon zooming into Leo on Tuesday afternoon and trining Mars early Wednesday, the mood will brighten temporarily, but don't start decking the halls just yet. A stubborn T-square between the Moon, Saturn, and Uranus that same day will play out for the umpteenth fixed-sign T-square of the year, dragging up the usual stubbornness. Don't be surprised if there are petty disputes over observing traditional Christmas practices versus opting for celebrations with a more modern flair.

Christmas Eve is a doozy, with the third and final square between Saturn and Uranus. This rare, heavy-hitting aspect will infuse the entire week with a tense, anxious energy. Take extra precautions when driving in snowy conditions to avoid accidents, and keep aware when out in Christmas markets and the like to be cognizant of security issues. The energy on Christmas Eve will be even tenser due to the Moon's opposition to Jupiter and square of Mars, leading to clashes in ideology and fights. Luckily, Christmas Day features festive trines from the Moon to Uranus and Mercury, creating a loose Grand Trine in the grounding earth signs, while a conjunction of Venus and Pluto will bring peace and goodwill. The day after Christmas sees a continuation of these upbeat vibes, with Mercury's sextile of dreamy Neptune and the Moon sending positive rays to Venus and Pluto.

December 27–January 2 (2022)

In a Mood for Play

For those who have to work during the week between Christmas and New Year's, it may be difficult to focus on the task at hand and get anything done, especially on Tuesday, when the Moon in chatty Libra dissipates the productive energies of the stellium of Mercury, Venus, and Pluto in Capricorn. Jupiter makes a return to its ruling sign of

Pisces on this same day, adding an extra dose of lilting, dreamy energy. Wednesday starts off with a social conjunction of Mercury and Venus, while the year's final fixed-sign T-square occurs between a Scorpio Moon, Uranus in Taurus, and Saturn in Aquarius, pitting the forces of innovation and change against tradition yet again. Luckily, Mars sextiles Saturn later in the day, bringing a much-needed jolt of energy to complete tasks. People will already be ringing in the new year on Thursday, with a mentally empowering conjunction between Mercury and Pluto that is sure to chase away any wintertime blues. The Scorpio Moon will be sending emotionally warm vibes to Neptune while sextiling the stellium of Venus, Pluto, and Mercury in Capricorn, bringing a joyous sense of love, understanding, and grounding. The final aspect of the year is Friday's extremely boisterous and dynamic conjunction of the Moon and Mars in Sagittarius. Sneak off early to get ready to ring in a promising 2022!

About the Astrologer

Michelle Perrin, aka Astrology Detective, has built a reputation as one of the world's most trusted and sought-after astrologers for more than ten years. Her work has appeared in some of the most influential titles online and in print, making her one of the few astrologers who has garnered respect from both a mass audience and the astrological community. Her horoscopes have appeared on the websites for Canada's W Dish and Slice TV Networks, Tarot.com's Daily Horoscope site, and Dell Horoscope Magazine, among others. Her writings have also been featured in *The Mountain Astrologer*, the leading trade journal for the astrological community, and astrology.com. For 2021, she has also contributed to Llewellyn's *Moon Sign Book* and *Moon Sign Datebook*. Her website is www.astrologydetective.com or follow her at https://www.instagram.com/hashtaghoroscopes/.

Finding Opportunity Periods

by Jim Shawvan

There are times when the most useful things you can do are ordinary tasks such as laundry, cooking, listening to music, reading, learning, or meditating. There are other times when the universe opens the gates of opportunity. Meetings, decisions, or commitments during these "Opportunity Periods" can lead to new and positive developments in your life. Most people are unaware of these subtle changes in the energies, so they wind up doing laundry when they could be signing an important contract, or they go out to try to meet a new sweetheart when the energies for such a thing are totally blocked.

I developed the Opportunity Periods system over more than thirty years, as I tested first one hypothesis and then another in real life. In about 1998, when I studied classical astrology with Lee Lehman, the system got some added zing, including William Lilly's idea that the Moon when void-of-course in the signs of the Moon and Jupiter "performeth somewhat." The signs of the Moon and Jupiter are Taurus, Cancer, Sagittarius, and Pisces. For those who want to understand the details of the system, they are explained here. If you simply want to use the system, all the information you need is on the calendar pages (you don't need to learn the technicalities).

An Opportunity Period (OP) is a period in which the aspects of the transiting Moon to other transiting planets show no interference with the free flow of decision and action.

Opportunity Periods apply to everyone in the world all at once; although, if the astrological influences on your own chart are putting blocks in your path, you may not be able to use every OP to the fullest. Nevertheless, you are always better off taking important actions and making crucial decisions during an Opportunity Period.

Signs of the Moon and Jupiter

Taurus: the Moon's exaltation
Cancer: the Moon's domicile and Jupiter's exaltation
Sagittarius: Jupiter's fiery domicile
Pisces: Jupiter's watery domicile

Steps to Find Your Opportunity Periods

Under Sun's Beams

Step 1: Determine whether the Moon is "under Sun's beams"; that is, less than 17 degrees from the Sun. If it is, go to step 7. If not, continue to step 2.

Moon Void-of-Course

Step 2: Determine when the Moon goes void-of-course (v/c). The Moon is said to be void-of-course from the time it makes the last Ptolemaic aspect (conjunction, sextile, square, trine, or opposition) in a sign until it enters the next sign.

In eight of the twelve signs of the zodiac, Moon-void periods are NOT Opportunity Periods. In the other four signs, however, they are! According to seventeenth-century astrologer William Lilly, the Moon in the signs of the Moon and Jupiter "performeth somewhat." Lee Lehman says that she has taken this to the bank many times—and so have I.

Stressful or Easy Aspect

Step 3: Determine whether the aspect on which the Moon goes void is a stressful or an easy aspect. Every square is stressful, and every trine and every sextile is easy. Conjunctions and oppositions require judgment according to the nature of the planet the Moon is aspecting, and according to your individual ability to cope with the energies of that planet. For example, the Moon applying to a conjunction of Jupiter, Venus, or Mercury is easy, whereas, for most purposes, the Moon applying to a conjunction of Saturn, Mars, Neptune, Pluto, or Uranus is stressful. However, if you are a person for whom Uranus or Pluto is a familiar and more or less comfortable energy, you may find that the period before the Moon's conjunction to that planet is an Opportunity Period for you. (Since this is true for relatively few people, such periods are not marked as OPs in this book.)

Oppositions can work if the Moon is applying to an opposition of Jupiter, Venus, Mercury, or the Sun (just before the Full Moon). The Moon applying to a conjunction with the Sun (New Moon) presents a whole set of issues on its own. See step 7.

Easy Equals Opportunity

Step 4: If the aspect on which the Moon goes void is an easy aspect, there is an Opportunity Period before the void period. If the aspect on which the Moon goes void is a stressful aspect, there is no Opportunity Period preceding the void period in that sign. To determine the beginning of the Opportunity Period, find the last stressful aspect the Moon makes in the sign. The Opportunity Period runs from the last stressful aspect to the last aspect (assuming that the last aspect is an easy one). If the Moon makes no stressful aspects at all while in the sign, then the Opportunity Period begins as soon as the Moon enters the sign, and ends at the last aspect.

When Is an Aspect Over?

Step 5: When is an aspect over? There are three different answers to this question, and I recommend observation to decide. I also recommend caution.

- An aspect is over (in electional astrology) as soon as it is no longer exact. For example, if the Moon's last stressful aspect in a sign is a square to Saturn at 1:51 p.m., the Opportunity Period (if there is one) would be considered to begin immediately. This is the way the Opportunity Periods are shown in this book.

- Lee Lehman says an aspect is effective (for electional purposes) until it is no longer partile. An aspect is said to be partile if the two planets are in the same degree numerically. For example, a planet at 0° Aries 00' 00" is in partile trine to a planet at 0° Leo 59' 59", but it is not in partile conjunction to a planet at 29° Pisces 59' 59", even though the orb of the conjunction is only one second of arc (1/3,600) of a degree.

- An aspect is effective until the Moon has separated from the exact aspect by a full degree, which takes about two hours. This is the most cautious viewpoint. If you have doubts about the wisdom of signing a major contract while the Moon is still within one degree of a nasty aspect, then for your own peace of mind you should give it two hours, to get the one-degree separating orb.

Translating Light and Translating Darkness

Step 6: One should avoid starting important matters when the Moon is translating light from a stressful aspect with a malefic planet to an ostensibly easy aspect with another malefic planet—or even a series of such aspects uninterrupted by any aspects to benefic planets. I refer to this as "translating darkness." Translation of light is a concept used primarily in horary astrology, and it is discussed in great detail in books and on websites on that subject. For example, the Moon's last difficult aspect is a square to Saturn, and there is an apparent Opportunity Period because the Moon's next aspect is a trine to Mars, on which the Moon goes void-of-course. The problem is this: the Moon is translating light from one malefic to another, and this vitiates what would otherwise be an Opportunity Period. The same would be true if the sequence were, for example, Moon square Saturn, then Moon trine Mars, then Moon sextile Neptune—an unbroken series of malefics.

For the purpose of this system, we may regard all of the following planets as malefics: Mars, Saturn, Uranus, Neptune, and Pluto. I can almost hear the howls of protest from the folks who believe there is no such thing as a malefic planet or a bad aspect. On the level of spiritual growth, that is doubtless true, but this book is meant to be used to make your everyday life easier. Anyone who urges others to suffer more than absolutely necessary in the name of spirituality is indulging in great spiritual arrogance themselves.

New Moon, Balsamic Phase, and Cazimi Notes

Step 7: Here are some notes on the period around the New Moon: waxing, waning, Balsamic, under beams, combust, and Cazimi.

As it separates from conjunction with the Sun (New Moon) and moves toward opposition (Full Moon), the Moon is said to be waxing, or increasing in light. Traditionally the period of the waxing Moon is considered favorable for electional purposes.

Then after the Full Moon, as the Moon applies to a conjunction with the Sun, the Moon is said to be waning, or decreasing in light. Traditionally this period is regarded as a poor choice for electional purposes, and the closer the Moon gets to the Sun, the worse it is said to be. In practice, I find that problems seem to occur only as the Moon gets very close to the Sun.

When the Moon is applying to a conjunction with the Sun (New Moon) and is less than 45 degrees away from the Sun, the Moon is said to be in its Balsamic phase. This phase is associated with giving things up and is considered especially unfavorable for starting things you wish to increase.

Any planet within 17 degrees of the Sun is said to be under Sun's beams. Traditionally this weakens the planet, particularly for electional and horary purposes.

Any planet within 8 degrees of the Sun is said to be combust. Traditionally this weakens the planet even more, particularly in electional and horary work.

Any planet whose center is within 17 minutes of arc of the center of the Sun in celestial longitude is said to be Cazimi. Oddly, this is considered the highest form of accidental dignity. In other words, a planet is thought to be weak when under Sun's beams, weaker still when combust, but—surprisingly—very powerful and benefic when Cazimi!

The average speed of the Moon is such that it remains Cazimi for about an hour; that is, half an hour before and half an hour after the exact conjunction with the Sun (New Moon). Other things being equal, you can use the Cazimi Moon to start something if you really want it to succeed.

However, please do not attempt to use the Cazimi Moon at the time of a Solar Eclipse, nor if the Moon is moving from the Cazimi into a stressful aspect. Cazimi is powerful, but it cannot override the difficulties shown by a Solar Eclipse, nor those shown by, say, the Moon's application to a square of Saturn.

If you really need to start something around the time of the New Moon, and you cannot use the Cazimi, it is a good idea to wait until the first Opportunity Period after the Moon has begun waxing. Even if the Moon is still under Sun's beams at that time, it is better than starting the new project while the Moon is still waning. However, if you can reasonably do so, it is best to wait for the first Opportunity Period after the Moon is no longer under Sun's beams; that is, after the Moon has separated from the Sun by at least 17 degrees. For the principles to use at that time, see step 2.

About the Astrologers

Paula Belluomini, CAP ISAR, began studying astrology as a teenager while living in Brazil. Growing up, she became fascinated with the movement of the stars and was passionate about learning how their positions affected life on Earth. She immersed herself in all the literature she could find on the subject, and moved to Southern California in the 1990s to continue her studies through independent coursework.

Paula completed the steps required to become a Certified Astrological Professional (CAP) by the International Society for Astrological Research (ISAR) in 2015, and participated in several astrological conferences promoted by ISAR and UAC. She was introduced to Jim Shawvan's Opportunity Periods system in Anaheim (ISAR 2003), and has followed his work ever since.

Paula's main areas of expertise and interest include modern astrology with predictive techniques, relationship analysis, and relocational astrology, as well as electional, mundane, and traditional astrology. More recently, horary astrology has piqued her interest because of its practicality and ability to answer questions in a more objective way.

In addition to providing astrology consulting services, Paula writes articles and posts about current astrological events, gives lectures about specific topics, participates in research and study groups, and continues educating herself on the stars.

Aside from astrology, Paula has a degree in marketing and is an experienced graphic and web designer who often creates artwork with astrological themes. For more information, please visit her website at astropaula.com.

Jim Shawvan developed the system of Opportunity Periods over a period of three decades, out of his interest in electional astrology—the art of picking times for important actions such as getting married, opening a business, or incorporating a company (or even matters of only medium importance). Jim began the study of astrology in 1969. He taught classes in predictive astrology and lectured numerous times to the San Diego Astrological Society and other astrological groups and conferences.

Jim's articles appeared in *The Mountain Astrologer* and other publications. He predicted the delay in the results of the US presidential election of 2000, and in early 2001 he predicted that, in response to anti-American terrorism, the US would be at war in Afghanistan in the first two years of George W. Bush's presidency.

Jim studied cultural anthropology and structural linguistics at Cornell University, and later became a computer programmer and systems analyst. From 1989 to 1997 he was the technical astrologer at Neil Michelsen's Astro Communications Services, handling the most difficult questions and orders. He held the Certified Astrological Professional certificate issued by the International Society for Astrological Research (ISAR). Jim passed away in 2019 and will be greatly missed.

Business Guide

Collections

Try to make collections on days when your Sun is well aspected. Avoid days when Mars or Saturn are aspected. If possible, the Moon should be in a cardinal sign: Aries, Cancer, Libra, or Capricorn. It is more difficult to collect when the Moon is in Taurus or Scorpio.

Employment, Promotion

Choose a day when your Sun is favorably aspected or the Moon is in your tenth house. Good aspects of Venus or Jupiter are beneficial.

Loans

Moon in the first and second quarters favors the lender; in the third and fourth it favors the borrower. Good aspects of Jupiter or Venus to the Moon are favorable to both, as is Moon in Leo, Sagittarius, Aquarius, or Pisces.

New Ventures

Things usually get off to a better start during the increase of the Moon. If there is impatience, anxiety, or deadlock, it can often be broken at the Full Moon. Agreements can be reached then.

Partnerships

Agreements and partnerships should be made on a day that is favorable to both parties. Mars, Neptune, Pluto, and Saturn should not be square or opposite the Moon. It is best to make an agreement or partnership when the Moon is in a mutable sign, especially Gemini or Virgo. The other signs are not favorable, with the possible exception of Leo or Capricorn. Begin partnerships when the Moon is increasing in light, as this is a favorable time for starting new ventures.

Public Relations

The Moon rules the public, so this must be well aspected, particularly by the Sun, Mercury, Uranus, or Neptune.

Selling

Selling is favored by good aspects of Venus, Jupiter, or Mercury to the Moon. Avoid aspects to Saturn. Try to get the planetary ruler of your product well aspected by Venus, Jupiter, or the Moon.

Signing Important Papers

Sign contracts or agreements when the Moon is increasing in a fruitful sign. Avoid days when Mars, Saturn, Neptune, or Pluto are afflicting the Moon. Don't sign anything if your Sun is badly afflicted.

Calendar Pages
How to Use Your *Daily Planetary Guide*

Both Eastern and Pacific times are given in the datebook. The Eastern times are listed in the left-hand column. The Pacific times are in the right-hand column in bold typeface. Note that adjustments have been made for Daylight Saving Time. The void-of-course Moon is listed to the right of the daily aspect at the exact time it occurs. It is indicated by "☽ v/c." On days when it occurs for only one time zone and not the other, it is indicated next to the appropriate column and then repeated on the next day for the other time zone. Note that the monthly ephemerides in the back of the book are shown for midnight Greenwich Mean Time (GMT). Opportunity Periods are designated by the letters "OP." See page 75 for a detailed discussion on how to use Opportunity Periods.

Symbol Key

Planets/	☉	Sun	♃	Jupiter
Asteroids	☽	Moon	♄	Saturn
	☿	Mercury	♅	Uranus
	♀	Venus	♆	Neptune
	♂	Mars	♇	Pluto
	⚷	Chiron		

Signs	♈	Aries	♎	Libra
	♉	Taurus	♏	Scorpio
	♊	Gemini	♐	Sagittarius
	♋	Cancer	♑	Capricorn
	♌	Leo	♒	Aquarius
	♍	Virgo	♓	Pisces

Aspects	♂	Conjunction (0°)	△	Trine (120°)
	✳	Sextile (60°)	⚻	Quincunx (150°)
	□	Square (90°)	☍	Opposition (180°)

Motion	℞	Retrograde	D	Direct

Moon Phases	●	New Moon	◑	2nd Quarter
	○	Full Moon	◑	4th Quarter

December 2020

---

28 Mon
2nd ♊

☽♊ ☌ ♀♐	1:47 am	
☽♊ □ ♆♓	6:59 am	**3:59 am**
☽♊ ⊼ ♇♑	6:03 pm	**3:03 pm**
☽♊ ⚹ ♂♈	10:01 pm	**7:01 pm** ☽ v/c

---

29 Tue
2nd ♊
○ Full Moon 8 ♋ 53

☽ enters ♋	5:28 am	**2:28 am**
☽♋ ⊼ ♄♒	8:04 am	**5:04 am**
☽♋ ⊼ ♃♒	9:47 am	**6:47 am**
☽♋ □ ⚷♈	3:07 pm	**12:07 pm**
☽♋ ⚹ ♅♉	6:32 pm	**3:32 pm**
☽♋ ☌ ☉♑	10:28 pm	**7:28 pm**

---

30 Wed
3rd ♋

♀♐ □ ♆♓	5:19 am	**2:19 am**
☽♋ ☌ ☿♑	11:04 am	**8:04 am**
☽♋ △ ♆♓	4:31 pm	**1:31 pm**
☽♋ ⊼ ♀♐	5:42 pm	**2:42 pm**

---

31 Thu
3rd ♋
New Year's Eve

☽♋ ☌ ♀♑	3:10 am	**12:10 am**
☽♋ □ ♂♈	8:45 am	**5:45 am** ☽ v/c
☽ enters ♌	1:58 pm	**10:58 am**
☽♌ ☌ ♄♒	4:56 pm	**1:56 pm**
☽♌ ☌ ♃♒	7:05 pm	**4:05 pm**
☽♌ △ ⚷♈	11:16 pm	**8:16 pm**
☽♌ □ ♅♉		**11:26 pm**

☽♌ □ ♅♉	2:26 am	
☿♑ ⚹ ♆♓	6:18 am	**3:18 am**
☽♌ ⚻ ☉♑	10:55 am	**7:55 am**
☽♌ ⚻ ♆♓	11:39 pm	**8:39 pm**
☽♌ ⚻ ☿♑		**11:02 pm**

OP: After Moon squares Uranus on Thursday or today until v/c Moon on Saturday. Self-motivation and initiative will produce very good results during this OP, with the fiery grand trine.

☽♌ ⚻ ☿♑	2:02 am	
☽♌ △ ♀♐	6:24 am	**3:24 am**
☽♌ ⚻ ♀♑	9:57 am	**6:57 am**
☽♌ △ ♂♈	5:00 pm	**2:00 pm** ☽ v/c
☽ enters ♍	8:13 pm	**5:13 pm**
☽♍ ⚻ ♄≈	11:32 pm	**8:32 pm**
☽♍ ⚻ ♃≈		**11:05 pm**

☽♍ ⚻ ♃≈	2:05 am	
☽♍ ⚻ ♂♈	5:14 pm	**2:14 am**
☽♍ △ ♅♉	8:12 am	**5:12 am**
☽♍ △ ☉♑	8:44 pm	**5:44 pm**

Eastern Time plain / **Pacific Time bold**

DECEMBER 2020						
S	M	T	W	T	F	S
		1	2	3	4	5
6	7	8	9	10	11	12
13	14	15	16	17	18	19
20	21	22	23	24	25	26
27	28	29	30	31		

JANUARY						
S	M	T	W	T	F	S
					1	2
3	4	5	6	7	8	9
10	11	12	13	14	15	16
17	18	19	20	21	22	23
24	25	26	27	28	29	30
31						

FEBRUARY						
S	M	T	W	T	F	S
	1	2	3	4	5	6
7	8	9	10	11	12	13
14	15	16	17	18	19	20
21	22	23	24	25	26	27
28						

4 Mon
3rd ♏

☽♍ ☌ ♆♓	4:50 am	**1:50 am**
☽♍ △ ☿♑	2:11 pm	**11:11 am**
☽♍ △ ♀♑	2:52 pm	**11:52 am**
☽♍ □ ♀♐	4:34 pm	**1:34 pm** ☽ v/c
☿♑ ☌ ♀♑	7:58 pm	**4:58 pm**
☽♍ ⊼ ♂♈	11:19 pm	**8:19 pm**
☽ enters ♎		**9:42 pm**

5 Tue
3rd ♏

☽ enters ♎	12:42 am	
☽♎ △ ♄≈	4:22 am	**1:22 am**
☽♎ △ ♃≈	7:17 am	**4:17 am**
☽♎ ☍ ♅♈	9:33 am	**6:33 am**
☽♎ ⊼ ♅♉	12:19 pm	**9:19 am**

6 Wed
3rd ♎

◑ 4th Quarter 16 ♎ 17

OP: After Moon squares Mercury today or Thursday until v/c Moon today or Thursday. Short OP during the Last Quarter Moon that leaves you just enough time to wrap up ongoing projects.

☽♎ □ ☉♑	4:37 am	**1:37 am**
☽♎ ⊼ ♆♓	8:32 am	**5:32 am**
♂ enters ♉	5:27 pm	**2:27 pm**
☽♎ □ ♀♑	6:23 pm	**3:23 pm**
☽♎ □ ☿♑		**9:21 pm**
☽♎ ✶ ♀♐		**9:55 pm** ☽ v/c

7 Thu
4th ♎

OP: After Moon opposes Uranus today until v/c Moon on Friday. Wait two hours after the opposition. Seize this opportunity to connect with your intuition and complete unfinished tasks.

☽♎ □ ☿♑	12:21 am	
☽♎ ✶ ♀♐	12:55 am	☽ v/c
☽ enters ♏	3:53 am	**12:53 am**
☽♏ ☍ ♂♉	4:14 am	**1:14 am**
☽♏ □ ♄≈	7:54 am	**4:54 am**
☽♏ □ ♃≈	11:11 am	**8:11 am**
☽♏ ⊼ ♅♈	12:38 pm	**9:38 am**
☽♏ ☍ ♅♉	3:16 pm	**12:16 pm**

☿ enters ♒	7:00 am	**4:00 am**
♀ enters ♑	10:41 am	**7:41 am**
☽♏ ✶ ☉♑	11:11 am	**8:11 am**
☽♏ △ ♆♓	11:14 am	**8:14 am**
☉♑ ✶ ♆♓	11:53 am	**8:53 am**
☽♏ ✶ ♀♑	8:59 pm	**5:59 pm** ☽ v/c
☿♒ □ ♂♉	9:44 pm	**6:44 pm**

FRI 8
4th ♏

☽ enters ♐	6:15 am	**3:15 am**
☽♐ ☍ ♂♉	8:17 am	**5:17 am**
☽♐ ✶ ☿♒	9:15 am	**6:15 am**
☽♐ ✶ ♄♒	10:38 am	**7:38 am**
♀♑ △ ♂♉	10:53 am	**7:53 am**
☽♐ ✶ ♃♒	2:18 pm	**11:18 am**
☽♐ △ ⚷♈	2:59 pm	**11:59 am**
☽♐ ☍ ♅♉	5:30 pm	**2:30 pm**
☿♒ ☌ ♄♒	10:17 pm	**7:17 pm**

SAT 9
4th ♏

☽♐ □ ♆♓	1:29 pm	**10:29 am** ☽ v/c

SUN 10
4th ♐

Eastern Time plain / **Pacific Time bold**

DECEMBER 2020						
S	M	T	W	T	F	S
		1	2	3	4	5
6	7	8	9	10	11	12
13	14	15	16	17	18	19
20	21	22	23	24	25	26
27	28	29	30	31		

JANUARY						
S	M	T	W	T	F	S
					1	2
3	4	5	6	7	8	9
10	11	12	13	14	15	16
17	18	19	20	21	22	23
24	25	26	27	28	29	30
31						

FEBRUARY						
S	M	T	W	T	F	S
	1	2	3	4	5	6
7	8	9	10	11	12	13
14	15	16	17	18	19	20
21	22	23	24	25	26	27
28						

11 Mon
4th ♐

☽ enters ♑	8:30 am	**5:30 am**	
☽♑ △ ♂♉	12:16 pm	**9:16 am**	
☿≈ ♂ ♃≈	12:19 pm	**9:19 am**	
☿≈ ✶ ♅♈	12:23 pm	**9:23 am**	
♃≈ ✶ ♅♈	12:48 pm	**9:48 am**	
☽♑ ♂ ♀♑	3:14 pm	**12:14 pm**	
☽♑ □ ♅♈	5:24 pm	**2:24 pm**	
☽♑ △ ♅♉	7:51 pm	**4:51 pm**	

12 Tue
4th ♑
● New Moon 23 ♑ 13 (Pacific)

☿≈ □ ♅♉	10:00 am	**7:00 am**	
♀♑ □ ♅♈	4:04 pm	**1:04 pm**	
☽♑ ✶ ♆♓	4:17 pm	**1:17 pm**	
☽♑ ♂ ☉♑		**9:00 pm**	
☽♑ ♂ ♀♑		**11:22 pm** ☽ v/c	

13 Wed
4th ♑
● New Moon 23 ♑ 13 (Eastern)

☽♑ ♂ ☉♑	12:00 am		
☽♑ ♂ ♀♑	2:22 am		☽ v/c
♂♉ □ ♄≈	6:02 am	**3:02 am**	
☽ enters ≈	11:44 am	**8:44 am**	
☽≈ ♂ ♄≈	5:11 pm	**2:11 pm**	
☽≈ □ ♂♉	5:30 pm	**2:30 pm**	
♀♑ △ ♅♉	7:22 pm	**4:22 pm**	
☽≈ ✶ ♅♈	9:02 pm	**6:02 pm**	
☽≈ ♂ ♃≈	9:55 pm	**6:55 pm**	
☽≈ □ ♅♉	11:29 pm	**8:29 pm**	

14 Thu
1st ≈
Uranus direct

♅ D	3:36 am	**12:36 am**	
☽≈ ♂ ☿≈	4:28 am	**1:28 am** ☽ v/c	
☉♑ ♂ ♀♑	9:19 am	**6:19 am**	

☽ enters ♓	5:17 pm	**2:17 pm**
☽♓ ✶ ♂♉		**10:29 pm**

Fri 15
1st ≈

☽♓ ✶ ♂♉	1:29 am	
☽♓ ✶ ♅♉	5:43 am	**2:43 am**
☽♓ ✶ ♀♑	12:02 pm	**9:02 am**

Sat 16
1st ♓

☽♓ ♂ ♆♓	4:35 am	**1:35 am**	
☽♓ ✶ ♀♑	3:55 pm	**12:55 pm**	
♃≈ □ ♅♉	5:50 pm	**2:50 pm**	
☽♓ ✶ ☉♑	10:44 pm	**7:44 pm**	☽ v/c
☽ enters ♈		**11:07 pm**	

Sun 17
1st ♓

OP: After Moon sextiles Pluto today (see "Translating Darkness" on page 78) until Moon enters Aries today or Monday. A great time to be inspired and embark on new adventures or projects.

Eastern Time plain / **Pacific Time bold**

DECEMBER 2020						
S	M	T	W	T	F	S
		1	2	3	4	5
6	7	8	9	10	11	12
13	14	15	16	17	18	19
20	21	22	23	24	25	26
27	28	29	30	31		

JANUARY						
S	M	T	W	T	F	S
					1	2
3	4	5	6	7	8	9
10	11	12	13	14	15	16
17	18	19	20	21	22	23
24	25	26	27	28	29	30
31						

FEBRUARY						
S	M	T	W	T	F	S
	1	2	3	4	5	6
7	8	9	10	11	12	13
14	15	16	17	18	19	20
21	22	23	24	25	26	27
28						

January

18 Mon

1st ♓

Martin Luther King Jr. Day

☽ enters ♈	2:07 am	
☽♈ ⚹ ♄♒	9:20 am	**6:20 am**
☽♈ ☌ ⚷♈	12:49 pm	**9:49 am**
☽♈ ⚹ ♃♒	3:45 pm	**12:45 pm**

19 Tue

1st ♈

Sun enters Aquarius

☽♈ □ ♀♑	4:43 am	**1:43 am**
☽♈ ⚹ ☿♒	12:54 pm	**9:54 am**
☉ enters ♒	3:40 pm	**12:40 pm**

20 Wed

1st ♈

◐ 2nd Quarter 1 ♉ 02

Inauguration Day

☽♈ □ ♇♑	3:29 am	**12:29 am**	☽ v/c
☽ enters ♉	1:56 pm	**10:56 am**	
♂♉ ☌ ♅♉	3:38 pm	**12:38 pm**	
☽♉ □ ☉♒	4:02 pm	**1:02 pm**	
☽♉ □ ♄♒	10:00 pm	**7:00 pm**	

21 Thu

2nd ♉

☽♉ ☌ ♅♉	3:37 am	**12:37 am**
☽♉ ☌ ♂♉	4:08 am	**1:08 am**
☽♉ □ ♃♒	5:15 am	**2:15 am**
☽♉ △ ♀♑		**9:28 pm**

Fri 22
2nd ♉

☽♉ △ ♀♑	12:28 am	
☽♉ ⚹ ♆♓	4:27 am	**1:27 am**
☽♉ □ ☿♒	8:59 am	**5:59 am**
☽♉ △ ♇♑	4:28 pm	**1:28 pm** ☽ v/c
☽ enters ♊		**11:43 pm**
♂♉ □ ♃♒		**11:49 pm**

OP: After Moon squares Mercury until Moon enters Gemini. (Taurus is one of the four signs in which the v/c Moon is a good thing. See page 75.) Reliable energy that favors constructive activities.

Sat 23
2nd ♉

☽ enters ♊	2:43 am	
♂♉ □ ♃♒	2:49 am	
☽♊ △ ☉♒	10:27 am	**7:27 am**
☽♊ △ ♄♒	11:19 am	**8:19 am**
☽♊ ⚹ ⚷♈	1:59 pm	**10:59 am**
♀♑ ⚹ ♆♓	2:49 pm	**11:49 am**
☽♊ △ ♃♒	7:04 pm	**4:04 pm**
☉♒ ☌ ♄♒	10:01 pm	**7:01 pm**

Sun 24
2nd ♊

☽♊ □ ♆♓	4:36 pm	**1:36 pm**
☽♊ ⚻ ♀♑	7:28 pm	**4:28 pm**
☽♊ △ ☿♒		**11:17 pm** ☽ v/c

OP: After Moon squares Neptune today until v/c Moon today or Monday. Wait two hours after the square and use this time to communicate and connect. Act quickly—this is your last chance before Mercury turns retrograde.

Eastern Time plain / **Pacific Time bold**

DECEMBER 2020

S	M	T	W	T	F	S
		1	2	3	4	5
6	7	8	9	10	11	12
13	14	15	16	17	18	19
20	21	22	23	24	25	26
27	28	29	30	31		

JANUARY

S	M	T	W	T	F	S
					1	2
3	4	5	6	7	8	9
10	11	12	13	14	15	16
17	18	19	20	21	22	23
24	25	26	27	28	29	30
31						

FEBRUARY

S	M	T	W	T	F	S
	1	2	3	4	5	6
7	8	9	10	11	12	13
14	15	16	17	18	19	20
21	22	23	24	25	26	27
28						

January

Mercury Note: Mercury enters its Storm (moving less than 40 minutes of arc per day) on Wednesday, as it slows down before going retrograde. The Storm acts like the retrograde. Not favorable for new projects—just follow through with the items that are already on your plate. Write down new ideas with date and time they occurred.

25 Mon
2nd ♊

☽♊ △ ☿ ≈	2:17 am		☽ v/c
☽♊ ⊼ ♀♑	4:12 am	**1:12 am**	
☉≈ ⚹ ♂ ♈	5:29 am	**2:29 am**	
☽ enters ♋	1:52 pm	**10:52 am**	
☽♋ ⊼ ♄ ≈	10:38 pm	**7:38 pm**	
☽♋ □ ♂ ♈		**9:46 pm**	
☽♋ ⊼ ☉≈		**11:23 pm**	
☽♋ ⚹ ♅ ♉		**11:49 pm**	

26 Tue
2nd ♋

☽♋ □ ♂ ♈	12:46 am	
☽♋ ⊼ ☉≈	2:23 am	
☽♋ ⚹ ♅ ♉	2:49 am	
☽♋ ⊼ ♃ ≈	6:32 am	**3:32 am**
☉≈ □ ♅ ♉	7:48 am	**4:48 am**
☽♋ ⚹ ♂ ♉	8:17 am	**5:17 am**
☽♋ △ ♆ ♓		**10:57 pm**

27 Wed
2nd ♋

☽♋ △ ♆ ♓	1:57 am		
☽♋ ☍ ♀♑	10:37 am	**7:37 am**	
☽♋ ☍ ♀♑	12:55 pm	**9:55 am**	☽ v/c
☽♋ ⊼ ☿ ≈	2:09 pm	**11:09 am**	
☽ enters ♌	9:54 pm	**6:54 pm**	

28 Thu
2nd ♌
○ Full Moon 9 ♌ 06

☽♌ ☍ ♄ ≈	6:41 am	**3:41 am**
☽♌ △ ♂ ♈	8:21 am	**5:21 am**
☽♌ □ ♅ ♉	10:11 am	**7:11 am**
♀♑ ♂ ♀♑	11:18 am	**8:18 am**
☽♌ ☍ ☉≈	2:16 pm	**11:16 am**
☽♌ ☍ ♃ ≈	2:39 pm	**11:39 am**
☽♌ □ ♂ ♉	5:32 pm	**2:32 pm**
☉≈ ♂ ♃ ≈	8:40 pm	**5:40 pm**

Mercury Note: Mercury goes retrograde on Saturday, January 30, and remains so until February 20, after which it will still be in its Storm until February 26. Projects initiated during this entire period may not work out as planned. It's best to use this time for reviews, editing, escrows, and so forth.

☽♌ ⊼ ♆♓	8:10 am	**5:10 am**
☽♌ ⊼ ♀♑	6:36 pm	**3:36 pm**
☽♌ ☍ ☿≈	8:53 pm	**5:53 pm** ☽ v/c
☽♌ ⊼ ♀♑	9:39 pm	**6:39 pm**

FRI 29
3rd ♌

☽ enters ♍	3:02 am	**12:02 am**
☿℞	10:52 am	**7:52 am**
☽♍ ⊼ ♄≈	11:54 am	**8:54 am**
☽♍ ⊼ ♅♈	1:11 pm	**10:11 am**
☽♍ △ ♅♉	2:52 pm	**11:52 am**
☽♍ ⊼ ♃≈	8:01 pm	**5:01 pm**
☽♍ ⊼ ☉≈	10:51 pm	**7:51 pm**
☽♍ △ ♂♉	11:57 pm	**8:57 pm**

SAT 30
3rd ♌
MERCURY RETROGRADE

☽♍ ☍ ♆♓	12:09 pm	**9:09 am**
☽♍ △ ♀♑	10:17 pm	**7:17 pm**
☽♍ ⊼ ☿≈		**9:05 pm**

SUN 31
3rd ♍

OP: After Moon trines Pluto today until v/c Moon on Monday. For those who enjoy staying up late on Sunday night, this is a good chance to be productive.

Eastern Time plain / **Pacific Time bold**

DECEMBER 2020						
S	M	T	W	T	F	S
		1	2	3	4	5
6	7	8	9	10	11	12
13	14	15	16	17	18	19
20	21	22	23	24	25	26
27	28	29	30	31		

JANUARY						
S	M	T	W	T	F	S
					1	2
3	4	5	6	7	8	9
10	11	12	13	14	15	16
17	18	19	20	21	22	23
24	25	26	27	28	29	30
31						

FEBRUARY						
S	M	T	W	T	F	S
	1	2	3	4	5	6
7	8	9	10	11	12	13
14	15	16	17	18	19	20
21	22	23	24	25	26	27
28						

February

1 Mon
3rd ♍

☽♍ ⚻ ☿≈	12:05 am	
☉≈ □ ♂♉	5:34 am	**2:34 am**
☽♍ △ ♀♈	6:10 am	**3:10 am** ☽ v/c
☽ enters ♎	6:25 am	**3:25 am**
♀ enters ≈	9:05 am	**6:05 am**
☽♎ △ ♄≈	3:32 pm	**12:32 pm**
☽♎ ☍ ♅♈	4:31 pm	**1:31 pm**
☽♎ ⚻ ♅♉	6:05 pm	**3:05 pm**
☽♎ △ ♃≈	11:58 pm	**8:58 pm**

2 Tue
3rd ♎

Groundhog Day

Imbolc

☽♎ ⚻ ♂♉	4:59 am	**1:59 am**
☽♎ △ ☉≈	5:50 am	**2:50 am**
☽♎ ⚻ ♆♓	3:10 pm	**12:10 pm**
☽♎ □ ♀♑		**10:15 pm**
☽♎ △ ☿≈		**10:15 pm** ☽ v/c

3 Wed
3rd ♎

☽♎ □ ♀♑	1:15 am	
☽♎ △ ☿≈	1:15 am	☽ v/c
☽ enters ♏	9:15 am	**6:15 am**
☽♏ □ ♀≈	1:55 pm	**10:55 am**
☽♏ □ ♄≈	6:47 pm	**3:47 pm**
☽♏ ⚻ ♅♈	7:29 pm	**4:29 pm**
☽♏ ☍ ♅♉	8:57 pm	**5:57 pm**

4 Thu
3rd ♏

◑ 4th Quarter 16 ♏ 08

OP: After Moon squares Mercury today or Friday until v/c Moon on Friday. Good opportunity to review and finish up ongoing projects.

☽♏ □ ♃≈	3:40 am	**12:40 am**
☽♏ ☍ ♂♉	9:51 am	**6:51 am**
☽♏ □ ☉≈	12:37 pm	**9:37 am**
☽♏ △ ♆♓	6:11 pm	**3:11 pm**
☽♏ □ ☿≈		**10:27 pm**

☽♏ □ ☿ ≈ 1:27 am

FRI 5
4th ♏

☽♏ ⚹ ♀♑ 4:20 am **1:20 am** ☽ v/c
☽ enters ♐ 12:16 pm **9:16 am**
☽♐ ⚹ ♀≈ 10:00 pm **7:00 pm**
☽♐ ⚹ ♄≈ 10:20 pm **7:20 pm**
☽♐ △ ♋♈ 10:45 pm **7:45 pm**
☽♐ ⚻ ♅♉   **9:10 pm**
♀≈ ♂ ♄≈   **11:07 pm**

☽♐ ⚻ ♅♉ 12:10 am

SAT 6
4th ♐

♀≈ ♂ ♄≈ 2:07 am
♀≈ ⚹ ♋♈ 6:43 am **3:43 am**
☽♐ ⚹ ♃♉ 7:45 am **4:45 am**
☽♐ ⚻ ♂♉ 3:12 pm **12:12 pm**
☽♐ ⚹ ☉≈ 7:56 pm **4:56 pm**
☽♐ □ ♆♓ 9:40 pm **6:40 pm**
♀≈ □ ♅♉ 10:33 pm **7:33 pm**
☽♐ ⚹ ☿≈   **10:16 pm** ☽ v/c

OP: After Moon squares Neptune today until Moon enters Capricorn on Sunday. (Sagittarius is one of the four signs in which the v/c Moon is a good thing. See page 75.) Great time to relax and have fun, as it's during the Last Quarter Moon and Mercury is retrograde.

☽♐ ⚹ ☿≈ 1:16 am ☽ v/c

SUN 7
4th ♐

☽ enters ♑ 3:52 pm **12:52 pm**
☽♑ □ ♋♈   **11:39 pm**

Eastern Time plain / **Pacific Time bold**

JANUARY						
S	M	T	W	T	F	S
					1	2
3	4	5	6	7	8	9
10	11	12	13	14	15	16
17	18	19	20	21	22	23
24	25	26	27	28	29	30
31						

FEBRUARY						
S	M	T	W	T	F	S
	1	2	3	4	5	6
7	8	9	10	11	12	13
14	15	16	17	18	19	20
21	22	23	24	25	26	27
28						

MARCH						
S	M	T	W	T	F	S
	1	2	3	4	5	6
7	8	9	10	11	12	13
14	15	16	17	18	19	20
21	22	23	24	25	26	27
28	29	30	31			

February

8 Mon
4th ♑

☽♑ □ ♎♈	2:39 am	
☽♑ △ ♅♉	4:00 am	**1:00 am**
☉≈ ♂ ☿≈	8:48 am	**5:48 am**
☽♑ △ ♂♉	9:21 pm	**6:21 pm**
☽♑ ⚹ ♆♓		**10:55 pm**

9 Tue
4th ♑

☽♑ ⚹ ♆♓	1:55 am	
♄≈ ⚹ ♎♈	5:59 am	**2:59 am**
☽♑ ♂ ♀♑	12:22 pm	**9:22 am** ☽ v/c
☽ enters ≈	8:20 pm	**5:20 pm**

10 Wed
4th ≈

☿≈ □ ♂♉	7:16 am	**4:16 am**
☽≈ ⚹ ♎♈	7:34 am	**4:34 am**
☽≈ ♂ ♄≈	7:42 am	**4:42 am**
☽≈ □ ♅♉	8:51 am	**5:51 am**
☽≈ ♂ ♀≈	5:11 pm	**2:11 pm**
☽≈ ♂ ♃≈	6:29 pm	**3:29 pm**
☽≈ ♂ ☿≈		**11:22 pm**

11 Thu
4th ≈

● New Moon 23 ≈ 17

OP: This Cazimi Moon is usable ½ hour before and ½ hour after the Sun-Moon conjunction. If you have something important to start around now that's part of a larger project started before January 27, this is a great time to do it.

☽≈ ♂ ☿≈	2:22 am	
☽≈ □ ♂♉	4:55 am	**1:55 am**
♀≈ ♂ ♃≈	10:00 am	**7:00 am**
☽≈ ♂ ☉≈	2:06 pm	**11:06 am** ☽ v/c
☽ enters ♓		**11:23 pm**

D enters ♓ 2:23 am
D♓ ✶ ♅ ♉ 3:30 pm **12:30 pm**
☿≈ ♂ ♀≈ **11:48 pm**

☿≈ ♂ ♀≈ 2:48 am
D♓ ✶ ♂♉ 2:55 pm **11:55 am**
D♓ ♂ ♆♓ 3:11 pm **12:11 pm**
♂♉ ✶ ♆♓ 9:13 pm **6:13 pm**
D♓ ✶ ♀♑ **11:29 pm** D v/c

OP: After Moon conjoins Neptune today until Moon enters Aries on Sunday. Wait two hours after the conjunction to get more clarity. This OP is favorable for the arts, meditation, and helping others.

D♓ ✶ ♀♑ 2:29 am D v/c
D enters ♈ 10:54 am **7:54 am**
☿≈ ♂ ♃≈ 4:40 pm **1:40 pm**
D♈ ♂ ♅♈ 11:36 pm **8:36 pm**
D♈ ✶ ♄≈ **9:23 pm**

Eastern Time plain / **Pacific Time bold**

JANUARY						
S	M	T	W	T	F	S
					1	2
3	4	5	6	7	8	9
10	11	12	13	14	15	16
17	18	19	20	21	22	23
24	25	26	27	28	29	30
31						

FEBRUARY						
S	M	T	W	T	F	S
	1	2	3	4	5	6
7	8	9	10	11	12	13
14	15	16	17	18	19	20
21	22	23	24	25	26	27
28						

MARCH						
S	M	T	W	T	F	S
	1	2	3	4	5	6
7	8	9	10	11	12	13
14	15	16	17	18	19	20
21	22	23	24	25	26	27
28	29	30	31			

FEBRUARY

15 MON
1st ♈
PRESIDENTS' DAY

☽♈ ✶ ♄≈ 12:23 am
☽♈ ✶ ☿≈ 11:50 am **8:50 am**
☽♈ ✶ ♃≈ 1:22 pm **10:22 am**
☽♈ ✶ ♀≈ 10:40 pm **7:40 pm**

16 TUE
1st ♈
MARDI GRAS (FAT TUESDAY)
OP: After Moon squares Pluto until v/c Moon. Mercury is retrograde, so use this time to review and push forward with projects you've already started.

☽♈ □ ♀♑ 1:32 pm **10:32 am**

☽♈ ✶ ☉≈ 7:17 pm **4:17 pm** ☽ v/c
☽ enters ♉ 10:12 pm **7:12 pm**

17 WED
1st ♉
ASH WEDNESDAY

☽♉ □ ♄≈ 12:48 pm **9:48 am**
☽♉ ♂ ♅♉ 12:48 pm **9:48 am**
♄≈ □ ♅♉ 2:08 pm **11:08 am**
☽♉ □ ☿≈ 9:32 pm **6:32 pm**
☽♉ □ ♃≈ **1:51 pm**

18 THU
1st ♉
SUN ENTERS PISCES
OP: After Moon conjoins Mars today until Moon enters Gemini on Friday. Use this OP to be practical and follow through on your existing projects.

☽♉ □ ♃≈ 2:51 am
☉ enters ♓ 5:44 am **2:44 am**
☽♉ ✶ ♆♓ 2:30 pm **11:30 am**
☽♉ ✶ ♀≈ 6:21 pm **3:21 pm**
☽♉ ♂ ♂♉ 7:48 pm **4:48 pm**
☽♉ △ ♀♑ **11:28 pm** ☽ v/c

Mercury Note: Mercury goes direct on Saturday, February 20, but remains in its Storm, moving slowly, until February 26.

FRI 19

1st ♉

◐ 2nd Quarter 1 ♊ 21

☽♉ △ ♇♑	2:28 am		☽ v/c
☽ enters ♊	11:04 am	**8:04 am**	
☽♊ □ ☉♓	1:47 pm	**10:47 am**	
♀≈ □ ♂♉	6:04 pm	**3:04 pm**	
☽♊ ⚹ ⚷♈		**9:47 pm**	
☽♊ △ ♄≈		**11:15 pm**	

SAT 20

2nd ♊

MERCURY DIRECT

☽♊ ⚹ ⚷♈	12:47 am		
☽♊ △ ♄≈	2:15 am		
☽♊ △ ☿≈	9:20 am	**6:20 am**	
☽♊ △ ♃≈	4:46 pm	**1:46 pm**	
☿ D	7:52 pm	**4:52 pm**	

SUN 21

2nd ♊

☽♊ □ ♆♓	3:10 am	**12:10 am**	
☽♊ △ ♀≈	1:39 pm	**10:39 am**	☽ v/c
☽♊ ⚻ ♇♑	2:45 pm	**11:45 am**	
☽ enters ♋	10:53 pm	**7:53 pm**	

OP: After Moon squares Neptune until v/c Moon. While this OP is good for communication and networking, with Mercury slow you can expect delays.

Eastern Time plain / **Pacific Time bold**

JANUARY

S	M	T	W	T	F	S
					1	2
3	4	5	6	7	8	9
10	11	12	13	14	15	16
17	18	19	20	21	22	23
24	25	26	27	28	29	30
31						

FEBRUARY

S	M	T	W	T	F	S
	1	2	3	4	5	6
7	8	9	10	11	12	13
14	15	16	17	18	19	20
21	22	23	24	25	26	27
28						

MARCH

S	M	T	W	T	F	S
	1	2	3	4	5	6
7	8	9	10	11	12	13
14	15	16	17	18	19	20
21	22	23	24	25	26	27
28	29	30	31			

February

22 Mon
2nd ♋

☽♋ △ ☉♓	6:47 am	**3:47 am**
☽♋ □ ♀♈	12:14 pm	**9:14 am**
☽♋ ✶ ♅♉	1:09 pm	**10:09 am**
☽♋ ⚻ ♄≈	1:55 pm	**10:55 am**
☽♋ ⚻ ☿≈	8:31 pm	**5:31 pm**

23 Tue
2nd ♋

☽♋ ⚻ ♃≈	4:14 am	**1:14 am**
☽♋ △ ♆♓	1:06 pm	**10:06 am**
☽♋ ✶ ♂♉	10:59 pm	**7:59 pm**
☽♋ ☍ ♀♑	11:54 pm	**8:54 pm** ☽ v/c

24 Wed
2nd ♋

☽♋ ⚻ ♀≈	4:47 am	**1:47 am**
☽ enters ♌	7:23 am	**4:23 am**
☽♌ ⚻ ☉♓	7:18 pm	**4:18 pm**
☽♌ △ ♀♈	8:03 pm	**5:03 pm**
☽♌ □ ♅♉	8:49 pm	**5:49 pm**
♂♉ △ ♀♑	8:52 pm	**5:52 pm**
☽♌ ☍ ♄≈	9:52 pm	**6:52 pm**

25 Thu
2nd ♌

☽♌ ☍ ☿≈	4:56 am	**1:56 am**
♀ enters ♓	8:11 am	**5:11 am**
☽♌ ☍ ♃≈	11:40 am	**8:40 am**
☉♓ ✶ ♅♉	4:13 pm	**1:13 pm**
☽♌ ⚻ ♆♓	7:09 pm	**4:09 pm**

Mercury Note: Mercury finally leaves its Storm on Saturday, February 27. Look over your notes on any ideas that occurred to you while Mercury was retrograde or slow. How do they look now?

☽♌ ⊼ ♀♑	5:12 am	**2:12 am**
☽♌ □ ♂♉	6:32 am	**3:32 am** ☽ v/c
☽ enters ♍	12:07 pm	**9:07 am**
☽♍ ☍ ♀♓	2:50 pm	**11:50 am**
☽♍ ⊼ ⚷♈		**9:14 pm**
☽♍ △ ♅♉		**9:54 pm**
☽♍ ⊼ ♄≈		**11:09 pm**

☽♍ ⊼ ⚷♈	12:14 am	
☽♍ △ ♅♉	12:54 am	
☽♍ ⊼ ♄≈	2:09 am	
☽♍ ☍ ☉♓	3:17 am	**12:17 am**
☽♍ ⊼ ☿≈	10:25 am	**7:25 am**
☽♍ ⊼ ♃≈	3:40 pm	**12:40 pm**
☽♍ ☍ ♆♓	10:06 pm	**7:06 pm**

☽♍ △ ♀♑	7:42 am	**4:42 am**
☽♍ △ ♂♉	10:58 am	**7:58 am** ☽ v/c
☽ enters ♎	2:17 pm	**11:17 am**
☽♎ ⊼ ♀♓	9:36 pm	**6:36 pm**
☽♎ ☍ ⚷♈		**11:14 pm**
☽♎ ⊼ ♅♉		**11:49 pm**

OP: After Moon trines Pluto until v/c Moon. You'll get positive results with the focus and steadiness offered by this OP.

Eastern Time plain / **Pacific Time bold**

	JANUARY							FEBRUARY							MARCH					
S	M	T	W	T	F	S	S	M	T	W	T	F	S	S	M	T	W	T	F	S
					1	2		1	2	3	4	5	6		1	2	3	4	5	6
3	4	5	6	7	8	9	7	8	9	10	11	12	13	7	8	9	10	11	12	13
10	11	12	13	14	15	16	14	15	16	17	18	19	20	14	15	16	17	18	19	20
17	18	19	20	21	22	23	21	22	23	24	25	26	27	21	22	23	24	25	26	27
24	25	26	27	28	29	30	28							28	29	30	31			
31																				

March

1 Mon
3rd ♎

☽ ♎ ☌ ♅ ♈	2:14 am	
☽ ♎ ⚻ ♅ ♉	2:49 am	
☽ ♎ △ ♄ ♒	4:17 am	**1:17 am**
☽ ♎ ⚻ ☉ ♓	8:42 am	**5:42 am**
☽ ♎ △ ☿ ♒	2:27 pm	**11:27 am**
☽ ♎ △ ♃ ♒	5:57 pm	**2:57 pm**
☽ ♎ ⚻ ♆ ♓	11:40 pm	**8:40 pm**

2 Tue
3rd ♎

☽ ♎ □ ♀ ♑	9:09 am	**6:09 am**	☽ v/c
☽ ♎ ⚻ ♂ ♉	2:22 pm	**11:22 am**	
☽ enters ♏	3:38 pm	**12:38 pm**	

3 Wed
3rd ♏

OP: After Moon squares Jupiter today until v/c Moon on Thursday.
Aided by Venus in Pisces, this OP is fine for anything, from business
to romance.

☽ ♏ △ ♀ ♓	3:39 am	**12:39 am**
☽ ♏ ⚻ ♅ ♈	3:49 am	**12:49 am**
☽ ♏ ☌ ♅ ♉	4:22 am	**1:22 am**
☽ ♏ □ ♄ ♒	6:05 am	**3:05 am**
♀ ♓ ✶ ♅ ♉	12:09 pm	**9:09 am**
☽ ♏ △ ☉ ♓	1:52 pm	**10:52 am**
☽ ♏ □ ☿ ♒	7:01 pm	**4:01 pm**
☽ ♏ □ ♃ ♒	8:22 pm	**5:22 pm**
♂ enters ♊	10:30 pm	**7:30 pm**
☽ ♏ △ ♆ ♓		**10:30 pm**

4 Thu
3rd ♏

☽ ♏ △ ♆ ♓	1:30 am		
☽ ♏ ✶ ♀ ♑	11:10 am	**8:10 am**	☽ v/c
☽ enters ♐	5:43 pm	**2:43 pm**	
☽ ♐ ☌ ♂ ♊	6:32 pm	**3:32 pm**	
☿ ♒ ☌ ♃ ♒	10:27 pm	**7:27 pm**	

☽♐ △ ⚷♈	6:26 am	**3:26 am**	
☽♐ ⚹ ♅♉	6:55 am	**3:55 am**	
☽♐ ⚹ ♄≈	8:56 am	**5:56 am**	
☽♐ □ ♀♓	10:58 am	**7:58 am**	
☽♐ □ ☉♓	8:30 pm	**5:30 pm**	
☽♐ ⚹ ♃≈		**9:07 pm**	
☽♐ ⚹ ☿≈		**10:36 pm**	

FRI 5
3rd ♐
◑ 4th Quarter 15 ♐ 42

☽♐ ⚹ ♃≈	12:07 am		
☽♐ ⚹ ☿≈	1:36 am		
☽♐ □ ♆♓	4:44 am	**1:44 am** ☽ v/c	
☽ enters ♑	9:20 pm	**6:20 pm**	
☽♑ ⚻ ♂♊		**9:29 pm**	

SAT 6
4th ♐

☽♑ ⚻ ♂♊	12:29 am		
☽♑ □ ⚷♈	10:42 am	**7:42 am**	
☽♑ △ ♅♉	11:09 am	**8:09 am**	
☽♑ ⚹ ♀♓	8:29 pm	**5:29 pm**	

SUN 7
4th ♑

Eastern Time plain / **Pacific Time bold**

FEBRUARY								MARCH								APRIL					
S	M	T	W	T	F	S		S	M	T	W	T	F	S		S	M	T	W	T	F	S
	1	2	3	4	5	6			1	2	3	4	5	6						1	2	3
7	8	9	10	11	12	13		7	8	9	10	11	12	13		4	5	6	7	8	9	10
14	15	16	17	18	19	20		14	15	16	17	18	19	20		11	12	13	14	15	16	17
21	22	23	24	25	26	27		21	22	23	24	25	26	27		18	19	20	21	22	23	24
28								28	29	30	31					25	26	27	28	29	30	

8 Mon
4th ♑

☽♑ ✶ ☉♓	5:15 am	**2:15 am**
☽♑ ✶ ♆♓	9:41 am	**6:41 am**
☽♑ ☌ ♀♑	7:52 pm	**4:52 pm** ☽ v/c
☽ enters ♒		**11:41 pm**

9 Tue
4th ♑

☽ enters ♒	2:41 am	
☽♒ △ ♂♊	8:23 am	**5:23 am**
☽♒ ✶ ♀♈	4:42 pm	**1:42 pm**
☽♒ ☐ ♅♉	5:06 pm	**2:06 pm**
☽♒ ☌ ♄♒	7:45 pm	**4:45 pm**

10 Wed
4th ♒

OP: After Moon conjoins Jupiter until v/c Moon. An entire day to finish up and release your ongoing projects during this Last Quarter Moon.

☽♒ ☌ ♃♒	12:58 pm	**9:58 am**
☉♓ ☌ ♆♓	7:01 pm	**4:01 pm**
☽♒ ☌ ☿♒	10:32 pm	**7:32 pm** ☽ v/c

11 Thu
4th ♒

☽ enters ♓	9:44 am	**6:44 am**
☽♓ ☐ ♂♊	6:16 pm	**3:16 pm**
☽♓ ✶ ♅♉		**9:50 pm**

FRI 12
4th ♓

☽♓ ✶ ♅♉ 12:50 am
☽♓ ☌ ♀♓ 10:29 pm **7:29 pm**
☽♓ ☌ ♆♓ **9:52 pm**

SAT 13
4th ♓

☽♓ ☌ ♆♓ 12:52 am
☽♓ ☌ ☉♓ 5:21 am **2:21 am**
☽♓ ✶ ♇♑ 11:38 am **8:38 am** ☽ v/c
☽ enters ♈ 6:44 pm **3:44 pm**
♀♓ ☌ ♆♓ 11:08 pm **8:08 pm**

● New Moon 23 ♓ 04

OP: This Cazimi Moon is usable ½ hour before and ½ hour after the Sun-Moon conjunction. Intuition is heightened, and if you have something important to start around now, this is a great time to do it.

SUN 14
1st ♈

☽♈ ✶ ♂♊ 7:28 am **4:28 am**
☽♈ ☌ ⚷♈ 11:18 am **8:18 am**
☽♈ ✶ ♄♒ 2:58 pm **11:58 am**

DAYLIGHT SAVING TIME BEGINS AT 2:00 A.M.

Eastern Time plain / **Pacific Time bold**

FEBRUARY

S	M	T	W	T	F	S
	1	2	3	4	5	6
7	8	9	10	11	12	13
14	15	16	17	18	19	20
21	22	23	24	25	26	27
28						

MARCH

S	M	T	W	T	F	S
	1	2	3	4	5	6
7	8	9	10	11	12	13
14	15	16	17	18	19	20
21	22	23	24	25	26	27
28	29	30	31			

APRIL

S	M	T	W	T	F	S
				1	2	3
4	5	6	7	8	9	10
11	12	13	14	15	16	17
18	19	20	21	22	23	24
25	26	27	28	29	30	

15 Mon
1st ♈

☽♈ ⚹ ♃≈	10:40 am	**7:40 am**	
☿ enters ♓	6:26 pm	**3:26 pm**	
☽♈ □ ♀♑	11:40 pm	**8:40 pm**	☽ v/c

16 Tue
1st ♈

☽ enters ♉	6:56 am	**3:56 am**	
☽♉ ⚹ ☿♓	8:31 am	**5:31 am**	
☉♓ ⚹ ♀♑	2:26 pm	**11:26 am**	
☽♉ ☌ ♅♉	11:37 pm	**8:37 pm**	

17 Wed
1st ♉
St. Patrick's Day

☽♉ □ ♄≈	3:20 am	**12:20 am**
♂♊ ⚹ ♅♈	11:35 pm	**8:35 pm**
☽♉ □ ♃≈		**9:14 pm**
☽♉ ⚹ ♆♓		**10:16 pm**

18 Thu
1st ♉

OP: After Moon squares Jupiter on Wednesday or today until Moon enters Gemini today. This OP is the last for a while and is an excellent opportunity to start turning your plans into reality.

☽♉ □ ♃≈	12:14 am		
☽♉ ⚹ ♆♓	1:16 am		
☽♉ ⚹ ♀♓	12:24 pm	**9:24 am**	
☽♉ △ ♀♑	12:30 pm	**9:30 am**	
♀♓ ⚹ ♀♑	1:20 pm	**10:20 am**	
☽♉ ⚹ ☉♓	4:40 pm	**1:40 pm**	☽ v/c
☽ enters ♊	7:47 pm	**4:47 pm**	

☽♊ □ ☿♓	5:28 am	**2:28 am**
☽♊ ⚹ ⚷♈	12:39 pm	**9:39 am**
☽♊ ☌ ♂♊	2:25 pm	**11:25 am**
☽♊ △ ♄♒	4:50 pm	**1:50 pm**

Fri 19
1st ♊

☉ enters ♈	5:37 am	**2:37 am**
☽♊ △ ♃♒	2:14 pm	**11:14 am**
☽♊ □ ♆♓	2:20 pm	**11:20 am**
☽♊ ⚻ ♇♑		**10:17 pm**

Sat 20
1st ♊
Spring Equinox
Ostara
Sun enters Aries
International Astrology Day

☽♊ ⚻ ♇♑	1:17 am		
☽♊ □ ♀♓	8:04 am	**5:04 am**	☽ v/c
☽ enters ♋	8:18 am	**5:18 am**	
♀ enters ♈	10:16 am	**7:16 am**	
☽♋ □ ☉♈	10:40 am	**7:40 am**	
☿♓ ⚹ ♅♉	7:35 pm	**4:35 pm**	
♂♊ △ ♄♒	10:35 pm	**7:35 pm**	
☽♋ □ ⚷♈		**9:53 pm**	
☽♋ ⚹ ♅♉		**10:02 pm**	
☽♋ △ ☿♓		**10:46 pm**	

Sun 21
1st ♊
◐ 2nd Quarter 1 ♋ 12

Eastern Time plain / **Pacific Time bold**

FEBRUARY

S	M	T	W	T	F	S
	1	2	3	4	5	6
7	8	9	10	11	12	13
14	15	16	17	18	19	20
21	22	23	24	25	26	27
28						

MARCH

S	M	T	W	T	F	S
	1	2	3	4	5	6
7	8	9	10	11	12	13
14	15	16	17	18	19	20
21	22	23	24	25	26	27
28	29	30	31			

APRIL

S	M	T	W	T	F	S
				1	2	3
4	5	6	7	8	9	10
11	12	13	14	15	16	17
18	19	20	21	22	23	24
25	26	27	28	29	30	

March

22 Mon
2nd ♋

☽♋ □ ⚷♈	12:53 am	
☽♋ ⚹ ♅♉	1:02 am	
☽♋ △ ☿♓	1:46 am	
☽♋ ⚻ ♄≈	5:02 am	**2:02 am**
☽♋ △ ♆♓		**10:14 pm**
☽♋ ⚻ ♃≈		**10:56 pm**

23 Tue
2nd ♋

☽♋ △ ♆♓	1:14 am	
☽♋ ⚻ ♃≈	1:56 am	
☽♋ ☍ ♀♑	11:26 am	**8:26 am** ☽ v/c
☽ enters ♌	5:56 pm	**2:56 pm**
☿♓ □ ♂♊	11:26 pm	**8:26 pm**
☽♌ △ ♀♈	11:50 pm	**8:50 pm**
☽♌ △ ☉♈		**9:54 pm**

24 Wed
2nd ♌

☽♌ △ ☉♈	12:54 am	
☽♌ △ ⚷♈	9:39 am	**6:39 am**
☽♌ □ ♅♉	9:45 am	**6:45 am**
☽♌ ☍ ♄≈	1:38 pm	**10:38 am**
☽♌ ⚹ ♂♊	4:08 pm	**1:08 pm**
☽♌ ⚻ ☿♓	5:28 pm	**2:28 pm**

25 Thu
2nd ♌

☽♌ ⚻ ♆♓	8:07 am	**5:07 am**
☽♌ ☍ ♃≈	9:27 am	**6:27 am** ☽ v/c
☽♌ ⚻ ♀♑	5:28 pm	**2:28 pm**
☽ enters ♍	11:25 pm	**8:25 pm**
☉♈ ☌ ♀♈		**11:58 pm**

☉♈ ☌ ♀♈	2:58 am	
☽♍ ⚻ ☉♈	9:52 am	**6:52 am**
☽♍ ⚻ ♀♈	10:00 am	**7:00 am**
☽♍ ⚻ ⚷♈	2:13 pm	**11:13 am**
☽♍ △ ♅♉	2:17 pm	**11:17 am**
☽♍ ⚻ ♄≈	6:00 pm	**3:00 pm**
☽♍ ☐ ♂♊	10:16 pm	**7:16 pm**

Fri 26
2nd ♍

☽♍ ☍ ☿♓	3:37 am	**12:37 am**	
☽♍ ☍ ♆♓	11:05 am	**8:05 am**	
☽♍ ⚻ ♃≈	12:55 pm	**9:55 am**	
☽♍ △ ♀♑	7:48 pm	**4:48 pm**	☽ v/c
☽ enters ♎		**10:22 pm**	

Sat 27
2nd ♍
Passover begins at sundown

☽ enters ♎	1:22 am	
♀♈ ☌ ⚷♈	12:28 pm	**9:28 am**
☽♎ ☍ ☉♈	2:48 pm	**11:48 am**
☽♎ ☍ ⚷♈	3:38 pm	**12:38 pm**
☽♎ ⚻ ♅♉	3:40 pm	**12:40 pm**
☽♎ ☍ ♀♈	3:55 pm	**12:55 pm**
☽♎ △ ♄≈	7:21 pm	**4:21 pm**
☽♎ △ ♂♊		**10:12 pm**

Sun 28
2nd ♍
○ Full Moon 8 ♎ 18
Palm Sunday

Eastern Time plain / **Pacific Time bold**

	FEBRUARY							MARCH							APRIL					
S	M	T	W	T	F	S	S	M	T	W	T	F	S	S	M	T	W	T	F	S
	1	2	3	4	5	6		1	2	3	4	5	6					1	2	3
7	8	9	10	11	12	13	7	8	9	10	11	12	13	4	5	6	7	8	9	10
14	15	16	17	18	19	20	14	15	16	17	18	19	20	11	12	13	14	15	16	17
21	22	23	24	25	26	27	21	22	23	24	25	26	27	18	19	20	21	22	23	24
28							28	29	30	31				25	26	27	28	29	30	

29 MON
3rd ♎

☽☌△♂Ⅱ	1:12 am	
☉♈☌ ⚷♈	4:09 am	**1:09 am**
☽☌ ⊼ ☿♓	10:16 am	**7:16 am**
☽☌ ⊼ ♆♓	11:42 am	**8:42 am**
☽☌ △ ♃≈	2:01 pm	**11:01 am**
☽☌ □ ♀♑	8:08 pm	**5:08 pm** ☽ v/c
☿♓ ☌ ♆♓	11:24 pm	**8:24 pm**
☽ enters ♏		**10:33 pm**

30 TUE
3rd ♎

☽ enters ♏	1:33 am	
♀♈ ✶ ♄≈	11:47 am	**8:47 am**
☽♏ ⊼ ⚷♈	3:53 pm	**12:53 pm**
☽♏ ☍ ♅♉	3:54 pm	**12:54 pm**
☽♏ ⊼ ☉♈	6:16 pm	**3:16 pm**
☽♏ □ ♄≈	7:39 pm	**4:39 pm**
☽♏ ⊼ ♀♈	8:20 pm	**5:20 pm**

31 WED
3rd ♏

OP: After Moon squares Jupiter until v/c Moon. The difficult becomes easy during this highly affirming OP.

☽♏ ⊼ ♂Ⅱ	3:17 am	**12:17 am**
☽♏ △ ♆♓	11:59 am	**8:59 am**
☽♏ □ ♃≈	2:52 pm	**11:52 am**
☽♏ △ ☿♓	4:35 pm	**1:35 pm**
☉♈ ✶ ♄≈	5:04 pm	**2:04 pm**
☽♏ ✶ ♀♑	8:29 pm	**5:29 pm** ☽ v/c
☽ enters ♐		**10:59 pm**

1 THU
3rd ♏
APRIL FOOLS' DAY

☽ enters ♐	1:59 am	
☽♐ ⊼ ♅♉	4:54 pm	**1:54 pm**
☽♐ △ ⚷♈	4:55 pm	**1:55 pm**
☽♐ ✶ ♄≈	8:53 pm	**5:53 pm**
☽♐ △ ☉♈	10:46 pm	**7:46 pm**
☽♐ △ ♀♈		**10:56 pm**
☿♓ ✶ ♀♑		**11:04 pm**

☽♐ △ ♀♈ 1:56 am
☿♓ ⚹ ♇♑ 2:04 am
☽♐ ☍ ♂♊ 6:40 am **3:40 am**
☽♐ □ ♆♓ 1:42 pm **10:42 am**
☽♐ ⚹ ♃≈ 5:17 pm **2:17 pm**
☽♐ □ ☿♓ **10:24 pm** ☽ v/c

FRI 2
3rd ♐
GOOD FRIDAY

☽♐ □ ☿♓ 1:24 am ☽ v/c
☽ enters ♑ 4:13 am **1:13 am**
☽♑ △ ♅♉ 8:05 pm **5:05 pm**
☽♑ □ ♁♈ 8:07 pm **5:07 pm**
☿ enters ♈ 11:41 pm **8:41 pm**

SAT 3
3rd ♐
PASSOVER ENDS

☽♑ □ ☉♈ 6:02 am **3:02 am**
☽♑ □ ♀♈ 10:33 am **7:33 am**
☽♑ ⚺ ♂♊ 12:46 pm **9:46 am**
☽♑ ⚹ ♆♓ 5:55 pm **2:55 pm**

SUN 4
3rd ♑
◑ 4th Quarter 14 ♑ 51
EASTER

Eastern Time plain / **Pacific Time bold**

	MARCH					
S	M	T	W	T	F	S
	1	2	3	4	5	6
7	8	9	10	11	12	13
14	15	16	17	18	19	20
21	22	23	24	25	26	27
28	29	30	31			

	APRIL					
S	M	T	W	T	F	S
				1	2	3
4	5	6	7	8	9	10
11	12	13	14	15	16	17
18	19	20	21	22	23	24
25	26	27	28	29	30	

	MAY					
S	M	T	W	T	F	S
						1
2	3	4	5	6	7	8
9	10	11	12	13	14	15
16	17	18	19	20	21	22
23	24	25	26	27	28	29
30	31					

April

5 Mon
4th ♑

☽♑ ☌ ♇♑	3:05 am	**12:05 am** ☽ v/c
☽ enters ♒	9:04 am	**6:04 am**
☽♒ ⚹ ☿♈	2:19 pm	**11:19 am**
☽♒ □ ♅♉		**10:58 pm**
☽♒ ⚹ ⚷♈		**11:01 pm**

6 Tue
4th ♒

OP: After Moon conjoins Saturn today until v/c Moon on Wednesday. A favorable time to strengthen connections, make sales calls, schedule meetings, etc.

☽♒ □ ♅♉	1:58 am	
☽♒ ⚹ ⚷♈	2:01 am	
☽♒ ☌ ♄♒	6:32 am	**3:32 am**
♀♈ ⚹ ♂♊	7:18 am	**4:18 am**
☽♒ ⚹ ☉♈	4:40 pm	**1:40 pm**
☽♒ △ ♂♊	9:55 pm	**6:55 pm**
☽♒ ⚹ ♀♈	10:44 pm	**7:44 pm**

7 Wed
4th ♒

☽♒ ☌ ♃♒	6:05 am	**3:05 am** ☽ v/c
☽ enters ♓	4:30 pm	**1:30 pm**

8 Thu
4th ♓

☽♓ ⚹ ♅♉	10:24 am	**7:24 am**

☿♈ ☌ ♇♈	3:08 am	**12:08 am**
☽♓ □ ♂♊	9:49 am	**6:49 am**
☽♓ ☌ ♆♓	10:04 am	**7:04 am**
♂♊ □ ♆♓	3:18 pm	**12:18 pm**
☽♓ ⚹ ♀♑	7:48 pm	**4:48 pm** ☽ v/c
☽ enters ♈		**11:11 pm**

Fri 9
4th ♓

☽ enters ♈	2:11 am	
☿♈ ⚹ ♄♒	11:09 am	**8:09 am**
♀♈ ⚹ ♃♒	2:53 pm	**11:53 am**
☽♈ ☌ ♇♈	9:03 pm	**6:03 pm**
☽♈ ⚹ ♄♒		**11:01 pm**

Sat 10
4th ♓

☽♈ ⚹ ♄♒	2:01 am	
☽♈ ☌ ☿♈	4:46 am	**1:46 am**
☽♈ ☌ ☉♈	10:31 pm	**7:31 pm**
♀♈ □ ♀♑	11:20 pm	**8:20 pm**
☽♈ ⚹ ♂♊		**9:00 pm**

Sun 11
4th ♈

● New Moon 22 ♈ 25

OP: This Cazimi Moon is usable ½ hour before and ½ hour after the Sun-Moon conjunction. If you have something important to start around now, this is a great time to do it.

Eastern Time plain / **Pacific Time bold**

	MARCH					
S	M	T	W	T	F	S
	1	2	3	4	5	6
7	8	9	10	11	12	13
14	15	16	17	18	19	20
21	22	23	24	25	26	27
28	29	30	31			

	APRIL					
S	M	T	W	T	F	S
				1	2	3
4	5	6	7	8	9	10
11	12	13	14	15	16	17
18	19	20	21	22	23	24
25	26	27	28	29	30	

	MAY					
S	M	T	W	T	F	S
						1
2	3	4	5	6	7	8
9	10	11	12	13	14	15
16	17	18	19	20	21	22
23	24	25	26	27	28	29
30	31					

12 Mon
1st ♈

☽♈ ⚹ ♂Ⅱ	12:00 am	
☽♈ ⚹ ♃≈	4:24 am	**1:24 am**
☽♈ □ ♀♑	7:12 am	**4:12 am**
☽♈ ♂ ♀♈	8:06 am	**5:06 am** ☽ v/c
☽ enters ♉	1:44 pm	**10:44 am**

13 Tue
1st ♉
RAMADAN BEGINS

☽♉ ♂ ♅♉	9:18 am	**6:18 am**
☽♉ □ ♄≈	2:30 pm	**11:30 am**
☉♈ ⚹ ♂Ⅱ	7:09 pm	**4:09 pm**

14 Wed
1st ♉

OP: After Moon squares Jupiter today until Moon enters Gemini today or Thursday. (Taurus is one of the four signs in which the v/c Moon is a good thing. See page 75.) Now is an excellent time to invest in what you want to see grow.

☽♉ ⚹ ♆♓	10:03 am	**7:03 am**
♀ enters ♉	2:22 pm	**11:22 am**
☽♉ □ ♃≈	6:02 pm	**3:02 pm**
☽♉ △ ♀♑	8:00 pm	**5:00 pm** ☽ v/c
☽ enters Ⅱ		**11:35 pm**

15 Thu
1st ♉

☽ enters Ⅱ	2:35 am	
☉♈ ⚹ ♃≈	12:59 pm	**9:59 am**
☽Ⅱ ⚹ ♇♈	10:44 pm	**7:44 pm**

☽♊ △ ♄≈	3:53 am	**12:53 am**
☉♈ □ ♀♑	9:27 am	**6:27 am**
☽♊ □ ♆♓	11:15 pm	**8:15 pm**
♂♊ △ ♃≈		**10:14 pm**

Fri 16
1st ♊

♂♊ △ ♃≈	1:14 am	
☽♊ ⚹ ☿♈	7:05 am	**4:05 am**
☽♊ △ ♃≈	7:53 am	**4:53 am**
☽♊ ☌ ♂♊	8:08 am	**5:08 am**
☽♊ ⚻ ♀♑	8:58 am	**5:58 am**
☽♊ ⚹ ☉♈	11:03 am	**8:03 am** ☽ v/c
☿♈ ⚹ ♃≈	12:00 pm	**9:00 am**
☿♈ ⚹ ♂♊	3:09 pm	**12:09 pm**
☽ enters ♋	3:25 pm	**12:25 pm**
☿♈ □ ♀♑	5:49 pm	**2:49 pm**
☽♋ ⚹ ♀♉	11:49 pm	**8:49 pm**
♂♊ ⚻ ♀♑		**9:26 pm**

Sat 17
1st ♊

OP: After Moon conjoins Mars until v/c Moon. Although this OP is short, use it to communicate in a clear, effective way.

♂♊ ⚻ ♀♑	12:26 am	
☽♋ ⚹ ♅♉	11:19 am	**8:19 am**
☽♋ □ ♇♈	11:25 am	**8:25 am**
☽♋ ⚻ ♄≈	4:24 pm	**1:24 pm**
☉♈ ☌ ☿♈	9:50 pm	**6:50 pm**

Sun 18
1st ♋

MARCH						
S	M	T	W	T	F	S
	1	2	3	4	5	6
7	8	9	10	11	12	13
14	15	16	17	18	19	20
21	22	23	24	25	26	27
28	29	30	31			

APRIL						
S	M	T	W	T	F	S
				1	2	3
4	5	6	7	8	9	10
11	12	13	14	15	16	17
18	19	20	21	22	23	24
25	26	27	28	29	30	

MAY						
S	M	T	W	T	F	S
						1
2	3	4	5	6	7	8
9	10	11	12	13	14	15
16	17	18	19	20	21	22
23	24	25	26	27	28	29
30	31					

April

19 Mon

1st ♋
◐ 2nd Quarter 0 ♌ 25 (Pacific)
SUN ENTERS TAURUS

☿ enters ♉	6:29 am	**3:29 am**
☽♋ △ ♆ ♓	10:56 am	**7:56 am**
☉ enters ♉	4:33 pm	**1:33 pm**
☽♋ ⊼ ♃ ≈	7:49 pm	**4:49 pm**
☽♋ ☌ ♀ ♇ ♑	8:03 pm	**5:03 pm** ☽ v/c
☽ enters ♌		**11:11 pm**
☽♌ □ ☉ ♉		**11:59 pm**

20 Tue

1st ♋
◐ 2nd Quarter 0 ♌ 25 (Eastern)

☽ enters ♌	2:11 am	
☽♌ □ ☉ ♉	2:59 am	
☽♌ □ ☿ ♉	6:08 am	**3:08 am**
☽♌ □ ♀ ♉	4:21 pm	**1:21 pm**
☽♌ □ ♅ ♉	9:11 pm	**6:11 pm**
☽♌ △ ♆ ♈	9:16 pm	**6:16 pm**
☽♌ ☌ ♄ ≈		**10:56 pm**

21 Wed

2nd ♌

☽♌ ☌ ♄ ≈	1:56 am	
☽♌ ⊼ ♆ ♓	7:07 pm	**4:07 pm**

22 Thu

2nd ♌
EARTH DAY

OP: After Moon opposes Jupiter until v/c Moon. Early birds can take advantage of this OP to focus on communication, social activities, and self-encouragement.

☽♌ ⊼ ♀ ♑	3:29 am	**12:29 am**
☽♌ ☌ ♃ ≈	3:54 am	**12:54 am**
☽♌ ⚹ ♂ ♊	8:05 am	**5:05 am** ☽ v/c
☽ enters ♍	9:08 am	**6:08 am**
☽♍ △ ☉ ♉	2:06 pm	**11:06 am**
♀ ♉ ♂ ♅ ♉	9:01 pm	**6:01 pm**
☽♍ △ ☿ ♉	10:47 pm	**7:47 pm**
☽♍ △ ♅ ♉		**11:57 pm**

☽♍△♅♉	2:57 am	
☽♍⚼♂♈	3:02 am	**12:02 am**
☽♍△♀♉	3:30 am	**12:30 am**
☽♍⚼♄≈	7:19 am	**4:19 am**
♂ enters ♋	7:49 am	**4:49 am**
☽♍☍♆♓	11:10 pm	**8:10 pm**
☿♉♂♅♉		**11:42 pm**

Fri 23
2nd ♍

OP: After Moon opposes Neptune today until v/c Moon on Saturday. Night owls should wait for two hours after the opposition to clear their minds and reset for maximum productivity.

☿♉♂♅♉	2:42 am	
☽♍△♀♑	6:50 am	**3:50 am** ☽ v/c
☽♍⚼♃≈	7:47 am	**4:47 am**
☽ enters ♎	12:06 pm	**9:06 am**
☽♎□♂♋	1:19 pm	**10:19 am**
☽♎⚼☉♉	8:19 pm	**5:19 pm**
♀♉□♄≈		**9:22 pm**

Sat 24
2nd ♍

♀♉□♄≈	12:22 am	
☽♎⚼♅♉	4:58 am	**1:58 am**
☽♎☍♂♈	5:02 am	**2:02 am**
☿♉□♄≈	7:58 am	**4:58 am**
☽♎△♄≈	9:02 am	**6:02 am**
☽♎⚼☿♉	9:13 am	**6:13 am**
☽♎⚼♀♉	9:48 am	**6:48 am**
☿♉♂♀♉	6:19 pm	**3:19 pm**
☽♎⚼♆♓		**9:01 pm**

Sun 25
2nd ♎

Eastern Time plain / **Pacific Time bold**

MARCH						
S	M	T	W	T	F	S
	1	2	3	4	5	6
7	8	9	10	11	12	13
14	15	16	17	18	19	20
21	22	23	24	25	26	27
28	29	30	31			

APRIL						
S	M	T	W	T	F	S
				1	2	3
4	5	6	7	8	9	10
11	12	13	14	15	16	17
18	19	20	21	22	23	24
25	26	27	28	29	30	

MAY						
S	M	T	W	T	F	S
						1
2	3	4	5	6	7	8
9	10	11	12	13	14	15
16	17	18	19	20	21	22
23	24	25	26	27	28	29
30	31					

26 MON

2nd ♎︎

○ Full Moon 7 ♏︎ 06

OP: After Moon squares Pluto until v/c Moon. Another short OP for early birds, good for sending out important communication or anything that interests you.

☽︎ ♎︎ ⊼ ♆ ♓︎	12:01 am	
☽︎ ♎︎ □ ♀ ♑︎	7:15 am	**4:15 am**
☽︎ ♎︎ △ ♃ ♒︎	8:40 am	**5:40 am** ☽︎ v/c
☽︎ enters ♏︎	12:18 pm	**9:18 am**
☽︎ ♏︎ △ ♂ ♋︎	3:29 pm	**12:29 pm**
☽︎ ♏︎ ☍ ☉ ♉︎	11:32 pm	**8:32 pm**

27 TUE

3rd ♏︎

PLUTO RETROGRADE

☽︎ ♏︎ ☍ ♅ ♉︎	4:51 am	**1:51 am**
☽︎ ♏︎ ⊼ ♁ ♈︎	4:54 am	**1:54 am**
☽︎ ♏︎ □ ♄ ♒︎	8:47 am	**5:47 am**
☽︎ ♏︎ ☍ ♀ ♉︎	1:35 pm	**10:35 am**
♀℞	4:04 pm	**1:04 pm**
☽︎ ♏︎ ☍ ☿ ♉︎	4:24 pm	**1:24 pm**
☽︎ ♏︎ △ ♆ ♓︎	11:31 pm	**8:31 pm**

28 WED

3rd ♏︎

☽︎ ♏︎ ✶ ♀ ♑︎	6:38 am	**3:38 am**
☽︎ ♏︎ □ ♃ ♒︎	8:31 am	**5:31 am** ☽︎ v/c
☽︎ enters ♐︎	11:42 am	**8:42 am**
☽︎ ♐︎ ⊼ ♂ ♋︎	4:54 pm	**1:54 pm**
☽︎ ♐︎ ⊼ ☉ ♉︎		**11:20 pm**

29 THU

3rd ♐︎

OP: After Moon squares Neptune today until Moon enters Capricorn on Friday. The path is clear to setting lofty goals and sparking inspiration.

☽︎ ♐︎ ⊼ ☉ ♉︎	2:20 am	
☽︎ ♐︎ ⊼ ♅ ♉︎	4:38 am	**1:38 am**
☽︎ ♐︎ △ ♁ ♈︎	4:40 am	**1:40 am**
☽︎ ♐︎ ✶ ♄ ♒︎	8:36 am	**5:36 am**
☽︎ ♐︎ ⊼ ♀ ♉︎	5:44 pm	**2:44 pm**
☿ ♉︎ ✶ ♆ ♓︎	10:27 pm	**7:27 pm**
☽︎ ♐︎ □ ♆ ♓︎	11:42 pm	**8:42 pm**
☽︎ ♐︎ ⊼ ☿ ♉︎	11:54 pm	**8:54 pm**

Fri 30
3rd ♐
Orthodox Good Friday

☽♐ ✶ ♃♒	9:27 am	**6:27 am**	☽ v/c
☽ enters ♑	12:16 pm	**9:16 am**	
☉♉ ☌ ♅♉	3:54 pm	**12:54 pm**	
☽♑ ☍ ♂♋	7:51 pm	**4:51 pm**	

Sat 1
3rd ♑
Beltane

☽♑ △ ♅♉	6:13 am	**3:13 am**
☽♑ □ ⚷♈	6:14 am	**3:14 am**
☽♑ △ ☉♉	7:12 am	**4:12 am**
☽♑ △ ♀♉		**9:42 pm**
☽♑ ✶ ♆♓		**11:16 pm**

OP: After Moon trines Uranus today (see "Translating Darkness" on page 78) until v/c Moon on Sunday. This productive OP is good for ambitious projects, especially if you're familiar with strong Pluto energy.

Sun 2
3rd ♑
Orthodox Easter

☽♑ △ ♀♉	12:42 am		
☽♑ ✶ ♆♓	2:16 am		
☿♉ △ ♇♑	5:19 am	**2:19 am**	
☽♑ ☌ ♇♑	9:54 am	**6:54 am**	
☽♑ △ ☿♉	10:38 am	**7:38 am**	☽ v/c
☽ enters ♒	3:31 pm	**12:31 pm**	
♀♉ ✶ ♆♓	6:38 pm	**3:38 pm**	
☽♒ ⚻ ♂♋		**11:02 pm**	

Eastern Time plain / **Pacific Time bold**

APRIL

S	M	T	W	T	F	S
				1	2	3
4	5	6	7	8	9	10
11	12	13	14	15	16	17
18	19	20	21	22	23	24
25	26	27	28	29	30	

MAY

S	M	T	W	T	F	S
						1
2	3	4	5	6	7	8
9	10	11	12	13	14	15
16	17	18	19	20	21	22
23	24	25	26	27	28	29
30	31					

JUNE

S	M	T	W	T	F	S
		1	2	3	4	5
6	7	8	9	10	11	12
13	14	15	16	17	18	19
20	21	22	23	24	25	26
27	28	29	30			

MAY

3 MON

3rd ≈≈
◐ 4th Quarter 13 ≈≈ 35

☽≈≈ ⊼ ♂⊛	2:02 am	
☿♉ □ ♃≈≈	5:33 am	**2:33 am**
⊙♉ □ ♄≈≈	6:02 am	**3:02 am**
☽≈≈ ⚹ ⚷♈	10:52 am	**7:52 am**
☽≈≈ □ ♅♉	10:52 am	**7:52 am**
☽≈≈ ♂ ♄≈≈	3:08 pm	**12:08 pm**
☽≈≈ □ ⊙♉	3:50 pm	**12:50 pm**
☿ enters ♊	10:49 pm	**7:49 pm**

4 TUE

4th ≈≈

OP: After Moon squares Venus until v/c Moon. With the Moon between benefic planets, this OP is good for anything that catches your interest.

☽≈≈ □ ♀♉	12:00 pm	**9:00 am**	
☽≈≈ ♂ ♃≈≈	8:05 pm	**5:05 pm** ☽ v/c
☽ enters ♓	10:09 pm	**7:09 pm**	
☽♓ □ ☿♊		**10:54 pm**	

5 WED

4th ♓
CINCO DE MAYO

☽♓ □ ☿♊	1:54 am	
☽♓ △ ♂⊛	12:07 pm	**9:07 am**
☽♓ ⚹ ♅♉	6:57 pm	**3:57 pm**

6 THU

4th ♓

OP: After Moon sextiles Pluto today or Friday until Moon enters Aries on Friday. Take advantage of this OP to finish projects or clear away unnecessary clutter during the Last Quarter Moon.

☽♓ ⚹ ⊙♉	4:41 am	**1:41 am**
♀♉ △ ♇♑	7:25 am	**4:25 am**
☽♓ ♂ ♆♓	5:17 pm	**2:17 pm**
☽♓ ⚹ ♀♑		**10:34 pm**

FRI 7
4th ♓

☽♓ ⚹ ♇♑	1:34 am	
☽♓ ⚹ ♀♉	3:36 am	**12:36 am** ☽ v/c
☽ enters ♈	7:52 am	**4:52 am**
☽♈ ⚹ ☿♊	9:01 pm	**6:01 pm**
☽♈ □ ♂♋		**10:35 pm**

SAT 8
4th ♈

☽♈ □ ♂♋	1:35 am	
☽♈ ☌ ⚷♈	5:48 am	**2:48 am**
♀♉ □ ♃♒	9:38 am	**6:38 am**
☽♈ ⚹ ♄♒	10:18 am	**7:18 am**
♀ enters ♊	10:01 pm	**7:01 pm**

SUN 9
4th ♈
MOTHER'S DAY

☽♈ □ ♇♑	1:16 pm	**10:16 am**
☽♈ ⚹ ♃♒	6:50 pm	**3:50 pm** ☽ v/c
☽ enters ♉	7:46 pm	**4:46 pm**

OP: After Moon squares Pluto until v/c Moon. Same advice as for last Thursday.

Eastern Time plain / **Pacific Time bold**

APRIL

S	M	T	W	T	F	S
				1	2	3
4	5	6	7	8	9	10
11	12	13	14	15	16	17
18	19	20	21	22	23	24
25	26	27	28	29	30	

MAY

S	M	T	W	T	F	S
						1
2	3	4	5	6	7	8
9	10	11	12	13	14	15
16	17	18	19	20	21	22
23	24	25	26	27	28	29
30	31					

JUNE

S	M	T	W	T	F	S
		1	2	3	4	5
6	7	8	9	10	11	12
13	14	15	16	17	18	19
20	21	22	23	24	25	26
27	28	29	30			

10 Mon
4th ☌

☽ ☿ ⚹ ♂ ⏣	5:12 pm	**2:12 pm**
☽ ☿ ♂ ♅ ☿	6:35 pm	**3:35 pm**
☿ ♊ ⚹ ☙ ♈	10:44 pm	**7:44 pm**
☽ ☿ □ ♄ ≈	10:55 pm	**7:55 pm**

11 Tue
4th ☿

● New Moon 21 ☿ 18

RAMADAN ENDS

OP: **This Cazimi Moon is usable ½ hour before and ½ hour after the Sun-Moon conjunction.** If you have something important to start around now, this is a great time to do it.

☽ ☿ ♂ ☉ ☿	3:00 pm	**12:00 pm**
☽ ☿ ⚹ ♆ ♓	5:47 pm	**2:47 pm**
♂ ⏣ □ ☙ ♈	7:54 pm	**4:54 pm**
♂ ⏣ ⚹ ♅ ☿	10:48 pm	**7:48 pm**
☽ ☿ △ ♀ ♑		**11:07 pm**

12 Wed
1st ☿

☽ ☿ △ ♀ ♑	2:07 am	
☽ ☿ □ ♃ ≈	8:23 am	**5:23 am** ☽ v/c
☽ enters ♊	8:43 am	**5:43 am**
☿ ♊ △ ♄ ≈	2:34 pm	**11:34 am**
☽ ♊ ♂ ♀ ♊	6:20 pm	**3:20 pm**
☉ ☿ ⚹ ♆ ♓		**10:45 pm**

13 Thu
1st ♊

☉ ☿ ⚹ ♆ ♓	1:45 am	
☽ ♊ ⚹ ☙ ♈	7:45 am	**4:45 am**
☽ ♊ △ ♄ ≈	12:03 pm	**9:03 am**
☽ ♊ ♂ ☿ ♊	2:32 pm	**11:32 am**
♃ enters ♓	6:36 pm	**3:36 pm**

Fri 14
1st ♊

☽♊ □ ♆♓	6:51 am	**3:51 am**	☽ v/c
☽♊ ⚻ ♇♑	2:57 pm	**11:57 am**	
☽ enters ♋	9:30 pm	**6:30 pm**	
☽♋ △ ♃♓	9:45 pm	**6:45 pm**	

Sat 15
1st ♋

♂♋ ⚻ ♄♒	10:49 am	**7:49 am**	
☽♋ □ ⚷♈	8:22 pm	**5:22 pm**	
☽♋ ⚹ ♅♉	8:35 pm	**5:35 pm**	
☽♋ ⚻ ♄♒		**9:24 pm**	
☽♋ ☌ ♂♋		**10:06 pm**	

Sun 16
1st ♋
Shavuot begins at sundown

☽♋ ⚻ ♄♒	12:24 am		
☽♋ ☌ ♂♋	1:06 am		
☽♋ △ ♆♓	6:42 pm	**3:42 pm**	
☽♋ ⚹ ☉♉		**11:05 pm**	
☽♋ ☍ ♇♑		**11:23 pm**	☽ v/c

Eastern Time plain / **Pacific Time bold**

APRIL

S	M	T	W	T	F	S
				1	2	3
4	5	6	7	8	9	10
11	12	13	14	15	16	17
18	19	20	21	22	23	24
25	26	27	28	29	30	

MAY

S	M	T	W	T	F	S
						1
2	3	4	5	6	7	8
9	10	11	12	13	14	15
16	17	18	19	20	21	22
23	24	25	26	27	28	29
30	31					

JUNE

S	M	T	W	T	F	S
		1	2	3	4	5
6	7	8	9	10	11	12
13	14	15	16	17	18	19
20	21	22	23	24	25	26
27	28	29	30			

17 MON
1st ⊙

☽ ⊙ ⚹ ☉ ♉	2:05 am	
☽ ⊙ ☍ ♀ ♑	2:23 am	☽ v/c
☉ ♉ △ ♀ ♑	5:49 am	**2:49 am**
☽ enters ♌	8:44 am	**5:44 am**
☽ ♌ ⚻ ♃ ♓	9:29 am	**6:29 am**

18 TUE
1st ♌

OP: After Moon opposes Saturn today until v/c Moon on Wednesday. Wait two hours after the opposition to tap into this OP good for building rapport.

☽ ♌ ⚹ ♀ ♊	6:43 am	**3:43 am**
☽ ♌ △ ♅ ♈	6:48 am	**3:48 am**
☽ ♌ □ ♅ ♉	7:04 am	**4:04 am**
♀ ♊ ⚹ ♅ ♈	7:44 am	**4:44 am**
☽ ♌ ☍ ♄ ≈	10:29 am	**7:29 am**
☽ ♌ ⚹ ☿ ♊	10:55 pm	**7:55 pm**

19 WED
1st ♌
◗ 2nd Quarter 29 ♌ 01

☽ ♌ ⚻ ♆ ♓	3:51 am	**12:51 am**
☽ ♌ ⚻ ♀ ♑	10:58 am	**7:58 am**
☽ ♌ □ ⊙ ♉	3:13 pm	**12:13 pm** ☽ v/c
☽ enters ♍	4:59 pm	**1:59 pm**
☽ ♍ ☍ ♃ ♓	6:07 pm	**3:07 pm**
♀ ♊ △ ♄ ≈	9:58 pm	**6:58 pm**

20 THU
2nd ♍
SUN ENTERS GEMINI

☽ ♍ ⚻ ♅ ♈	1:51 pm	**10:51 am**
☽ ♍ △ ♅ ♉	2:09 pm	**11:09 am**
⊙ enters ♊	3:37 pm	**12:37 pm**
☽ ♍ ⚻ ♄ ≈	5:08 pm	**2:08 pm**
☽ ♍ □ ♀ ♊	7:01 pm	**4:01 pm**
☽ ♍ ⚹ ♂ ⊙	10:57 pm	**7:57 pm**

Mercury Note: Mercury enters its Storm (moving less than 40 minutes of arc per day) on Saturday, as it slows down before going retrograde. The Storm acts like the retrograde. Not favorable for new projects—just follow through with the items that are already on your plate. Write down new ideas with date and time they occurred.

☽♍ □ ☿ ♊	7:47 am	**4:47 am**
☽♍ ☍ ♆ ♓	9:24 am	**6:24 am**
☉♊ □ ♃ ♓	11:03 am	**8:03 am**
☽♍ △ ♀ ♑	3:56 pm	**12:56 pm** ☽ v/c
☽ enters ♎	9:35 pm	**6:35 pm**
☽♎ ⊼ ♃ ♓	10:59 pm	**7:59 pm**
☽♎ △ ☉ ♊	11:46 pm	**8:46 pm**

FRI 21
2nd ♍

☽♎ ☍ ⚷ ♈	5:15 pm	**2:15 pm**
☽♎ ⊼ ♅ ♉	5:34 pm	**2:34 pm**
☽♎ △ ♄ ♒	8:11 pm	**5:11 pm**
☿♊ □ ♆ ♓	10:43 pm	**7:43 pm**
☽♎ △ ♀ ♊		**11:36 pm**

SAT 22
2nd ♎

☽♎ △ ♀ ♊	2:36 am	
☽♎ □ ♂♋	3:51 am	**12:51 am**
♄℞	5:21 am	**2:21 am**
☽♎ ⊼ ♆ ♓	11:33 am	**8:33 am**
☽♎ △ ☿ ♊	11:59 am	**8:59 am**
☽♎ □ ♀ ♑	5:36 pm	**2:36 pm** ☽ v/c
☽ enters ♏	11:00 pm	**8:00 pm**
☽♏ △ ♃ ♓		**9:37 pm**

SUN 23
2nd ♎
SATURN RETROGRADE

Eastern Time plain / **Pacific Time bold**

	APRIL					
S	M	T	W	T	F	S
				1	2	3
4	5	6	7	8	9	10
11	12	13	14	15	16	17
18	19	20	21	22	23	24
25	26	27	28	29	30	

	MAY					
S	M	T	W	T	F	S
						1
2	3	4	5	6	7	8
9	10	11	12	13	14	15
16	17	18	19	20	21	22
23	24	25	26	27	28	29
30	31					

	JUNE					
S	M	T	W	T	F	S
		1	2	3	4	5
6	7	8	9	10	11	12
13	14	15	16	17	18	19
20	21	22	23	24	25	26
27	28	29	30			

MAY

24 Mon
2nd ♏
Victoria Day (Canada)

☽♏ △ ♃ ♓	12:37 am	
☽♏ ⊼ ☉ ♊	4:28 am	**1:28 am**
☽♏ ⊼ ♅ ♈	5:54 am	**2:54 pm**
☽♏ ☍ ♅ ♉	6:15 am	**3:15 pm**
☽♏ □ ♄ ≈	8:35 pm	**5:35 pm**

25 Tue
2nd ♏

☽♏ △ ♂ ♋	6:01 am	**3:01 am**
☽♏ ⊼ ♀ ♊	7:01 am	**4:01 am**
☽♏ △ ♆ ♓	11:30 am	**8:30 am**
☽♏ ⊼ ☿ ♊	1:13 pm	**10:13 am**
☽♏ ✶ ♀ ♑	5:20 pm	**2:20 pm** ☽ v/c
☽ enters ♐	10:39 pm	**7:39 pm**
☽♐ □ ♃ ♓		**9:30 pm**

26 Wed
2nd ♐
Lunar Eclipse | ◯ Full Moon 5 ♐ 26

☽♐ □ ♃ ♓	12:30 am	
☽♐ ☍ ☉ ♊	7:14 am	**4:14 am**
☽♐ △ ♅ ♈	5:29 pm	**2:29 pm**
☽♐ ⊼ ♅ ♉	5:52 pm	**2:52 pm**
☽♐ ✶ ♄ ≈	8:01 pm	**5:01 pm**

27 Thu
3rd ♐

☽♐ ⊼ ♂ ♋	7:31 am	**4:31 am**
☽♐ ☍ ♀ ♊	10:43 am	**7:43 am**
☽♐ □ ♆ ♓	11:06 am	**8:06 am**
☽♐ ☍ ☿ ♊	1:35 pm	**10:35 am** ☽ v/c
♀♊ □ ♆ ♓	3:25 pm	**12:25 pm**
☽ enters ♑	10:23 pm	**7:23 pm**
☽♑ ✶ ♃ ♓		**9:31 pm**

MAY

Mercury Note: Mercury goes retrograde on Saturday, May 29, and remains so until June 22, after which it will still be in its Storm until June 30. Projects initiated during this entire period may not work out as planned. It's best to use this time for reviews, editing, escrows, and so forth.

FRI 28
3rd ♑

☽♑ ⚹ ♃♓	12:31 am	
☽♑ ⊼ ☉♊	10:32 am	**7:32 am**
☽♑ □ ♂♈	5:54 pm	**2:54 pm**
☽♑ △ ♅♉	6:22 pm	**3:22 pm**
☿♊ ♂ ♀♊		**10:13 pm**

SAT 29
3rd ♑
MERCURY RETROGRADE

☿♊ ♂ ♀♊	1:13 am	
☽♑ ☍ ♂♋	10:36 am	**7:36 am**
☽♑ ⚹ ♆♓	12:13 pm	**9:13 am**
☽♑ ⊼ ☿♊	3:07 pm	**12:07 pm**
☽♑ ⊼ ♀♊	4:23 pm	**1:23 pm**
☽♑ ♂ ♀♑	6:15 pm	**3:15 pm** ☽ v/c
☿ ℞	6:34 pm	**3:34 pm**
☽ enters ♒		**9:04 pm**

SUN 30
3rd ♑

☽ enters ♒	12:04 am	
♀♊ ⊼ ♀♑	1:47 pm	**10:47 am**
☽♒ △ ☉♊	4:43 pm	**1:43 pm**
☽♒ ⚹ ♂♈	8:57 pm	**5:57 pm**
☽♒ □ ♅♉	9:30 pm	**6:30 pm**
☽♒ ♂ ♄♒	11:25 pm	**8:25 pm**
♂♋ △ ♆♓		**10:15 pm**

OP: After Moon conjoins Saturn today until v/c Moon on Monday or Tuesday. Wait two hours after the conjunction for this very positive OP. As we're between eclipses and Mercury is retrograde, use it to attend to matters started before May 22.

Eastern Time plain / **Pacific Time bold**

	APRIL					
S	M	T	W	T	F	S
				1	2	3
4	5	6	7	8	9	10
11	12	13	14	15	16	17
18	19	20	21	22	23	24
25	26	27	28	29	30	

	MAY					
S	M	T	W	T	F	S
						1
2	3	4	5	6	7	8
9	10	11	12	13	14	15
16	17	18	19	20	21	22
23	24	25	26	27	28	29
30	31					

	JUNE					
S	M	T	W	T	F	S
		1	2	3	4	5
6	7	8	9	10	11	12
13	14	15	16	17	18	19
20	21	22	23	24	25	26
27	28	29	30			

31 Mon
3rd ♒
Memorial Day

♂♋ △ ♆♓	1:15 am	
☽♒ ⚻ ♂♋	5:11 pm	**2:11 pm**
☽♒ △ ☿♊	7:13 pm	**4:13 pm**
☽♒ △ ♀♊		**11:14 pm** ☽ v/c

1 Tue
3rd ♒

☽♒ △ ♀♊	2:14 am	☽ v/c
☽ enters ♓	5:07 am	**2:07 am**
☽♓ ☌ ♃♓	8:04 am	**5:04 am**

2 Wed
3rd ♓
◑ 4th Quarter 11 ♓ 59

☽♓ □ ☉♊	3:24 am	**12:24 am**
☽♓ ⚹ ♅♉	4:22 am	**1:22 am**
☉♊ ⚹ ⚷♈	7:23 am	**4:23 am**
♀ enters ♋	9:19 am	**6:19 am**
☽♓ ☌ ♆♓		**9:31 pm**
☽♓ □ ☿♊		**11:24 pm**

3 Thu
4th ♓

OP: After Moon squares Mercury on Wednesday or today until Moon enters Aries today. Great OP to let go of toxic emotions and create harmony within, helped by the trine between Venus and Jupiter. Same warning as for last Sunday.

☽♓ ☌ ♆♓	12:31 am	
☽♓ □ ☿♊	2:24 am	
☽♓ △ ♂♋	4:08 am	**1:08 am**
☽♓ ⚹ ♇♑	7:10 am	**4:10 am** ☽ v/c
☽ enters ♈	1:59 pm	**10:59 am**
☉♊ △ ♄♒	3:05 pm	**12:05 pm**
☽♈ □ ♀♋	5:09 pm	**2:09 pm**
♀♋ △ ♃♓	7:33 pm	**4:33 pm**

Fri 4
4th ♈

☽♈ ☌ ⚷♈ 2:05 pm **11:05 am**
☽♈ ⚹ ♄♒ 4:24 pm **1:24 pm**
☽♈ ⚹ ☉♊ 6:38 pm **3:38 pm**

Sat 5
4th ♈

☽♈ ⚹ ☿♊ 11:56 am **8:56 am**
☿♊ □ ♆♓ 3:05 pm **12:05 pm**
♂♋ ☍ ♇♑ 3:45 pm **12:45 pm**
☽♈ □ ♇♑ 6:37 pm **3:37 pm**
☽♈ □ ♂♋ 6:47 pm **3:47 pm** ☽ v/c
☽ enters ♉ **10:46 pm**

Sun 6
4th ♈

☽ enters ♉ 1:46 am
☽♉ ⚹ ♃♓ 5:32 am **2:32 am**
☽♉ ⚹ ♀♋ 11:57 am **8:57 am**

Eastern Time plain / **Pacific Time bold**

MAY

S	M	T	W	T	F	S
						1
2	3	4	5	6	7	8
9	10	11	12	13	14	15
16	17	18	19	20	21	22
23	24	25	26	27	28	29
30	31					

JUNE

S	M	T	W	T	F	S
		1	2	3	4	5
6	7	8	9	10	11	12
13	14	15	16	17	18	19
20	21	22	23	24	25	26
27	28	29	30			

JULY

S	M	T	W	T	F	S
				1	2	3
4	5	6	7	8	9	10
11	12	13	14	15	16	17
18	19	20	21	22	23	24
25	26	27	28	29	30	31

JUNE

7 MON
4th ♉

☽♉ ♂ ♅♉	3:39 am	**12:39 am**
☽♉ □ ♄≈	4:51 am	**1:51 am**
☽♉ ⚹ ♆♓		**9:47 pm**

8 TUE
4th ♉

☽♉ ⚹ ♆♓	12:47 am	
☽♉ △ ♀♑	7:30 am	**4:30 am**
☽♉ ⚹ ♂♋	11:07 am	**8:07 am** ☽ v/c
☽ enters ♊	2:47 pm	**11:47 am**
☽♊ □ ♃♓	6:47 pm	**3:47 pm**

9 WED
4th ♊

☽♊ ⚹ ♁♈	3:56 pm	**12:56 pm**
☽♊ △ ♄≈	5:44 pm	**2:44 pm**

10 THU
4th ♊
Solar Eclipse | ● New Moon 19 ♊ 47

☽♊ ♂ ☉♊	6:53 am	**3:53 am**
☽♊ ♂ ☿♊	8:37 am	**5:37 am**
☽♊ □ ♆♓	1:38 pm	**10:38 am** ☽ v/c
☽♊ ⊼ ♀♑	8:07 pm	**5:07 pm**
☉♊ ♂ ☿♊	9:13 pm	**6:13 pm**

Fri 11
1st ♊

☽ enters ♋ 3:23 am **12:23 am**
☽♋ △ ♃♓ 7:28 am **4:28 am**
♂ enters ♌ 9:34 am **6:34 am**
☽♋ ☌ ♀♋ **11:59 pm**

Sat 12
1st ♋

☽♋ ☌ ♀♋ 2:59 am
☽♋ □ ⚷♈ 4:07 am **1:07 am**
☽♋ ⚹ ♅♉ 5:11 am **2:11 am**
☽♋ ⚻ ♄♒ 5:35 am **2:35 am**
♀♋ □ ⚷♈ 2:28 pm **11:28 am**
☽♋ △ ♆♓ **10:06 pm**
♀♋ ⚹ ♅♉ **10:38 pm**

Sun 13
1st ♋

☽♋ △ ♆♓ 1:06 am
♀♋ ⚹ ♅♉ 1:38 am
♀♋ ⚻ ♄♒ 4:15 am **1:15 am**
☽♋ ☍ ♇♑ 7:16 am **4:16 am** ☽ v/c
☽ enters ♌ 2:22 pm **11:22 am**
☽♌ ☌ ♂♌ 5:08 pm **2:08 pm**
☽♌ ⚻ ♃♓ 6:27 pm **3:27 pm**
☉♊ □ ♆♓ 7:40 pm **4:40 pm**

Eastern Time plain / **Pacific Time bold**

MAY

S	M	T	W	T	F	S
						1
2	3	4	5	6	7	8
9	10	11	12	13	14	15
16	17	18	19	20	21	22
23	24	25	26	27	28	29
30	31					

JUNE

S	M	T	W	T	F	S
		1	2	3	4	5
6	7	8	9	10	11	12
13	14	15	16	17	18	19
20	21	22	23	24	25	26
27	28	29	30			

JULY

S	M	T	W	T	F	S
				1	2	3
4	5	6	7	8	9	10
11	12	13	14	15	16	17
18	19	20	21	22	23	24
25	26	27	28	29	30	31

14 Mon
1st ♌
FLAG DAY

OP: After Moon opposes Saturn today until v/c Moon on Tuesday. Wait two hours after the opposition, then use this favorable OP for ongoing projects. With Mercury retrograde, keep your focus on reviews and repairs.

☽♌ △ ♂♈	2:20 pm	**11:20 am**	
☽♌ □ ♅♉	3:27 pm	**12:27 pm**	
☽♌ ☌ ♄≈	3:28 pm	**12:28 pm**	
♄≈ □ ♅♉	6:01 pm	**3:01 pm**	
♂♌ ⚻ ♃♓	8:39 pm	**5:39 pm**	
☽♌ ⚹ ☿♊		**9:58 pm**	

15 Tue
1st ♌

☽♌ ⚹ ☿♊	12:58 am		
☽♌ ⚻ ♆♓	10:22 am	**7:22 am**	
☽♌ ⚹ ☉♊	1:27 pm	**10:27 am**	☽ v/c
☽♌ ⚻ ♀♑	4:10 pm	**1:10 pm**	
☽ enters ♍	11:02 pm	**8:02 pm**	

16 Wed
1st ♍

☽♍ ☌ ♃♓	3:00 am	**12:00 am**	
☽♍ ⚻ ♂♈	9:58 pm	**6:58 pm**	
☽♍ ⚻ ♄≈	10:47 pm	**7:47 pm**	
☽♍ △ ♅♉	11:07 pm	**8:07 pm**	
☉♊ ⚻ ♀♑		**10:24 pm**	

17 Thu
1st ♍
● 2nd Quarter 27 ♍ 09

☉♊ ⚻ ♀♑	1:24 am		
☽♍ □ ☿♊	6:16 am	**3:16 am**	
☽♍ ⚹ ♀♋	8:07 am	**5:07 am**	
☽♍ ☌ ♆♓	4:55 pm	**1:55 pm**	
☽♍ △ ♀♑	10:18 pm	**7:18 pm**	
☽♍ □ ☉♊	11:54 pm	**8:54 pm**	☽ v/c

☽ enters ♎	4:54 am	**1:54 am**
☽♎☍ ♃ ♓	8:41 am	**5:41 am**
☽♎⚹ ♂♌	12:32 pm	**9:32 am**
☽♎☍ ⚷ ♈		**11:43 pm**

Fri 18
2nd ♍

☽♎☍ ⚷ ♈	2:43 am	
☽♎△ ♄ ≈	3:15 am	**12:15 am**
☽♎☌ ♅ ♉	3:53 am	**12:53 am**
☽♎△ ☿ ♊	9:22 am	**6:22 am**
☽♎□ ♀♋	5:07 pm	**2:07 pm**
☽♎☍ ♆ ♓	8:36 pm	**5:36 pm**
☽♎□ ♀♑		**10:37 pm**

Sat 19
2nd ♎

OP: After Moon squares Pluto today or Sunday until v/c Moon on Sunday. Good for networking and reaching out to important people. Same Mercury retrograde warning as last Monday.

☽♎□ ♀♑	1:37 am	

☽♎△☉♊	6:52 am	**3:52 am** ☽ v/c
☽ enters ♏	7:58 am	**4:58 am**
♃℞	11:06 am	**8:06 am**
☽♏△ ♃ ♓	11:35 am	**8:35 am**
☽♏□ ♂♌	5:29 pm	**2:29 pm**
☉ enters ♋	11:32 pm	**8:32 pm**

Sun 20
2nd ♎
Father's Day
Jupiter retrograde
Summer Solstice
Litha
Sun enters Cancer

Eastern Time plain / **Pacific Time bold**

	MAY								JUNE								JULY				
S	M	T	W	T	F	S		S	M	T	W	T	F	S		S	M	T	W	T	F	S
						1				1	2	3	4	5						1	2	3
2	3	4	5	6	7	8		6	7	8	9	10	11	12		4	5	6	7	8	9	10
9	10	11	12	13	14	15		13	14	15	16	17	18	19		11	12	13	14	15	16	17
16	17	18	19	20	21	22		20	21	22	23	24	25	26		18	19	20	21	22	23	24
23	24	25	26	27	28	29		27	28	29	30					25	26	27	28	29	30	31
30	31																					

June

Mercury Note: Mercury goes direct on Tuesday, June 22, but remains in its Storm, moving slowly, until June 30.

21 Mon

2nd ♏

OP: After Moon opposes Uranus today until v/c Moon today or Tuesday. Aided by the grand trine in watery signs, this OP inspires emotions and intuition.

☽♏ ⚻ ⚷♈	4:51 am	**1:51 am**	
☽♏ □ ♄♒	5:09 am	**2:09 am**	
☽♏ ☍ ♅♉	6:02 am	**3:02 am**	
♀♋ △ ♆♓	9:57 am	**6:57 am**	
☽♏ ⚻ ☿♊	10:35 am	**7:35 am**	
☽♏ △ ♆♓	9:57 pm	**6:57 pm**	
☽♏ △ ♀♋	11:01 pm	**8:01 pm**	
☽♏ ⚹ ♇♑		**11:43 pm**	☽ v/c

22 Tue

2nd ♏

Mercury direct

☽♏ ⚹ ♇♑	2:43 am		☽ v/c
☽ enters ♐	8:55 am	**5:55 am**	
☽♐ ⚻ ☉♋	11:12 am	**8:12 am**	
☽♐ □ ♃♓	12:26 pm	**9:26 am**	
☿ D	6:00 pm	**3:00 pm**	
☽♐ △ ♂♌	8:17 pm	**5:17 pm**	

23 Wed

2nd ♐

☽♐ △ ⚷♈	5:20 am	**2:20 am**	
☽♐ ⚹ ♄♒	5:25 am	**2:25 am**	
☉♋ △ ♃♓	6:11 am	**3:11 am**	
☽♐ ⚻ ♅♉	6:35 am	**3:35 am**	
☽♐ ☍ ☿♊	10:50 am	**7:50 am**	
♀♋ ☍ ♇♑	7:39 pm	**4:39 pm**	
☽♐ □ ♆♓	10:09 pm	**7:09 pm**	☽ v/c
♄♒ ⚹ ⚷♈		**9:30 pm**	

24 Thu

2nd ♐

○ Full Moon 3 ♑ 28

♄♒ ⚹ ⚷♈	12:30 am	
☽♐ ⚻ ♀♋	3:28 am	**12:28 am**
☽ enters ♑	9:05 am	**6:05 am**
☽♑ ⚹ ♃♓	12:33 pm	**9:33 am**
☽♑ ☍ ☉♋	2:40 pm	**11:40 am**
☽♑ ⚻ ♂♌	10:35 pm	**7:35 pm**

☽♑ □ ⚷♈ 5:43 am **2:43 am**
☽♑ △ ♅♉ 7:04 am **4:04 am**
☽♑ ⊼ ☿♊ 11:42 am **8:42 am**
♆℞ 3:21 pm **12:21 pm**
☽♑ ✶ ♆♓ 10:51 pm **7:51 pm**

FRI 25
3rd ♑
NEPTUNE RETROGRADE

☽♑ ☌ ♇♑ 3:36 am **12:36 am**
☽♑ ☍ ♀♋ 8:49 am **5:49 am** ☽ v/c
☽ enters ♒ 10:09 am **7:09 am**
☽♒ ⊼ ☉♋ 7:29 pm **4:29 pm**
♀ enters ♌ **9:27 pm**
☽♒ ☍ ♂♌ **11:30 pm**

SAT 26
3rd ♑

♀ enters ♌ 12:27 am
☽♒ ☍ ♂♌ 2:30 am
☽♒ ☌ ♄♒ 7:23 am **4:23 am**
☽♒ ✶ ⚷♈ 7:46 am **4:46 am**
☽♒ □ ♅♉ 9:16 am **6:16 am**
☽♒ △ ☿♊ 3:08 pm **12:08 pm** ☽ v/c

SUN 27
3rd ♒

Eastern Time plain / **Pacific Time bold**

		MAY								JUNE								JULY			
S	M	T	W	T	F	S		S	M	T	W	T	F	S		S	M	T	W	T	F	S
						1				1	2	3	4	5						1	2	3
2	3	4	5	6	7	8		6	7	8	9	10	11	12		4	5	6	7	8	9	10
9	10	11	12	13	14	15		13	14	15	16	17	18	19		11	12	13	14	15	16	17
16	17	18	19	20	21	22		20	21	22	23	24	25	26		18	19	20	21	22	23	24
23	24	25	26	27	28	29		27	28	29	30					25	26	27	28	29	30	31
30	31																					

Mercury Note: Mercury finally leaves its Storm on Thursday, July 1. Look over your notes on any ideas that occurred to you while Mercury was retrograde or slow. How do they look now?

28 Mon
3rd ≈

☽ enters ♓		1:51 pm	**10:51 am**
♀♌ ⊼ ♃♓		5:31 pm	**2:31 pm**
☽♓ ♂ ♃♓		5:33 pm	**2:33 pm**
☽♓ ⊼ ♀♌		5:34 pm	**2:34 pm**

29 Tue
3rd ♓

☽♓ △ ☉♋		3:54 am	**12:54 am**
☽♓ ⊼ ♂♌		9:58 am	**6:58 am**
☽♓ ⚹ ♅♉		2:47 pm	**11:47 am**
☽♓ □ ☿♊		11:00 pm	**8:00 pm**

30 Wed
3rd ♓

OP: After Moon conjoins Neptune until Moon enters Aries. A good time for helping others, but be mindful of the stressful aspect between Mars and Saturn. Find a balance between drive and reality.

☽♓ ♂ ♆♓		8:25 am	**5:25 am**
☽♓ ⚹ ♀♑		1:40 pm	**10:40 am** ☽ v/c
☽ enters ♈		9:21 pm	**6:21 pm**

1 Thu
3rd ♈
◑ 4th Quarter 10 ♈ 14
Canada Day

☽♈ △ ♀♌		7:22 am	**4:22 am**
♂♌ ☍ ♄≈		9:08 am	**6:08 am**
☽♈ □ ☉♋		5:11 pm	**2:11 pm**
☽♈ ⚹ ♄≈		9:16 pm	**6:16 pm**
☽♈ △ ♂♌		9:58 pm	**6:58 pm**
☽♈ ♂ ⚷♈		10:18 pm	**7:18 pm**

FRI 2
4th ♈

♂♌ △ ⚷♈	4:41 am	**1:41 am**	
☽♈ ⚹ ☿♊	12:12 pm	**9:12 am**	
☽♈ □ ♇♑		**9:15 pm**	☽ v/c

SAT 3
4th ♈

☽♈ □ ♇♑	12:15 am		☽ v/c
☽ enters ♉	8:28 am	**5:28 am**	
☽♉ ⚹ ♃♓	12:19 pm	**9:19 am**	
☉♋ ⚻ ♄♒	6:51 pm	**3:51 pm**	
♂♌ □ ♅♉	9:40 pm	**6:40 pm**	
☽♉ □ ♀♌		**10:44 pm**	

SUN 4
4th ♉
INDEPENDENCE DAY

☽♉ □ ♀♌	1:44 am	
☽♉ □ ♄♒	9:06 am	**6:06 am**
☽♉ ⚹ ☉♋	10:26 am	**7:26 am**
☉♋ □ ⚷♈	11:39 am	**8:39 am**
☽♉ ☌ ♅♉	12:41 pm	**9:41 am**
☽♉ □ ♂♌	1:28 pm	**10:28 am**

Eastern Time plain / **Pacific Time bold**

JUNE

S	M	T	W	T	F	S
		1	2	3	4	5
6	7	8	9	10	11	12
13	14	15	16	17	18	19
20	21	22	23	24	25	26
27	28	29	30			

JULY

S	M	T	W	T	F	S
				1	2	3
4	5	6	7	8	9	10
11	12	13	14	15	16	17
18	19	20	21	22	23	24
25	26	27	28	29	30	31

AUGUST

S	M	T	W	T	F	S
1	2	3	4	5	6	7
8	9	10	11	12	13	14
15	16	17	18	19	20	21
22	23	24	25	26	27	28
29	30	31				

5 Mon
4th ☿

☽ ♉ ⚹ ♆ ♓	7:30 am	**4:30 am**
☽ ♉ △ ♀ ♑	12:57 pm	**9:57 am** ☽ v/c
☉ ♋ ⚹ ♅ ♉	3:14 pm	**12:14 pm**
☽ enters ♊	9:24 pm	**6:24 pm**
☽ ♊ □ ♃ ♓		**10:03 pm**

6 Tue
4th ♊

☽ ♊ □ ♃ ♓	1:03 am	
☿ ♊ □ ♆ ♓	3:39 am	**12:39 am**
☽ ♊ ⚹ ♀ ♌	9:41 pm	**6:41 pm**
☽ ♊ △ ♄ ♒	9:47 pm	**6:47 pm**
♀ ♌ ☍ ♄ ♒	10:36 pm	**7:36 pm**
☽ ♊ ⚹ ⚷ ♈	11:33 pm	**8:33 pm**

7 Wed
4th ♊

OP: After Moon squares Neptune today until v/c Moon today or Thursday. This short OP during the Balsamic phase of the Moon is favorable for wrapping up projects.

☽ ♊ ⚹ ♂ ♌	5:47 am	**2:47 am**
♀ ♌ △ ⚷ ♈	4:09 pm	**1:09 pm**
☽ ♊ □ ♆ ♓	8:12 pm	**5:12 pm**
☽ ♊ ☌ ☿ ♊		**9:20 pm** ☽ v/c
☽ ♊ ⚻ ♇ ♑		**10:28 pm**

8 Thu
4th ♊

☽ ♊ ☌ ☿ ♊	12:20 am	☽ v/c
☽ ♊ ⚻ ♇ ♑	1:28 am	
☽ enters ♋	9:51 am	**6:51 am**
☿ ♊ ⚻ ♇ ♑	11:36 am	**8:36 am**
☽ ♋ △ ♃ ♓	1:09 pm	**10:09 am**
♀ ♌ □ ♅ ♉	3:25 pm	**12:25 pm**

☽⊗ ⊼ ♄≈	9:15 am	**6:15 am**	
☽⊗ ☐ ♅♈	11:19 am	**8:19 am**	
☽⊗ ✶ ♅♉	1:38 pm	**10:38 am**	
☽⊗ ♂ ☉⊗	9:17 pm	**6:17 pm**	

FRI 9

4th ⊗

● New Moon 18 ⊗ 02

OP: This Cazimi Moon is usable ½ hour before and ½ hour after the Sun-Moon conjunction. If you have something important to start around now, this is a great time to do it.

☽⊗ △ ♆♓	7:11 am	**4:11 am**	
☽⊗ ♂ ♀♑	12:10 pm	**9:10 am** ☽ v/c
☽ enters ♌	8:21 pm	**5:21 pm**	
☽♌ ⊼ ♃♓	11:14 pm	**8:14 pm**	

SAT 10

1st ⊗

☿ enters ⊗	4:35 pm	**1:35 pm**
☽♌ ♂ ♄≈	6:32 pm	**3:32 pm**
☽♌ △ ♅♈	8:49 pm	**5:49 pm**
☽♌ ☐ ♅♉	11:11 pm	**8:11 pm**

SUN 11

1st ♌

Eastern Time plain / **Pacific Time bold**

		JUNE				
S	M	T	W	T	F	S
		1	2	3	4	5
6	7	8	9	10	11	12
13	14	15	16	17	18	19
20	21	22	23	24	25	26
27	28	29	30			

		JULY				
S	M	T	W	T	F	S
				1	2	3
4	5	6	7	8	9	10
11	12	13	14	15	16	17
18	19	20	21	22	23	24
25	26	27	28	29	30	31

		AUGUST				
S	M	T	W	T	F	S
1	2	3	4	5	6	7
8	9	10	11	12	13	14
15	16	17	18	19	20	21
22	23	24	25	26	27	28
29	30	31				

12 Mon
1st ♌

☽♌ ☌ ♀♌	7:14 am	**4:14 am**	
☽♌ ☌ ♂♌	8:29 am	**5:29 am**	☽ v/c
☿♋ △ ♃♓	3:45 pm	**12:45 pm**	
☽♌ ⚻ ♆♓	3:50 pm	**12:50 pm**	
☽♌ ⚻ ♀♑	8:33 pm	**5:33 pm**	

13 Tue
1st ♌

☽ enters ♍	4:30 am	**1:30 am**
☽♍ ☍ ♃♓	7:00 am	**4:00 am**
☽♍ ⚹ ☿♋	9:05 am	**6:05 am**
♀♌ ☌ ♂♌	9:33 am	**6:33 am**
☽♍ ⚻ ♄≈		**10:33 pm**

14 Wed
1st ♍

OP: After Moon opposes Neptune today until v/c Moon today or Thursday. Wait two hours after the opposition for a window of opportunity for night owls.

☽♍ ⚻ ♄≈	1:33 am		
☽♍ ⚻ ♅♈	4:02 am	**1:02 am**	
☽♍ △ ♅♉	6:25 am	**3:25 am**	
☽♍ ⚹ ☉♋	9:46 pm	**6:46 pm**	
☽♍ ☍ ♆♓	10:17 pm	**7:17 pm**	
☽♍ △ ♀♑		**11:46 pm**	☽ v/c

15 Thu
1st ♍

Chiron retrograde

☽♍ △ ♀♑	2:46 am		☽ v/c
☉♋ △ ♆♓	4:49 am	**1:49 am**	
☽ enters ♎	10:32 am	**7:32 am**	
☽♎ ⚻ ♃♓	12:38 pm	**9:38 am**	
♅ ℞	12:41 pm	**9:41 am**	
☽♎ □ ☿♋	10:09 pm	**7:09 pm**	
♀♌ ⚻ ♆♓		**11:41 pm**	

♀♌ ⊼ ♆ ♓	2:41 am	
☽⚍ △ ♄ ≈	6:33 am	**3:33 am**
☽⚍ ☌ ♂ ♈	9:12 am	**6:12 am**
☽⚍ ⊼ ♅ ♉	11:37 am	**8:37 am**
☽⚍ ✶ ♂♌		**10:04 pm**
☽⚍ ⊼ ♆ ♓		**11:46 pm**

☽⚍ ✶ ♂♌	1:04 am	
☽⚍ ⊼ ♆ ♓	2:46 am	
☽⚍ ✶ ♀♌	5:04 am	**2:04 am**
☽⚍ ☐ ☉♋	6:11 am	**3:11 am**
☽⚍ ☐ ♀♑	7:03 am	**4:03 am** ☽ v/c
☽ enters ♏	2:38 pm	**11:38 pm**
☽♏ △ ♃ ♓	4:23 pm	**1:23 pm**
☉♋ ☌ ♀♑	6:46 pm	**3:46 pm**

♀♌ ⊼ ♀♑	3:48 am	**12:48 am**
☽♏ △ ☿♋	9:13 am	**6:13 am**
☽♏ ☐ ♄ ≈	9:45 am	**6:45 am**
☽♏ ⊼ ♂ ♈	12:34 pm	**9:34 am**
☿♋ ⊼ ♄ ≈	1:13 pm	**10:13 am**
♂♌ ⊼ ♆ ♓	2:22 pm	**11:22 am**
☽♏ ☌ ♅ ♉	3:00 pm	**12:00 pm**

Eastern Time plain / **Pacific Time bold**

	JUNE					
S	M	T	W	T	F	S
		1	2	3	4	5
6	7	8	9	10	11	12
13	14	15	16	17	18	19
20	21	22	23	24	25	26
27	28	29	30			

	JULY					
S	M	T	W	T	F	S
				1	2	3
4	5	6	7	8	9	10
11	12	13	14	15	16	17
18	19	20	21	22	23	24
25	26	27	28	29	30	31

	AUGUST					
S	M	T	W	T	F	S
1	2	3	4	5	6	7
8	9	10	11	12	13	14
15	16	17	18	19	20	21
22	23	24	25	26	27	28
29	30	31				

July

19 Mon
2nd ♏

OP: After Moon squares Mars until v/c Moon. Constructive action and precision reign during this OP.

☽♏ △ ♆♓	5:33 am	**2:33 am**
☽♏ □ ♂♌	6:15 am	**3:15 am**
☽♏ ✶ ♀♑	9:40 am	**6:40 am**
☿♋ □ ♅♈	10:52 am	**7:52 am**
☽♏ □ ♀♌	12:27 pm	**9:27 am**
☽♏ △ ☉♋	12:30 pm	**9:30 am** ☽ v/c
☽ enters ♐	5:08 pm	**2:08 pm**
☽♐ □ ♃♓	6:32 pm	**3:32 pm**

20 Tue
2nd ♐

☿♋ ✶ ♅♉	5:38 am	**2:38 am**
☽♐ ✶ ♄≈	11:31 am	**8:31 am**
☽♐ △ ♅♈	2:30 pm	**11:30 am**
☽♐ ⚻ ♅♉	4:59 pm	**1:59 pm**
☽♐ ⚻ ☿♋	6:42 pm	**3:42 pm**

21 Wed
2nd ♐

OP: After Moon trines Mars until Moon enters Capricorn. During this very positive OP, you're set up to succeed at anything, from arts to finances to romance.

☽♐ □ ♆♓	7:08 am	**4:08 am**
☽♐ △ ♂♌	10:06 am	**7:06 am**
☽♐ ⚻ ☉♋	5:30 pm	**2:30 pm**
☽♐ △ ♀♌	6:26 pm	**3:26 pm** ☽ v/c
☽ enters ♑	6:36 pm	**3:36 pm**
☽♑ ✶ ♃♓	7:41 pm	**4:41 pm**
♀ enters ♍	8:37 pm	**5:37 pm**

22 Thu
2nd ♑
Sun enters Leo

♀♍ ☍ ♃♓	8:45 am	**5:45 am**
♂♌ ⚻ ♀♑	10:09 am	**7:09 am**
☉ enters ♌	10:26 am	**7:26 am**
☽♑ □ ♅♈	3:51 pm	**12:51 pm**
☽♑ △ ♅♉	6:25 pm	**3:25 pm**
☉♌ ⚻ ♃♓		**9:10 pm**

142

Fri 23
2nd ♑
○ Full Moon 1 ♒ 26

☉♌ ⚻ ♃♓	12:10 am	
☽♑ ☍ ☿♋	3:53 am	**12:53 am**
☽♑ ⚹ ♆♓	8:32 am	**5:32 am**
☽♑ ☌ ♇♑	12:34 pm	**9:34 am** ☽ v/c
☽♑ ⚻ ♂♌	1:49 pm	**10:49 am**
☽ enters ♒	8:12 pm	**5:12 pm**
☽♒ ☍ ☉♌	10:37 pm	**7:37 pm**
☽♒ ⚻ ♀♍		**9:34 pm**

Sat 24
3rd ♒

☽♒ ⚻ ♀♍	12:34 am	
☿♋ △ ♆♓	12:35 pm	**9:35 am**
☽♒ ☌ ♄♒	2:25 pm	**11:25 am**
☽♒ ⚹ ⚷♈	5:57 pm	**2:57 pm**
☽♒ □ ♅♉	8:43 pm	**5:43 pm**

Sun 25
3rd ♒

☽♒ ⚻ ☿♋	3:15 pm	**12:15 pm**
☿♋ ☍ ♇♑	4:15 pm	**1:15 pm**
☽♒ ☍ ♂♌	7:14 pm	**4:14 pm** ☽ v/c
☽ enters ♓	11:30 pm	**8:30 pm**
☽♓ ☌ ♃♓	11:56 pm	**8:56 pm**

Eastern Time plain / **Pacific Time bold**

JUNE

S	M	T	W	T	F	S
		1	2	3	4	5
6	7	8	9	10	11	12
13	14	15	16	17	18	19
20	21	22	23	24	25	26
27	28	29	30			

JULY

S	M	T	W	T	F	S
				1	2	3
4	5	6	7	8	9	10
11	12	13	14	15	16	17
18	19	20	21	22	23	24
25	26	27	28	29	30	31

AUGUST

S	M	T	W	T	F	S
1	2	3	4	5	6	7
8	9	10	11	12	13	14
15	16	17	18	19	20	21
22	23	24	25	26	27	28
29	30	31				

July

26 Mon
3rd ♓

☽♓ ⊼ ☉♌	5:55 am	**2:55 am**
☽♓ ☍ ♀♍	9:04 am	**6:04 am**
☽♓ ⚹ ♅♉		**10:28 pm**

27 Tue
3rd ♓

☽♓ ⚹ ♅♉	1:28 am	
☽♓ ☌ ♆♓	4:47 pm	**1:47 pm**
☿ enters ♌	9:12 pm	**6:12 pm**
☽♓ ⚹ ♀♑	9:13 pm	**6:13 pm** ☽ v/c
☿♌ ⊼ ♃♓	9:45 pm	**6:45 pm**

28 Wed
3rd ♓

☽♓ ⊼ ♂♌	4:11 am	**1:11 am**
☽ enters ♈	5:58 am	**2:58 am**
☽♈ △ ☿♌	7:42 am	**4:42 am**
♃ enters ♒	8:43 am	**5:43 am**
☽♈ △ ☉♌	5:19 pm	**2:19 pm**
☽♈ ⊼ ♀♍	10:00 pm	**7:00 pm**
☽♈ ⚹ ♄♒		**10:53 pm**

29 Thu
3rd ♈

☽♈ ⚹ ♄♒	1:53 am	
☽♈ ☌ ⚷♈	6:27 am	**3:27 am**
♂♌ ☍ ♃♒	11:50 am	**8:50 am**
♂ enters ♍	4:32 pm	**1:32 pm**

☽♈ □ ♀♑	6:44 am	**3:44 am**
♀♍ ⊼ ♄≈	12:27 pm	**9:27 am**
☽♈ ⚹ ♃≈	3:38 pm	**12:38 pm** ☽ v/c
☽ enters ♉	4:08 pm	**1:08 pm**
☽♉ △ ♂♍	5:26 pm	**2:26 pm**

Fri 30
3rd ♈

OP: After Moon squares Pluto until v/c Moon. Good energy that you can use for any project you're involved with.

☽♉ □ ☿♌	6:24 am	**3:24 am**
☽♉ □ ☉♌	9:16 am	**6:16 am**
☽♉ □ ♄≈	12:48 pm	**9:48 am**
☽♉ △ ♀♍	3:41 pm	**12:41 pm**
☽♉ ☌ ♅♉	9:34 pm	**6:34 pm**

Sat 31
3rd ♉
◑ 4th Quarter 8 ♉ 33

☉♌ ☌ ☿♌	10:08 am	**7:08 am**
♀♍ ⊼ ♆♈	1:17 pm	**10:17 am**
☽♉ ⚹ ♆♓	2:13 pm	**11:13 am**
☿♌ ☍ ♄≈	5:50 pm	**2:50 pm**
☽♉ △ ♀♑	7:01 pm	**4:01 pm**
☉♌ ☍ ♄≈		**11:14 pm**

Sun 1
4th ♉
Lammas

Eastern Time plain / **Pacific Time bold**

JULY / AUGUST / SEPTEMBER calendars

145

2 MON
4th ♉

☉♌ ⚹ ♄≈	2:14 am
☽♉ □ ♃≈	3:41 am **12:41 am** ☽ v/c
☽ enters ♊	4:46 am **1:46 am**
☽♊ □ ♂♍	9:30 am **6:30 am**
☿♌ △ ♆♈	11:41 pm **8:41 pm**
☽♊ △ ♄≈	**10:19 pm**
♀♍ △ ♅♉	**11:53 pm**

3 TUE
4th ♊

☽♊ △ ♄≈	1:19 am
♀♍ △ ♅♉	2:53 am
☽♊ ⚹ ☉♌	3:30 am **12:30 am**
☽♊ ⚹ ♆♈	6:43 am **3:43 am**
☽♊ ⚹ ☿♌	8:12 am **5:12 am**
☽♊ □ ♀♍	11:25 am **8:25 am**
☿♌ □ ♅♉	9:57 pm **6:57 pm**
☽♊ □ ♆♓	**11:55 pm**

4 WED
4th ♊

OP: After Moon squares Neptune on Tuesday or today until v/c Moon today. This Last Quarter Moon OP is an excellent time to get in touch with others and finish up projects.

☽♊ □ ♆♓	2:55 am
☽♊ ⚻ ♀♑	7:37 am **4:37 am**
☽♊ △ ♃≈	3:38 pm **12:38 pm** ☽ v/c
☽ enters ♋	5:17 pm **2:17 pm**
☉♌ △ ♆♈	6:41 pm **3:41 pm**
☽♋ ⚹ ♂♍	**10:12 pm**

5 THU
4th ♋

☽♋ ⚹ ♂♍	1:12 am
☽♋ ⚻ ♄≈	12:52 pm **9:52 am**
☽♋ □ ♆♈	6:22 pm **3:22 pm**
☽♋ ⚹ ♅♉	10:12 pm **7:12 pm**

☽♋ ✶ ♀♍	5:17 am	**2:17 am**
☽♋ △ ♆♓	1:43 pm	**10:43 am**
☽♋ ☍ ♀♑	6:12 pm	**3:12 pm** ☽ v/c
☉♌ □ ♅♉	7:57 pm	**4:57 pm**
☽♋ ⚻ ♃≈		**10:23 pm**

FRI 6
4th ♋

☽♋ ⚻ ♃≈	1:23 am	
☽ enters ♌	3:31 am	**12:31 am**
☽♌ ☍ ♄≈	9:50 pm	**6:50 pm**
☿♌ ⚻ ♆♓	10:24 pm	**7:24 pm**

SAT 7
4th ♋

☽♌ △ ⚷♈	3:17 am	**12:17 am**
☽♌ □ ♅♉	7:04 am	**4:04 am**
☽♌ ☌ ☉♌	9:50 am	**6:50 am**
☽♌ ⚻ ♆♓	9:42 pm	**6:42 pm**
☽♌ ☌ ☿♌		**10:45 pm**
☽♌ ⚻ ♀♑		**10:57 pm**

SUN 8
4th ♌

● New Moon 16 ♌ 14
ISLAMIC NEW YEAR BEGINS AT SUNDOWN

Eastern Time plain / **Pacific Time bold**

	JULY								AUGUST								SEPTEMBER				
S	M	T	W	T	F	S		S	M	T	W	T	F	S		S	M	T	W	T	F	S
				1	2	3		1	2	3	4	5	6	7					1	2	3	4
4	5	6	7	8	9	10		8	9	10	11	12	13	14		5	6	7	8	9	10	11
11	12	13	14	15	16	17		15	16	17	18	19	20	21		12	13	14	15	16	17	18
18	19	20	21	22	23	24		22	23	24	25	26	27	28		19	20	21	22	23	24	25
25	26	27	28	29	30	31		29	30	31						26	27	28	29	30		

9 Mon

1st ♌

☽♌ ☌ ☿♌	1:45 am	
☽♌ ⚻ ♇♑	1:57 am	
☿♌ ⚻ ♇♑	3:03 am	**12:03 am**
☽♌ ☍ ♃♒	8:23 am	**5:23 am** ☽ v/c
☽ enters ♍	10:56 am	**7:56 am**
♀♍ ☍ ♆♓	8:20 pm	**5:20 pm**
☽♍ ☌ ♂♍	11:42 pm	**8:42 pm**

10 Tue

1st ♍

☽♍ ⚻ ♄♒	4:07 am	**1:07 am**
☽♍ ⚻ ⚷♈	9:34 am	**6:34 am**
☽♍ △ ♅♉	1:19 pm	**10:19 am**
☿♌ ☍ ♃♒	9:20 pm	**6:20 pm**

11 Wed

1st ♍

OP: After Moon opposes Neptune until v/c Moon. Wait two hours after the opposition for clarity. This OP is good for anything, from romance to practical matters.

☽♍ ☍ ♆♓	3:16 am	**12:16 am**
☽♍ ☌ ♀♍	6:15 am	**3:15 am**
☽♍ △ ♇♑	7:22 am	**4:22 am** ☽ v/c
☽♍ ⚻ ♃♒	1:10 pm	**10:10 am**
☽ enters ♎	4:08 pm	**1:08 pm**
☿ enters ♍	5:57 pm	**2:57 pm**
♀♍ △ ♇♑	6:46 pm	**3:46 pm**

12 Thu

1st ♎

☽♎ △ ♄♒	8:32 am	**5:32 am**
☽♎ ☍ ⚷♈	2:02 pm	**11:02 am**
☽♎ ⚻ ♅♉	5:48 pm	**2:48 pm**

☽♎︎⚹☉♌︎ 4:13 am **1:13 am**
☽♎︎⚻♆♓ 7:19 am **4:19 am**
☽♎︎□♀♑︎ 11:20 am **8:20 am**
♂♍︎⚻♄♒︎ 12:27 pm **9:27 am**
☽♎︎△♃♒︎ 4:39 pm **1:39 pm** ☽ v/c
☽ enters ♏︎ 8:01 pm **5:01 pm**

OP: After Moon squares Pluto until v/c Moon. An excellent waxing Moon OP for beauty-based projects, arts, networking, and more.

☽♏︎⚹☿♍︎ 3:33 am **12:33 am**
♀♍︎⚻♃♒︎ 6:58 am **3:58 am**
☽♏︎□♄♒︎ 11:54 am **8:54 am**
☽♏︎⚹♂♍︎ 1:08 pm **10:08 am**
☽♏︎⚻♇♈︎ 5:29 pm **2:29 pm**
☽♏︎☍♅♉︎ 9:18 pm **6:18 pm**
☉♌︎⚻♆♓ **9:14 pm**

☉♌︎⚻♆♓ 12:14 am
☽♏︎△♆♓ 10:33 am **7:33 am**
☽♏︎□☉♌︎ 11:20 am **8:20 am**
☽♏︎⚹♀♑︎ 2:32 pm **11:32 am**
☽♏︎□♃♒︎ 7:23 pm **4:23 pm**

☽♏︎⚹♀♍︎ 11:05 pm **8:05 pm** ☽ v/c
☽ enters ♐︎ 11:12 pm **8:12 pm**
♀ enters ♎︎ **9:27 pm**

OP: After Moon squares Jupiter until v/c Moon. This great OP aligns with the Moon enclosed between benefics and is good for everything.

Eastern Time plain / **Pacific Time bold**

		JULY				
S	M	T	W	T	F	S
				1	2	3
4	5	6	7	8	9	10
11	12	13	14	15	16	17
18	19	20	21	22	23	24
25	26	27	28	29	30	31

		AUGUST				
S	M	T	W	T	F	S
1	2	3	4	5	6	7
8	9	10	11	12	13	14
15	16	17	18	19	20	21
22	23	24	25	26	27	28
29	30	31				

		SEPTEMBER				
S	M	T	W	T	F	S
			1	2	3	4
5	6	7	8	9	10	11
12	13	14	15	16	17	18
19	20	21	22	23	24	25
26	27	28	29	30		

16 MON
2nd ♐

♀ enters ♎ 12:27 am
☽♐ □ ☿♍ 1:57 pm **10:57 am**
☽♐ ⚹ ♄≈ 2:40 pm **11:40 am**
☽♐ □ ♂♍ 6:31 pm **3:31 pm**
☿♍ ⚻ ♄≈ 7:35 pm **4:35 pm**
☽♐ △ ⚷♈ 8:22 pm **5:22 pm**
☽♐ ⚻ ♅♉ **9:15 pm**

17 TUE
2nd ♐

OP: After Moon squares Neptune until v/c Moon. Wait two hours after the square for another excellent opportunity to initiate big plans.

☽♐ ⚻ ♅♉ 12:15 am
☉♌ ⚻ ♀♑ 9:31 am **6:31 am**
☽♐ □ ♆♓ 1:19 pm **10:19 am**
☽♐ △ ☉♌ 5:51 pm **2:51 pm**
☽♐ ⚹ ♃≈ 9:43 pm **6:43 pm** ☽ v/c
☽ enters ♑ **10:58 pm**

18 WED
2nd ♐

☽ enters ♑ 1:58 am
☽♑ □ ♀♎ 6:27 am **3:27 am**
♂♍ ⚻ ⚷♈ 10:09 am **7:09 am**
☿♍ ⚻ ⚷♈ 6:19 pm **3:19 pm**
☽♑ □ ⚷♈ 10:59 pm **7:59 pm**
☿♍ ♂ ♂♍ 11:28 pm **8:28 pm**
☽♑ △ ♂♍ 11:37 pm **8:37 pm**
☽♑ △ ☿♍ 11:38 pm **8:38 pm**
☽♑ △ ♅♉ **11:59 pm**

19 THU
2nd ♑
URANUS RETROGRADE

☽♑ △ ♅♉ 2:59 am
☽♑ ⚹ ♆♓ 3:59 pm **12:59 pm**
☽♑ ♂ ♀♑ 7:59 pm **4:59 pm** ☽ v/c
☉♌ ♂ ♃≈ 8:29 pm **5:29 pm**
♅℞ 9:40 pm **6:40 pm**
☽♑ ⚻ ☉♌ **9:21 pm**

FRI 20
2nd ♑

☽♑ ⚻ ☉♌	12:21 am	
☿♍ △ ♅♉	4:06 am	**1:06 am**
☽ enters ♒	4:49 am	**1:49 am**
☽♒ △ ♀♎	2:01 pm	**11:01 am**
☽♒ ☌ ♄♒	7:55 pm	**4:55 pm**
☽♒ ⚹ ⚷♈		**11:01 pm**

SAT 21
2nd ♒

☽♒ ⚹ ⚷♈	2:01 am	
☽♒ ⚻ ♂♍	5:13 am	**2:13 am**
☽♒ □ ♅♉	6:12 am	**3:12 am**
☽♒ ⚻ ☿♍	9:41 am	**6:41 am**
♂♍ △ ♅♉		**11:38 pm**

OP: After Moon squares Uranus today until v/c Moon on Sunday. A good time to break out of a rut for innovative work and presentations.

SUN 22
2nd ♒

◯ Full Moon 29 ♒ 37

SUN ENTERS VIRGO

♂♍ △ ♅♉	2:38 am	
☽♒ ☌ ♃♒	3:19 am	**12:19 am**
☽♒ ☍ ☉♌	8:02 am	**5:02 am** ☽ v/c
☽ enters ♓	8:43 am	**5:43 am**
☉ enters ♍	5:35 pm	**2:35 pm**
☽♓ ⚻ ♀♎	11:14 pm	**8:14 pm**

Eastern Time plain / **Pacific Time bold**

JULY

S	M	T	W	T	F	S
				1	2	3
4	5	6	7	8	9	10
11	12	13	14	15	16	17
18	19	20	21	22	23	24
25	26	27	28	29	30	31

AUGUST

S	M	T	W	T	F	S
1	2	3	4	5	6	7
8	9	10	11	12	13	14
15	16	17	18	19	20	21
22	23	24	25	26	27	28
29	30	31				

SEPTEMBER

S	M	T	W	T	F	S
			1	2	3	4
5	6	7	8	9	10	11
12	13	14	15	16	17	18
19	20	21	22	23	24	25
26	27	28	29	30		

23 MON
3rd ♓

♀︎ ☌ △ ♄ ≈	8:48 am	**5:48 am**	
☽ ♓ ⚹ ♅ ♉	11:04 am	**8:04 am**	
☽ ♓ ☍ ♂ ♍	12:43 pm	**9:43 am**	
☽ ♓ ☍ ☿ ♍	10:03 pm	**7:03 pm**	
☽ ♓ ☌ ♆ ♓		**9:50 pm**	

24 TUE
3rd ♓

☽ ♓ ☌ ♆ ♓	12:50 am		
☽ ♓ ⚹ ♀︎ ♑	5:12 am	**2:12 am**	☽ v/c
☽ enters ♈	2:57 pm	**11:57 am**	
☽ ♈ ⚻ ☉ ♍	6:37 pm	**3:37 pm**	
☿ ♍ ☍ ♆ ♓	9:14 pm	**6:14 pm**	

25 WED
3rd ♈

☽ ♈ ⚹ ♄ ≈	6:58 am	**3:58 am**	
☽ ♈ ☍ ♀︎ ☌	11:57 am	**8:57 am**	
☽ ♈ ☌ ⚷ ♈	2:00 pm	**11:00 am**	
☽ ♈ ⚻ ♂ ♍	11:37 pm	**8:37 pm**	

26 THU
3rd ♈

OP: After Moon squares Pluto until v/c Moon. Suitable for anything, this OP is an excellent time to take the initiative.

♀︎ ☌ ☍ ⚷ ♈	9:24 am	**6:24 am**	
☿ ♍ △ ♀︎ ♑	10:23 am	**7:23 am**	
☽ ♈ ☐ ♀︎ ♑	2:02 pm	**11:02 am**	
☽ ♈ ⚻ ☿ ♍	2:33 pm	**11:33 am**	
☽ ♈ ⚹ ♃ ≈	5:14 pm	**2:14 pm**	☽ v/c
☽ enters ♉		**9:27 pm**	

☽ enters ♉ 12:27 am
☽♉ △ ☉♍ 9:19 am **6:19 am**
☿♍ ⊼ ♃≈ 11:05 am **8:05 am**
☽♉ □ ♄≈ 5:04 pm **2:04 pm**

Fri 27
3rd ♈

☽♉ ⊼ ♀♎ 5:00 am **2:00 am**
☽♉ ☌ ♅♉ 5:52 am **2:52 am**
♀♎ ⊼ ♅♉ 1:43 pm **10:43 am**
☽♉ △ ♂♍ 2:14 pm **11:14 am**
☽♉ ✶ ♆♓ 8:56 pm **5:56 pm**
☽♉ △ ♀♑ **10:50 pm**

Sat 28
3rd ♉

☽♉ △ ♀♑ 1:50 am
☽♉ □ ♃≈ 4:36 am **1:36 am**
☽♉ △ ☿♍ 10:59 am **7:59 am** ☽ v/c
☽ enters ♊ 12:42 pm **9:42 am**
☿ enters ♎ **10:10 pm**

Sun 29
3rd ♉

OP: After Moon squares Jupiter until Moon enters Gemini. Get up early to catch this highly productive OP.

Eastern Time plain / **Pacific Time bold**

	JULY							AUGUST							SEPTEMBER					
S	M	T	W	T	F	S	S	M	T	W	T	F	S	S	M	T	W	T	F	S
				1	2	3	1	2	3	4	5	6	7				1	2	3	4
4	5	6	7	8	9	10	8	9	10	11	12	13	14	5	6	7	8	9	10	11
11	12	13	14	15	16	17	15	16	17	18	19	20	21	12	13	14	15	16	17	18
18	19	20	21	22	23	24	22	23	24	25	26	27	28	19	20	21	22	23	24	25
25	26	27	28	29	30	31	29	30	31					26	27	28	29	30		

30 Mon
3rd ♊
◗ 4th Quarter 7 ♊ 09

☿ enters ♎	1:10 am	
☽♊ □ ☉♍	3:13 am	**12:13 am**
☽♊ △ ♄≈	5:26 am	**2:26 am**
☽♊ ✶ ♅♈	1:14 pm	**10:14 am**
☽♊ △ ♀♎		**9:30 pm**

31 Tue
4th ♊

OP: After Moon squares Neptune until v/c Moon. Wait two hours after the square for clarity, and use this OP to connect with others or anything you're involved with.

☽♊ △ ♀♎	12:30 am	
☉♍ ⚻ ♄≈	4:46 am	**1:46 am**
☽♊ □ ♂♍	6:36 am	**3:36 am**
☽♊ □ ♆♓	9:41 am	**6:41 am**
☽♊ ⚻ ⚳♑	2:37 pm	**11:37 am**
☽♊ △ ♃≈	4:48 pm	**1:48 pm** ☽ v/c
☽ enters ♋		**10:26 pm**

1 Wed
4th ♊

☽ enters ♋	1:26 am	
☽♋ □ ☿♎	7:46 am	**4:46 am**
☽♋ ⚻ ♄≈	5:30 pm	**2:30 pm**
☽♋ ✶ ☉♍	8:52 pm	**5:52 pm**
☽♋ □ ♅♈		**10:11 pm**

2 Thu
4th ♋

☽♋ □ ♅♈	1:11 am	
☽♋ ✶ ♅♉	6:33 am	**3:33 am**
♂♍ ☍ ♆♓	1:43 pm	**10:43 am**
☽♋ □ ♀♎	6:24 pm	**3:24 pm**
☽♋ △ ♆♓	8:52 pm	**5:52 pm**
☽♋ ✶ ♂♍	9:16 pm	**6:16 pm**
☽♋ ☍ ⚳♑		**10:37 pm** ☽ v/c

☽⊗ ☌ ♀♑	1:37 am	☽ v/c	
☽⊗ ⊼ ♃≈	3:12 am	**12:12 am**	
☽ enters ♌	11:58 am	**8:58 am**	
♀♎ ⊼ ♆♓	8:13 pm	**5:13 pm**	
☽♌ ✶ ☿♎		**9:45 pm**	
☉♍ ⊼ ♂♈		**10:20 pm**	
☽♌ ☌ ♄≈		**11:55 pm**	

Fri 3
4th ⊗

☽♌ ✶ ☿♎	12:45 am	
☉♍ ⊼ ♂♈	1:20 am	
☽♌ ☌ ♄≈	2:55 am	
☽♌ △ ♂♈	10:14 am	**7:14 am**
☽♌ □ ♅♉	3:23 pm	**12:23 pm**
☿♎ △ ♄≈	9:30 pm	**6:30 pm**

Sat 4
4th ♌

☽♌ ⊼ ♆♓	4:47 am	**1:47 am**	
☽♌ ✶ ♀♎	7:58 am	**4:58 am**	
☽♌ ⊼ ♀♑	9:18 am	**6:18 am**	
☽♌ ☌ ♃≈	10:22 am	**7:22 am**	☽ v/c
☽ enters ♍	7:06 pm	**4:06 pm**	
♀♎ □ ♀♑	11:07 pm	**8:07 pm**	

Sun 5
4th ♌

Eastern Time plain / **Pacific Time bold**

	AUGUST					
S	M	T	W	T	F	S
1	2	3	4	5	6	7
8	9	10	11	12	13	14
15	16	17	18	19	20	21
22	23	24	25	26	27	28
29	30	31				

	SEPTEMBER					
S	M	T	W	T	F	S
			1	2	3	4
5	6	7	8	9	10	11
12	13	14	15	16	17	18
19	20	21	22	23	24	25
26	27	28	29	30		

	OCTOBER					
S	M	T	W	T	F	S
					1	2
3	4	5	6	7	8	9
10	11	12	13	14	15	16
17	18	19	20	21	22	23
24	25	26	27	28	29	30
31						

6 Mon
4th ℳ

● New Moon 14 ℳ 38
Labor Day (US)
Labour Day (Canada)
Rosh Hashanah begins at sundown

OP: This Cazimi Moon is usable ½ hour before and ½ hour after the Sun-Moon conjunction. If you have something important to start around now, this is a great time to do it.

♂ℳ △ ♀ ♈	8:20 am	**5:20 am**
☽ℳ ⊼ ♄ ≈	8:57 am	**5:57 am**
♀♎ △ ♃ ≈	9:05 am	**6:05 am**
☽ℳ ⊼ ♅ ♈	3:56 pm	**12:56 pm**
☽ℳ ♂ ☉ℳ	8:52 pm	**5:52 pm**
☽ℳ △ ♅ ♉	8:54 pm	**5:54 pm**
☉ℳ △ ♅ ♉	9:29 pm	**6:29 pm**
♂ℳ ⊼ ♃ ≈	11:50 pm	**8:50 pm**

7 Tue
1st ℳ

☽ℳ ♋ ♆ ♓	9:34 am	**6:34 am**
☽ℳ △ ♀ ♈	1:56 pm	**10:56 am**
☽ℳ ⊼ ♃ ≈	2:33 pm	**11:33 am**
☽ℳ ♂ ♂ℳ	3:24 pm	**12:24 pm** ☽ v/c
☽ enters ♎	11:20 pm	**8:20 pm**
☿♎ ♋ ♅ ♈		**9:30 pm**

8 Wed
1st ♎

☿♎ ♋ ♅ ♈	12:30 am	
☽♎ △ ♄ ≈	12:29 pm	**9:29 am**
☽♎ ♋ ♅ ♈	7:16 pm	**4:16 pm**
☽♎ ♂ ☿♎	9:01 pm	**6:01 pm**
☽♎ ⊼ ♅ ♉		**9:11 pm**

9 Thu
1st ♎

OP: After Moon squares Pluto until v/c Moon. An awesome OP for starting new projects, working with groups, promotions, or other things that interest you.

☽♎ ⊼ ♅ ♉	12:11 am	
☽♎ ⊼ ♆ ♓	12:28 pm	**9:28 am**
☽♎ □ ♀ ♈	4:48 pm	**1:48 pm**
☽♎ △ ♃ ≈	5:03 pm	**2:03 pm**
☽♎ ♂ ♀♎		**9:48 pm** ☽ v/c
☽ enters ℳ		**11:05 pm**

☽⚊ ☌ ♀⚊	12:48 am	☽ v/c	
☽ enters ♏	2:05 am		
☿⚊ ⚻ ♅♉	12:17 pm	**9:17 am**	
☽♏ □ ♄≈	2:53 pm	**11:53 am**	
♀ enters ♏	4:39 pm	**1:39 pm**	
☽♏ ⚻ ♀♈	9:39 pm	**6:39 pm**	
☽♏ ☍ ♅♉		**11:37 pm**	

Fri 10
1st ⚊

☽♏ ☍ ♅♉	2:37 am		
☽♏ ⚹ ☉♏	10:08 am	**7:08 am**	
☽♏ △ ♆♓	2:50 pm	**11:50 am**	
☽♏ □ ♃≈	7:08 pm	**4:08 pm**	
☽♏ ⚹ ♀♈	7:13 pm	**4:13 pm**	
☽♏ ⚹ ♂♍		**10:33 pm** ☽ v/c	

Sat 11
1st ♏

OP: After Moon squares Jupiter until v/c Moon. Ease your worries during this great OP suitable for anything, from hard work to romance.

☽♏ ⚹ ♂♍	1:33 am	☽ v/c	
☽ enters ♐	4:34 am	**1:34 am**	
☽♐ ⚹ ♄≈	5:18 pm	**2:18 pm**	
☽♐ △ ♀♈		**9:08 pm**	

Sun 12
1st ♏

Eastern Time plain / **Pacific Time bold**

AUGUST						
S	M	T	W	T	F	S
1	2	3	4	5	6	7
8	9	10	11	12	13	14
15	16	17	18	19	20	21
22	23	24	25	26	27	28
29	30	31				

SEPTEMBER						
S	M	T	W	T	F	S
			1	2	3	4
5	6	7	8	9	10	11
12	13	14	15	16	17	18
19	20	21	22	23	24	25
26	27	28	29	30		

OCTOBER						
S	M	T	W	T	F	S
					1	2
3	4	5	6	7	8	9
10	11	12	13	14	15	16
17	18	19	20	21	22	23
24	25	26	27	28	29	30
31						

September

13 Mon
1st ♐
◐ 2nd Quarter 21 ♐ 16

☽♐ △ ♗♈	12:08 am	
☽♐ ⊼ ♅♉	5:13 am	**2:13 am**
☽♐ ✶ ☿♎	10:31 am	**7:31 am**
☽♐ □ ☉♍	4:39 pm	**1:39 pm**
☽♐ □ ♆♓	5:33 pm	**2:33 pm**
☽♐ ✶ ♃≈	9:38 pm	**6:38 pm**

14 Tue
2nd ♐

☉♍ ☍ ♆♓	5:21 am	**2:21 am**
☽♐ □ ♂♍	6:57 am	**3:57 am** ☽ v/c
☽ enters ♑	7:34 am	**4:34 am**
☽♑ ✶ ♀♏	3:21 pm	**12:21 pm**
♂ enters ♎	8:14 pm	**5:14 pm**

15 Wed
2nd ♑
Yom Kippur begins at sundown

☽♑ □ ♗♈	3:15 am	**12:15 am**
☽♑ △ ♅♉	8:31 am	**5:31 am**
☽♑ □ ☿♎	5:41 pm	**2:41 pm**
☽♑ ✶ ♆♓	9:01 pm	**6:01 pm**
☽♑ △ ☉♍		**9:07 pm**
☽♑ ☌ ♀♑		**10:40 pm** ☽ v/c

16 Thu
2nd ♑

☽♑ △ ☉♍	12:07 am	
☽♑ ☌ ♀♑	1:40 am	☽ v/c
☉♍ ⊼ ♃≈	10:18 am	**7:18 am**
☽ enters ≈	11:23 am	**8:23 am**
☽≈ △ ♂♎	1:19 pm	**10:19 am**
☉♍ △ ♀♑	9:53 pm	**6:53 pm**
☽≈ □ ♀♏		**9:03 pm**
☽≈ ☌ ♄≈		**9:14 pm**
♀♏ □ ♄≈		**11:15 pm**

☽≈ □ ♀♏,	12:03 am	
☽≈ ♂ ♄≈	12:14 am	
♀♏, □ ♄≈	2:15 am	
☽≈ ⚹ ♅♈	7:18 am	**4:18 am**
☽≈ □ ♅♉	12:45 pm	**9:45 am**
☿♎ ⚻ ♆♓		**9:18 pm**
☽≈ △ ☿♎		**10:36 pm**

Fri 17
2nd ≈

OP: After Moon squares Uranus today until v/c Moon on Saturday. Very versatile OP. Take full advantage of it before Mercury turns retrograde next week.

☿♎ ⚻ ♆♓	12:18 am	
☽≈ △ ☿♎	1:36 am	
☽≈ ♂ ♃≈	5:14 am	**2:14 am** ☽ v/c
☽≈ ⚻ ☉♍	8:55 am	**5:55 am**
☽ enters ♓	4:22 pm	**1:22 pm**
☽♓ ⚻ ♂♎	9:04 pm	**6:04 pm**

Sat 18
2nd ≈

☽♓ △ ♀♏,	10:26 am	**7:26 am**
☽♓ ⚹ ♅♉	6:26 pm	**3:26 pm**

Sun 19
2nd ♓

Eastern Time plain / **Pacific Time bold**

AUGUST								SEPTEMBER								OCTOBER					
S	M	T	W	T	F	S		S	M	T	W	T	F	S		S	M	T	W	T	F	S
1	2	3	4	5	6	7					1	2	3	4							1	2
8	9	10	11	12	13	14		5	6	7	8	9	10	11		3	4	5	6	7	8	9
15	16	17	18	19	20	21		12	13	14	15	16	17	18		10	11	12	13	14	15	16
22	23	24	25	26	27	28		19	20	21	22	23	24	25		17	18	19	20	21	22	23
29	30	31						26	27	28	29	30				24	25	26	27	28	29	30
																31						

September

Mercury Note: Mercury enters its Storm (moving less than 40 minutes of arc per day) on Monday, as it slows down before going retrograde. The Storm acts like the retrograde. Not favorable for new projects—just follow through with the items that are already on your plate. Write down new ideas with date and time they occurred.

20 Mon
2nd ♓
○ Full Moon 28 ♓ 14
Sukkot begins at sundown

☽♓	♂	♆♓	7:39 am	**4:39 am**
☽♓	⚻	☿♎	10:50 am	**7:50 am**
♀♏	⚻	♅♈	12:12 pm	**9:12 am**
☽♓	⚹	♀♑	12:45 pm	**9:45 am**
☿♎	△	♃≈	6:53 pm	**3:53 pm**
☽♓	☌	☉♍	7:55 pm	**4:55 pm** ☽ v/c
☽ enters ♈			11:13 pm	**8:13 pm**

21 Tue
3rd ♈
UN International Day of Peace

☽♈	☍	♂♎	7:03 am	**4:03 am**
☽♈	⚹	♄≈	12:43 pm	**9:43 am**
☽♈	☌	♅♈	8:16 pm	**5:16 pm**
☽♈	⚻	♀♏	11:34 pm	**8:34 pm**

22 Wed
3rd ♈
Fall Equinox
Mabon
Sun enters Libra

☿♎	□	♀♑	9:12 am	**6:12 am**
☉ enters ♎			3:21 pm	**12:21 pm**
☽♈	⚹	♃≈	7:42 pm	**4:42 pm**
☽♈	□	♀♑	9:37 pm	**6:37 pm**
☽♈	☍	☿♎	10:05 pm	**7:05 pm** ☽ v/c

23 Thu
3rd ♈

♀♏	☍	♅♉	5:41 am	**2:41 am**
☽ enters ♉			8:38 am	**5:38 am**
☽♉	⚻	☉♎	10:08 am	**7:08 am**
☽♉	⚻	♂♎	8:07 pm	**5:07 pm**
☽♉	□	♄≈	10:40 pm	**7:40 pm**

Mercury Note: Mercury goes retrograde on Sunday, September 26 (Pacific) or Monday, September 27 (Eastern), and remains so until October 18, after which it will still be in its Storm until October 22. Projects initiated during this entire period may not work out as planned. It's best to use this time for reviews, editing, escrows, and so forth.

☽♉ ♂ ☿♉	12:56 pm	**9:56 am**
☽♉ ☌ ♀♏	4:16 pm	**1:16 pm**

FRI 24
3rd ♉

☽♉ ✳ ♆♓	3:23 am	**12:23 am**	
☽♉ □ ♃ ≈	6:49 am	**3:49 am**	
☽♉ △ ♀♑	9:09 am	**6:09 am**	☽ v/c
☽♉ ⊼ ☿♎	11:10 am	**8:10 am**	
♂♎ △ ♄ ≈	5:50 pm	**2:50 pm**	
☽ enters ♊	8:36 pm	**5:36 pm**	

SAT 25
3rd ♉

OP: After Moon squares Jupiter until Moon enters Gemini. Good, constructive OP, but with Mercury in its Storm, it's best to use this time for work you've already started.

☽♊ △ ☉♎	3:35 am	**12:35 am**
☽♊ △ ♄ ≈	10:57 am	**7:57 am**
☽♊ △ ♂♎	11:59 am	**8:59 am**
☽♊ ✳ ♅♈	6:53 pm	**3:53 pm**
☿℞		**10:10 pm**

SUN 26
3rd ♊

MERCURY RETROGRADE (PACIFIC)

Eastern Time plain / **Pacific Time bold**

	AUGUST							SEPTEMBER							OCTOBER					
S	M	T	W	T	F	S	S	M	T	W	T	F	S	S	M	T	W	T	F	S
1	2	3	4	5	6	7			1	2	3	4							1	2
8	9	10	11	12	13	14	5	6	7	8	9	10	11	3	4	5	6	7	8	9
15	16	17	18	19	20	21	12	13	14	15	16	17	18	10	11	12	13	14	15	16
22	23	24	25	26	27	28	19	20	21	22	23	24	25	17	18	19	20	21	22	23
29	30	31					26	27	28	29	30			24	25	26	27	28	29	30
														31						

27 Mon
3rd ♊

Sukkot ends

Mercury retrograde (Eastern)

OP: After Moon squares Neptune today until v/c Moon today or Tuesday. Good OP for relaxing or socializing while the Moon is waning and Mercury is retrograde.

☿ R		1:10 am	
☽ ♊ ⊼ ♀ ♏	11:28 am	**8:28 am**	
☽ ♊ □ ♆ ♓	4:11 pm	**1:11 pm**	
☽ ♊ △ ♃ ♒	7:25 pm	**4:25 pm**	
☽ ♊ ⊼ ♇ ♑	10:06 pm	**7:06 pm**	
☽ ♊ △ ☿ ♎		**9:18 pm**	☽ v/c

28 Tue
3rd ♊

◑ 4th Quarter 6 ♋ 09

☽ ♊ △ ☿ ♎	12:18 am		☽ v/c
☽ enters ♋	9:34 am	**6:34 am**	
☽ ♋ □ ☉ ♎	9:57 pm	**6:57 pm**	
☽ ♋ ⊼ ♄ ♒	11:39 pm	**8:39 pm**	

29 Wed
4th ♋

☽ ♋ □ ♂ ♎	4:17 am	**1:17 am**
☽ ♋ □ ♅ ♈	7:20 am	**4:20 am**
♀ ♏ △ ♆ ♓	12:14 pm	**9:14 am**
☽ ♋ ✶ ♅ ♉	1:54 pm	**10:54 am**
☉ ♎ △ ♄ ♒	6:19 pm	**3:19 pm**

30 Thu
4th ♋

☽ ♋ △ ♆ ♓	4:06 am	**1:06 am**	
☽ ♋ △ ♀ ♏	5:44 am	**2:44 am**	
☽ ♋ ⊼ ♃ ♒	7:02 am	**4:02 am**	
☽ ♋ ☍ ♇ ♑	9:54 am	**6:54 am**	
☽ ♋ □ ☿ ♎	10:49 am	**7:49 am**	☽ v/c
♀ ♏ □ ♃ ♒	7:31 pm	**4:31 pm**	
☽ enters ♌	8:53 pm	**5:53 pm**	

♂︎♎︎ ☍ ♃ ♈︎ 9:00 am **6:00 am**
☽♌︎ ☍ ♄ ♒︎ 10:10 am **7:10 am**
☿♎︎ □ ♀ ♑︎ 10:26 am **7:26 am**
☽♌︎ ✶ ☉♎︎ 1:34 pm **10:34 am**
☽♌︎ △ ♃ ♈︎ 5:17 pm **2:17 pm**
☽♌︎ ✶ ♂︎♎︎ 5:46 pm **2:46 pm**
☽♌︎ □ ♅ ♉︎ 11:32 pm **8:32 pm**

FRI 1
4th ♌︎

♀♏︎ ✶ ♀ ♑︎ 3:48 am **12:48 am**
☽♌︎ ⚻ ♆ ♓︎ 12:51 pm **9:51 am**
☽♌︎ ☍ ♃ ♒︎ 3:29 pm **12:29 pm**
☽♌︎ ✶ ☿ ♎︎ 4:57 pm **1:57 pm**
☽♌︎ ⚻ ♀ ♑︎ 6:22 pm **3:22 pm**
☽♌︎ □ ♀♏︎ 7:43 pm **4:43 pm** ☽ v/c

SAT 2
4th ♌︎

☽ enters ♍︎ 4:38 am **1:38 am**
☉♎︎ ☍ ♃ ♈︎ 11:51 am **8:51 am**
☽♍︎ ⚻ ♄ ♒︎ 4:56 pm **1:56 pm**
☿♎︎ △ ♃ ♒︎ 8:05 pm **5:05 pm**
☽♍︎ ⚻ ♃ ♈︎ 11:27 pm **8:27 pm**

SUN 3
4th ♌︎

Eastern Time plain / **Pacific Time bold**

SEPTEMBER						
S	M	T	W	T	F	S
			1	2	3	4
5	6	7	8	9	10	11
12	13	14	15	16	17	18
19	20	21	22	23	24	25
26	27	28	29	30		

OCTOBER						
S	M	T	W	T	F	S
					1	2
3	4	5	6	7	8	9
10	11	12	13	14	15	16
17	18	19	20	21	22	23
24	25	26	27	28	29	30
31						

NOVEMBER						
S	M	T	W	T	F	S
	1	2	3	4	5	6
7	8	9	10	11	12	13
14	15	16	17	18	19	20
21	22	23	24	25	26	27
28	29	30				

4 MON
4th ♍

OP: After Moon opposes Neptune today until v/c Moon on Tuesday. A good time to do repairs, finish projects, and reconnect with people from the past.

☽♍ △ ♅ ♉	5:19 am	**2:19 am**	
☽♍ ☍ ♆ ♓	5:48 pm	**2:48 pm**	
☽♍ ⚻ ♃ ♒	8:10 pm	**5:10 pm**	
☽♍ △ ♀ ♑	11:03 pm	**8:03 pm**	

5 TUE
4th ♍

☽♍ ⚹ ♀♏	4:46 am	**1:46 am**	☽ v/c
☽ enters ♎	8:41 am	**5:41 am**	
☿♎ ⚻ ♆ ♓	9:53 am	**6:53 am**	
☽♎ △ ♄ ♒	8:16 pm	**5:16 pm**	
☽♎ ☍ ♉ ♈		**11:19 pm**	

6 WED
4th ♎

● New Moon 13 ♎ 25
PLUTO DIRECT

☽♎ ☍ ♉ ♈	2:19 am		
♂♎ ⚻ ♅ ♉	5:27 am	**2:27 am**	
☽♎ ☌ ☉♎	7:05 am	**4:05 am**	
☽♎ ⚻ ♅ ♉	7:56 am	**4:56 am**	
☽♎ ☌ ♂♎	8:04 am	**5:04 am**	
♀D	2:29 pm	**11:29 am**	
☽♎ ☌ ☿♎	5:40 pm	**2:40 pm**	
☉♎ ⚻ ♅ ♉	7:11 pm	**4:11 pm**	
☽♎ ⚻ ♆ ♓	7:54 pm	**4:54 pm**	
☽♎ △ ♃ ♒	10:08 pm	**7:08 pm**	
☽♎ □ ♀ ♑		**10:03 pm**	☽ v/c

7 THU
1st ♎

☽♎ □ ♀ ♑	1:03 am		☽ v/c
♀ enters ♐	7:21 am	**4:21 am**	
☽ enters ♏	10:22 am	**7:22 am**	
☽♏ □ ♄ ♒	9:37 pm	**6:37 pm**	
☉♎ ☌ ♂♎		**9:01 pm**	

☉︎☌♂︎☍ 12:01 am
☽︎♏︎✶♃♈ 3:26 am **12:26 am**
☽︎♏︎☍♅♉ 9:00 am **6:00 am**
☽︎♏︎△♆♓ 8:53 pm **5:53 pm**
☽︎♏︎□ ♃♒ 11:04 pm **8:04 pm**

FRI 8
1st ♏︎

OP: After Moon squares Jupiter today until v/c Moon today or Saturday. Short window of opportunity for deep thinking and renovation.

☽︎♏︎✶ ♀♑ **11:05 pm** ☽︎ v/c

☽︎♏︎✶ ♀♑ 2:05 am ☽︎ v/c
☽︎ enters ♐ 11:24 am **8:24 am**
☉︎♎☌ ☿♎ 12:18 pm **9:18 am**
☽︎♐ ☌ ♀♐ 3:37 pm **12:37 pm**
☿♎ ☌ ♂♎ 6:48 pm **3:48 pm**
☽︎♐ ✶ ♄♒ 10:43 pm **7:43 pm**

SAT 9
1st ♏︎

☽︎♐ △ ♃♈ 4:27 am **1:27 am**
☽︎♐ ✶ ♅♉ 10:08 am **7:08 am**
☽︎♐ ✶ ☿♎ 12:49 pm **9:49 am**
☽︎♐ ✶ ♂♎ 3:12 pm **12:12 pm**
☽︎♐ ✶ ☉︎♎ 4:45 pm **1:45 pm**
☽︎♐ □ ♆♓ 10:17 pm **7:17 pm**
♄ D 10:17 pm **7:17 pm**
☽︎♐ ✶ ♃♒ **9:30 pm** ☽︎ v/c

SUN 10
1st ♐
SATURN DIRECT

OP: After Moon squares Neptune today until Moon enters Capricorn on Monday. (Sagittarius is one of the four signs in which the v/c Moon is a good thing. See page 75.) With Mercury retrograde, this very positive OP offers an ideal time for renewal.

Eastern Time plain / **Pacific Time bold**

SEPTEMBER						
S	M	T	W	T	F	S
			1	2	3	4
5	6	7	8	9	10	11
12	13	14	15	16	17	18
19	20	21	22	23	24	25
26	27	28	29	30		

OCTOBER						
S	M	T	W	T	F	S
					1	2
3	4	5	6	7	8	9
10	11	12	13	14	15	16
17	18	19	20	21	22	23
24	25	26	27	28	29	30
31						

NOVEMBER						
S	M	T	W	T	F	S
	1	2	3	4	5	6
7	8	9	10	11	12	13
14	15	16	17	18	19	20
21	22	23	24	25	26	27
28	29	30				

11 Mon
1st ♐

INDIGENOUS PEOPLES' DAY
COLUMBUS DAY
THANKSGIVING DAY (CANADA)

☽♐ ⚹ ♃≈	12:30 am		☽ v/c
☽ enters ♑	1:15 pm	**10:15 am**	
☿♎ ⚻ ♅♉		**10:29 pm**	

12 Tue
1st ♑
◑ 2nd Quarter 20 ♑ 01

☿♎ ⚻ ♅♉	1:29 am	
☽♑ □ ♂♈	6:39 am	**3:39 am**
☽♑ □ ☿♎	11:51 am	**8:51 am**
☽♑ △ ♅♉	12:34 pm	**9:34 am**
☽♑ □ ♂♎	8:27 pm	**5:27 pm**
☽♑ □ ☉♎	11:25 pm	**8:25 pm**
☽♑ ⚹ ♆♓		**10:11 pm**

13 Wed
2nd ♑

☽♑ ⚹ ♆♓	1:11 am		
☽♑ ☌ ♀♑	6:53 am	**3:53 am**	☽ v/c
♀♐ ⚹ ♄≈	3:26 pm	**12:26 pm**	
☽ enters ≈	4:47 pm	**1:47 pm**	
☉♎ ⚻ ♆♓	11:32 pm	**8:32 pm**	

14 Thu
2nd ≈

☽≈ ☌ ♄≈	4:54 am	**1:54 am**
☽≈ ⚹ ♀♐	6:03 am	**3:03 am**
☽≈ ⚹ ♂♈	10:42 am	**7:42 am**
☽≈ △ ☿♎	1:09 pm	**10:09 am**
☽≈ □ ♅♉	4:52 pm	**1:52 pm**

Fri 15
2nd ♒

☽♒ △ ♂♎	3:58 am	**12:58 am**	
☉♎ △ ♃♒	7:46 am	**4:46 am**	
☽♒ ☌ ♃♒	8:29 am	**5:29 am**	
☽♒ △ ☉♎	8:33 am	**5:33 am**	☽ v/c
☽ enters ♓	10:22 pm	**7:22 pm**	

OP: After Moon trines Mars (see "Translating Darkness" on page 78) until v/c Moon. An excellent time for reaching out to important people, but with Mercury retrograde be sure to double-check everything.

Sat 16
2nd ♓

♀♐ △ ⚷♈	2:49 pm	**11:49 am**
☽♓ □ ♀♐	4:59 pm	**1:59 pm**
☽♓ ⚻ ☿♎	5:27 pm	**2:27 pm**
♂♎ ⚻ ♆♓	8:32 pm	**5:32 pm**
☿♎ ⚹ ♀♐	9:24 pm	**6:24 pm**
☽♓ ⚹ ♅♉	11:14 pm	**8:14 pm**

Sun 17
2nd ♓

Jupiter direct (Pacific)

☉♎ □ ♇♑	8:12 am	**5:12 am**	
☽♓ ☌ ♆♓	1:00 pm	**10:00 am**	
☽♓ ⚻ ♂♎	1:56 pm	**10:56 am**	
☽♓ ⚹ ♇♑	7:24 pm	**4:24 pm**	☽ v/c
☽♓ ⚻ ☉♎	8:20 pm	**5:20 pm**	
♃ D		**10:30 pm**	

Eastern Time plain / **Pacific Time bold**

SEPTEMBER

S	M	T	W	T	F	S
			1	2	3	4
5	6	7	8	9	10	11
12	13	14	15	16	17	18
19	20	21	22	23	24	25
26	27	28	29	30		

OCTOBER

S	M	T	W	T	F	S
					1	2
3	4	5	6	7	8	9
10	11	12	13	14	15	16
17	18	19	20	21	22	23
24	25	26	27	28	29	30
31						

NOVEMBER

S	M	T	W	T	F	S
	1	2	3	4	5	6
7	8	9	10	11	12	13
14	15	16	17	18	19	20
21	22	23	24	25	26	27
28	29	30				

October

Mercury Note: Mercury goes direct on Monday, October 18, but remains in its Storm, moving slowly, until October 22.

18 Mon

2nd ♓

Jupiter direct (Eastern)

Mercury direct

♃ D	1:30 am	
☽ enters ♈	6:04 am	**3:04 am**
☿ D	11:17 am	**8:17 am**
☽♈ ⚹ ♄♒	7:15 pm	**4:15 pm**
♂♎ △ ♃♒	10:36 pm	**7:36 pm**
☽♈ ☌ ⚷♈		**10:03 pm**
☽♈ ☍ ☿♎		**10:26 pm**

19 Tue

2nd ♈

☽♈ ☌ ⚷♈	1:03 am	
☽♈ ☍ ☿♎	1:26 am	
☽♈ △ ♀♐	6:40 am	**3:40 am**
♀♐ ⚻ ♅♉	7:15 pm	**4:15 pm**
☽♈ ⚹ ♃♒		**9:59 pm**
☽♈ ☍ ♂♎		**11:28 pm**

20 Wed

2nd ♈

○ Full Moon 27 ♈ 26

☽♈ ⚹ ♃♒	12:59 am	
☽♈ ☍ ♂♎	2:28 am	
☽♈ □ ♇♑	4:56 am	**1:56 am**
☽♈ ☍ ☉♎	10:57 am	**7:57 am** ☽ v/c
☽ enters ♉	3:59 pm	**12:59 pm**

21 Thu

3rd ♉

☽♉ □ ♄♒	5:45 am	**2:45 am**
☽♉ ⚻ ☿♎	1:44 pm	**10:44 am**
☽♉ ☌ ♅♉	6:28 pm	**3:28 pm**
☽♉ ⚻ ♀♐	11:08 pm	**8:08 pm**
♂♎ □ ♇♑		**9:20 pm**

Mercury Note: Mercury finally leaves its Storm on Saturday. Look over your notes on any ideas that occurred to you while Mercury was retrograde or slow. How do they look now?

♂︎ ☌ ⚹ ♀ ♑	12:20 am	
☽ ♉ ⚹ ♆ ♓	9:26 am	**6:26 am**
☽ ♉ □ ♃ ♒	12:32 pm	**9:32 am**
☽ ♉ △ ♀ ♑	4:35 pm	**1:35 pm** ☽ v/c
☽ ♉ ⚻ ♂︎ ♎	5:33 pm	**2:33 pm**
☉ enters ♏		**9:51 pm**

FRI 22
3rd ♉
SUN ENTERS SCORPIO (PACIFIC)

OP: After Moon squares Jupiter today until Moon enters Gemini on Saturday. (Taurus is one of the four signs in which the v/c Moon is a good thing. See page 75.) Keep a steady pace during this productive OP.

☉ enters ♏	12:51 am	
☽ enters ♊	3:57 am	**12:57 am**
☽ ♊ ⚻ ☉ ♏	4:14 am	**1:14 am**
☽ ♊ △ ♄ ♒	6:12 pm	**3:12 pm**
☽ ♊ ⚹ ⚷ ♈	11:46 pm	**8:46 pm**

SAT 23
3rd ♉
SUN ENTERS SCORPIO (EASTERN)

☽ ♊ △ ☿ ♎	6:17 am	**3:17 am**
☿ ♎ ⚻ ♅ ♉	1:45 pm	**10:45 am**
☽ ♊ ☍ ♀ ♐	5:42 pm	**2:42 pm**
☽ ♊ □ ♆ ♓	10:14 pm	**7:14 pm**
☽ ♊ △ ♃ ♒		**10:33 pm**

SUN 24
3rd ♊

OP: After Moon squares Neptune today until v/c Moon on Monday. Wait two hours after the square for clarity. Very good time for communication and socializing as Mercury picks up speed.

Eastern Time plain / **Pacific Time bold**

SEPTEMBER						
S	M	T	W	T	F	S
			1	2	3	4
5	6	7	8	9	10	11
12	13	14	15	16	17	18
19	20	21	22	23	24	25
26	27	28	29	30		

OCTOBER						
S	M	T	W	T	F	S
					1	2
3	4	5	6	7	8	9
10	11	12	13	14	15	16
17	18	19	20	21	22	23
24	25	26	27	28	29	30
31						

NOVEMBER						
S	M	T	W	T	F	S
	1	2	3	4	5	6
7	8	9	10	11	12	13
14	15	16	17	18	19	20
21	22	23	24	25	26	27
28	29	30				

25 Mon
3rd ♊

☽♊ △ ♃≈	1:33 am	
☽♊ ⊼ ♀♑	5:36 am	**2:36 am**
☽♊ △ ♂♎	10:11 am	**7:11 am** ☽ v/c
☽ enters ♋	5:00 pm	**2:00 pm**
☽♋ △ ☉♏	10:54 pm	**7:54 pm**

26 Tue
3rd ♋

☽♋ ⊼ ♄≈	7:21 am	**4:21 am**
☽♋ □ ♅♈	12:33 pm	**9:33 am**
☽♋ ✶ ♅♉	7:37 pm	**4:37 pm**
♀♐ □ ♆♓	9:06 pm	**6:06 pm**
☽♋ □ ☿♎		**10:10 pm**

27 Wed
3rd ♋

☽♋ □ ☿♎	1:10 am	
☽♋ △ ♆♓	10:48 am	**7:48 am**
☽♋ ⊼ ♀♐	12:04 pm	**9:04 am**
☽♋ ⊼ ♃≈	2:16 pm	**11:16 am**
☽♋ ☍ ♀♑	6:08 pm	**3:08 pm**
☽♋ □ ♂♎		**11:02 pm** ☽ v/c

28 Thu
3rd ♋
◐ 4th Quarter 5 ♌ 37

☽♋ □ ♂♎	2:02 am	☽ v/c
☽ enters ♌	5:07 am	**2:07 am**
♀♐ ✶ ♃≈	3:15 pm	**12:15 pm**
☽♌ □ ☉♏	4:05 pm	**1:05 pm**
☽♌ ☍ ♄≈	7:03 pm	**4:03 pm**
☽♌ △ ♅♈	11:42 pm	**8:42 pm**

☽♌ □ ♅♉	6:25 am	**3:25 am**	
☽♌ ⚹ ☿♎	6:32 pm	**3:32 pm**	
☽♌ ⊼ ♆♓	8:53 pm	**5:53 pm**	
☽♌ ☍ ♃≈		**9:24 pm**	

FRI 29
4th ♌

OP: After Moon opposes Jupiter today or Saturday until v/c Moon on Saturday. Good time for purchases and to connect with others, accomplish goals, etc.

☽♌ ☍ ♃≈ 12:24 am		

SAT 30
4th ♌

☽♌ △ ♀♐	3:05 am	**12:05 am** ☽ v/c
☽♌ ⊼ ♀♑	3:54 am	**12:54 am**	
☉♏ □ ♄≈	5:53 am	**2:53 am**	
♂ enters ♏	10:21 am	**7:21 am**	
☽ enters ♍	2:09 pm	**11:09 am**	
☽♍ ⚹ ♂♏	2:22 pm	**11:22 am**	
☿♎ ⊼ ♆♓	3:40 pm	**12:40 pm**	

☽♍ ⊼ ♄≈	3:17 am	**12:17 am**
☽♍ ⚹ ☉♏	4:58 am	**1:58 am**
☽♍ ⊼ ♀♈	7:19 am	**4:19 am**
☽♍ △ ♅♉	1:33 pm	**10:33 am**
☿♎ △ ♃≈		**9:18 pm**

SUN 31
4th ♍
HALLOWEEN
SAMHAIN

Eastern Time plain / **Pacific Time bold**

SEPTEMBER						
S	M	T	W	T	F	S
			1	2	3	4
5	6	7	8	9	10	11
12	13	14	15	16	17	18
19	20	21	22	23	24	25
26	27	28	29	30		

OCTOBER						
S	M	T	W	T	F	S
					1	2
3	4	5	6	7	8	9
10	11	12	13	14	15	16
17	18	19	20	21	22	23
24	25	26	27	28	29	30
31						

NOVEMBER						
S	M	T	W	T	F	S
	1	2	3	4	5	6
7	8	9	10	11	12	13
14	15	16	17	18	19	20
21	22	23	24	25	26	27
28	29	30				

November

1 MON
4th ♍
ALL SAINTS' DAY

☿ ☌ △ ♃ ≈	12:18 am	
☽♍ ☍ ♆ ♓	3:05 am	**12:05 am**
☽♍ ⚻ ♃ ≈	6:35 am	**3:35 am**
☽♍ △ ♀ ♑	9:43 am	**6:43 am**
☉♏ ⚻ ♅ ♈	11:20 am	**8:20 am**
☽♍ □ ♀ ♐	1:00 pm	**10:00 am** ☽ v/c
☽ enters ♎	7:11 pm	**4:11 pm**

2 TUE
4th ♎
ELECTION DAY (GENERAL)

☿♎ □ ♀ ♑	5:39 am	**2:39 am**
☽♎ △ ♄ ≈	7:31 am	**4:31 am**
☽♎ ☍ ♅ ♈	11:01 am	**8:01 am**
☽♎ ⚻ ♅ ♉	4:50 pm	**1:50 pm**

3 WED
4th ♎

OP: After Moon squares Pluto until v/c Moon. Use this excellent OP for finishing up projects during the Balsamic Moon.

☽♎ ⚻ ♆ ♓	5:36 am	**2:36 am**
☽♎ △ ♃ ≈	9:08 am	**6:08 am**
☽♎ □ ♀ ♑	11:57 am	**8:57 am**
☽♎ ☌ ☿ ♎	3:27 pm	**12:27 pm**
☽♎ ✶ ♀ ♐	6:32 pm	**3:32 pm** ☽ v/c
☽ enters ♏	8:52 pm	**5:52 pm**
☽♏ ☌ ♂♏		**10:55 pm**

4 THU
4th ♏
● New Moon 12 ♏ 40

☽♏ ☌ ♂♏	1:55 am	
☽♏ □ ♄ ≈	8:46 am	**5:46 am**
☽♏ ⚻ ♅ ♈	11:51 am	**8:51 am**
☽♏ ☌ ☉♏	5:15 pm	**2:15 pm**
☽♏ ☍ ♅ ♉	5:26 pm	**2:26 pm**
☉♏ ☍ ♅ ♉	7:58 pm	**4:58 pm**

Fri 5
1st ♏

☽♏△♆♓	5:53 am	**2:53 am**
♀ enters ♑	6:44 am	**3:44 am**
☽♏□♃♒	9:33 am	**6:33 am**
☽♏⚹♇♑	12:10 pm	**9:10 am** ☽ v/c
☿ enters ♏	6:35 pm	**3:35 pm**
☽ enters ♐	8:52 pm	**5:52 pm**

OP: After Moon squares Jupiter until v/c Moon. A few good hours to accomplish goals.

Sat 6
1st ♐

☽♐⚹♄♒	8:46 am	**5:46 am**
☽♐△⚷♈	11:36 am	**8:36 am**
☿♏⚹♀♑	11:59 am	**8:59 am**
☽♐⚻♅♉	5:09 pm	**2:09 pm**

Sun 7
1st ♐

☽♐□♆♓	4:47 am	**1:47 am**
☽♐⚹♃♒	8:44 am	**5:44 am** ☽ v/c
☽ enters ♑	8:03 pm	**5:03 pm**
☽♑☌♀♑		**9:19 pm**
☽♑⚹☿♏		**11:13 pm**

Daylight Saving Time ends at 2:00 a.m.

OP: After Moon squares Neptune until Moon enters Capricorn. Sunday is yours to use for fun, adventure, mind expansion, or anything you choose.

Eastern Time plain / **Pacific Time bold**

OCTOBER

S	M	T	W	T	F	S
					1	2
3	4	5	6	7	8	9
10	11	12	13	14	15	16
17	18	19	20	21	22	23
24	25	26	27	28	29	30
31						

NOVEMBER

S	M	T	W	T	F	S
	1	2	3	4	5	6
7	8	9	10	11	12	13
14	15	16	17	18	19	20
21	22	23	24	25	26	27
28	29	30				

DECEMBER

S	M	T	W	T	F	S
			1	2	3	4
5	6	7	8	9	10	11
12	13	14	15	16	17	18
19	20	21	22	23	24	25
26	27	28	29	30	31	

8 Mon
1st ♑

☽♑ ♂ ♀♑	12:19 am	
☽♑ ⚹ ☿♏	2:13 am	
☽♑ ⚹ ♂♏	5:49 am	**2:49 am**
☽♑ □ ♅♈	11:05 am	**8:05 am**
☽♑ △ ♅♉	4:48 pm	**1:48 pm**
☽♑ ⚹ ☉♏		**9:06 pm**

9 Tue
1st ♑

☽♑ ⚹ ☉♏	12:06 am	
☽♑ ⚹ ♆♓	6:01 am	**3:01 am**
☽♑ ♂ ♀♑	12:51 pm	**9:51 am** ☽ v/c
☽ enters ♒	10:03 pm	**7:03 pm**

10 Wed
1st ♒

☿♏ ♂ ♂♏	7:57 am	**4:57 am**
☽♒ □ ♂♏	10:55 am	**7:55 am**
☽♒ □ ☿♏	11:08 am	**8:08 am**
☽♒ ♂ ♄♒	11:15 am	**8:15 am**
☿♏ □ ♄♒	12:04 pm	**9:04 am**
☽♒ ⚹ ♅♈	1:45 pm	**10:45 am**
♂♏ □ ♄♒	6:14 pm	**3:14 pm**
☽♒ □ ♅♉	7:45 pm	**4:45 pm**

11 Thu
1st ♒

● 2nd Quarter 19 ♒ 21

VETERANS DAY
REMEMBRANCE DAY (CANADA)

OP: **After Moon squares Sun until v/c Moon.** The Crescent Moon favors continual growth, so use this good OP for starting anything that interests you.

☽♒ □ ☉♏	7:46 am	**4:46 am**
☿♏ ⚻ ♅♈	9:06 am	**6:06 am**
☽♒ ♂ ♃♒	2:52 pm	**11:52 am** ☽ v/c
☽ enters ♓		**11:54 pm**

Fri 12
2nd ♒

☽ enters ♓	2:54 am	
☉♏ △ ♆♓	11:24 am	**8:24 am**
☽♓ ⚹ ♀♑	3:18 pm	**12:18 pm**
♂♏ ⚻ ⚷♈	6:19 pm	**3:19 pm**
☽♓ △ ♂♏	7:28 pm	**4:28 pm**
☽♓ △ ☿♏		**9:23 pm**
☽♓ ⚹ ♅♉		**10:44 pm**

Sat 13
2nd ♓

☽♓ △ ☿♏	12:23 am		
☽♓ ⚹ ♅♉	1:44 am		
☿♏ ☍ ♅♉	10:57 am	**7:57 am**	
☽♓ ☌ ♆♓	4:46 pm	**1:46 pm**	
☽♓ △ ☉♏	7:19 pm	**4:19 pm**	
☽♓ ⚹ ♇♑		**9:40 pm**	☽ v/c

OP: After Moon conjoins Neptune today until Moon enters Aries on Sunday. Intuition is heightened—use it to start creative projects that spark your interest.

Sun 14
2nd ♓

☽♓ ⚹ ♇♑	12:40 am		☽ v/c
☽ enters ♈	10:48 am	**7:48 am**	
☽♈ ⚹ ♄♒		**10:59 pm**	

Eastern Time plain / **Pacific Time bold**

OCTOBER

S	M	T	W	T	F	S
					1	2
3	4	5	6	7	8	9
10	11	12	13	14	15	16
17	18	19	20	21	22	23
24	25	26	27	28	29	30
31						

NOVEMBER

S	M	T	W	T	F	S
	1	2	3	4	5	6
7	8	9	10	11	12	13
14	15	16	17	18	19	20
21	22	23	24	25	26	27
28	29	30				

DECEMBER

S	M	T	W	T	F	S
			1	2	3	4
5	6	7	8	9	10	11
12	13	14	15	16	17	18
19	20	21	22	23	24	25
26	27	28	29	30	31	

November

15 Mon
2nd ♈

☽♈ ⚹ ♄≈	1:59 am		
♀♑ □ ♅♈	3:07 am	**12:07 am**	
☽♈ ♂ ♅♈	4:02 am	**1:02 am**	
☽♈ □ ♀♑	4:06 am	**1:06 am**	
☽♈ ⊼ ♂♏	7:32 am	**4:32 am**	
☉♏ □ ♃≈	2:58 pm	**11:58 am**	
☽♈ ⊼ ☿♏	5:58 pm	**2:58 pm**	

16 Tue
2nd ♈

☽♈ ⚹ ♃≈	8:55 am	**5:55 am**	
☽♈ ⊼ ☉♏	10:23 am	**7:23 am**	
☽♈ □ ♀♑	10:51 am	**7:51 am**	☽ v/c
☉♏ ⚹ ♀♑	4:01 pm	**1:01 pm**	
☽ enters ♉	9:18 pm	**6:18 pm**	

17 Wed
2nd ♉

♂♏ ☍ ♅♉	12:23 pm	**9:23 am**	
☽♉ □ ♄≈	1:19 pm	**10:19 am**	
☽♉ △ ♀♑	7:39 pm	**4:39 pm**	
☽♉ ♂ ♅♉	9:44 pm	**6:44 pm**	
☽♉ ☍ ♂♏	10:20 pm	**7:20 pm**	

18 Thu
2nd ♉

☿♏ △ ♆♓	10:38 am	**7:38 am**	
☽♉ ⚹ ♆♓	2:14 pm	**11:14 am**	
☽♉ ☍ ☿♏	2:48 pm	**11:48 am**	
☽♉ □ ♃≈	9:23 pm	**6:23 pm**	
☽♉ △ ♀♑	10:57 pm	**7:57 pm**	
♀♑ △ ♅♉		**10:08 pm**	

♀♍△♅♉ 1:08 am
☽♉ ☍☉♏ 3:57 am **12:57 am** ☽ v/c
☽ enters ♊ 9:33 am **6:33 am**
☽♊ △ ♄≈ **11:12 pm**

Lunar Eclipse | ○ Full Moon 27 ♉ 14

☽♊ △ ♄≈ 2:12 am
☽♊ ⚹ ♂♈ 3:27 am **12:27 am**
☽♊ ⊼ ♀♑ 12:43 pm **9:43 am**
☽♊ ⊼ ♂♏ 2:46 pm **11:46 am**
☿♏ □ ♃≈ 6:43 pm **3:43 pm**

☽♊ □ ♆♓ 3:05 am **12:05 am**
☿♏ ⚹ ♀♑ 4:14 am **1:14 am**
☽♊ △ ♃≈ 10:52 am **7:52 am** ☽ v/c
☽♊ ⊼ ♀♑ 12:01 pm **9:01 am**
☽♊ ⊼ ☿♏ 1:13 pm **10:13 am**
☉ enters ♐ 9:34 pm **6:34 pm**
☽ enters ♋ 10:33 pm **7:33 pm**
☽♋ ⊼ ☉♐ 10:38 pm **7:38 pm**

SUN ENTERS SAGITTARIUS
OP: After Moon squares Neptune until v/c Moon. Use this powerful OP for clever insights, but be open to change between the two eclipses.

Eastern Time plain / **Pacific Time bold**

	OCTOBER					
S	M	T	W	T	F	S
					1	2
3	4	5	6	7	8	9
10	11	12	13	14	15	16
17	18	19	20	21	22	23
24	25	26	27	28	29	30
31						

	NOVEMBER					
S	M	T	W	T	F	S
	1	2	3	4	5	6
7	8	9	10	11	12	13
14	15	16	17	18	19	20
21	22	23	24	25	26	27
28	29	30				

	DECEMBER					
S	M	T	W	T	F	S
			1	2	3	4
5	6	7	8	9	10	11
12	13	14	15	16	17	18
19	20	21	22	23	24	25
26	27	28	29	30	31	

22 Mon
3rd ♋

☽♋ ⊼ ♄≈	3:32 pm	**12:32 pm**
☽♋ □ ♋♈	4:19 pm	**1:19 pm**
☽♋ ✶ ♅♉	10:59 pm	**7:59 pm**

23 Tue
3rd ♋

☽♋ ☍ ♀♑	5:49 am	**2:49 am**
☽♋ △ ♂♏	7:24 am	**4:24 am**
☽♋ △ ♆♓	3:50 pm	**12:50 pm**
☽♋ ⊼ ♃≈		**9:06 pm**
☽♋ ☍ ♀♑		**9:46 pm** ☽ v/c

24 Wed
3rd ♋

☽♋ ⊼ ♃≈	12:06 am	
☽♋ ☍ ♀♑	12:46 am	☽ v/c
☿ enters ♐	10:36 am	**7:36 am**
☽ enters ♌	10:59 am	**7:59 am**
☽♌ △ ☿♐	11:02 am	**8:02 am**
☽♌ △ ☉♐	4:34 pm	**1:34 pm**

25 Thu
3rd ♌
Thanksgiving Day (US)

☽♌ ☍ ♄≈	3:52 am	**12:52 am**
☽♌ △ ♋♈	4:10 am	**1:10 am**
☽♌ □ ♅♉	10:32 am	**7:32 am**
☽♌ ⊼ ♀♑	8:57 pm	**5:57 pm**
☽♌ □ ♂♏	10:19 pm	**7:19 pm**
☽♌ ⊼ ♆♓		**11:55 pm**

Fri 26
3rd ♌

☽♌ ⚻ ♆♓	2:55 am	
☽♌ ☍ ♃♒	11:24 am	**8:24 am** ☽ v/c
☽♌ ⚻ ♇♑	11:35 am	**8:35 am**
♄♒ ⚹ ⚷♈	8:03 pm	**5:03 pm**
☽ enters ♍	9:12 pm	**6:12 pm**

Sat 27
3rd ♍

◑ 4th Quarter 5 ♍ 28

☽♍ □ ☿♐	5:27 am	**2:27 am**
☽♍ □ ☉♐	7:28 am	**4:28 am**
☽♍ ⚻ ⚷♈	1:22 pm	**10:22 am**
☽♍ ⚻ ♄♒	1:30 pm	**10:30 am**
☽♍ △ ♅♉	7:18 pm	**4:18 pm**

Sun 28
4th ♍

Hanukkah begins at sundown

☽♍ △ ♀♑	8:15 am	**5:15 am**
☽♍ ⚹ ♂♏	9:37 am	**6:37 am**
☽♍ ☍ ♆♓	10:50 am	**7:50 am**
☽♍ △ ♇♑	7:02 pm	**4:02 pm** ☽ v/c
☽♍ ⚻ ♃♒	7:17 pm	**4:17 pm**
☉♐ ☌ ☿♐	11:39 pm	**8:39 pm**

Eastern Time plain / **Pacific Time bold**

OCTOBER

S	M	T	W	T	F	S
					1	2
3	4	5	6	7	8	9
10	11	12	13	14	15	16
17	18	19	20	21	22	23
24	25	26	27	28	29	30
31						

NOVEMBER

S	M	T	W	T	F	S
	1	2	3	4	5	6
7	8	9	10	11	12	13
14	15	16	17	18	19	20
21	22	23	24	25	26	27
28	29	30				

DECEMBER

S	M	T	W	T	F	S
			1	2	3	4
5	6	7	8	9	10	11
12	13	14	15	16	17	18
19	20	21	22	23	24	25
26	27	28	29	30	31	

29 Mon
4th ♍

☽ enters ♎	3:55 am	**12:55 am**
♂♏△♆♓	9:10 am	**6:10 am**
☽♎✶☉♐	5:44 pm	**2:44 pm**
☽♎✶☿♐	6:33 pm	**3:33 pm**
☽♎☍♅♈	6:55 pm	**3:55 pm**
☽♎△♄≈	7:24 pm	**4:24 pm**
☿♐△♅♈	9:41 pm	**6:41 pm**
☽♎⚻♅♉		9:22 pm
☿♐✶♄≈		11:19 pm

30 Tue
4th ♎

OP: After Moon squares Pluto until v/c Moon. This short OP during the Last Quarter Moon is positive for delivering your completed project.

☽♎⚻♅♉	12:22 am	
☿♐✶♄≈	2:19 am	
☉♐△♅♈	9:38 am	**6:38 am**
☽♎□♀♑	2:56 pm	**11:56 am**
☽♎⚻♆♓	2:58 pm	**11:58 am**
♀♑✶♆♓	3:46 pm	**12:46 pm**
☉♐✶♄≈	6:14 pm	**3:14 pm**
☽♎□♀♑	10:43 pm	**7:43 pm**
☽♎△♃≈	11:20 pm	**8:20 pm** ☽ v/c

1 Wed
4th ♎
Neptune direct

☽ enters ♏	6:55 am	**3:55 am**
♆D	8:22 am	**5:22 am**
☽♏⚻♅♈	8:56 pm	**5:56 pm**
☿♐⚻♅♉	9:15 pm	**6:15 pm**
☽♏□♄≈	9:43 pm	**6:43 pm**
☽♏☍♅♉		11:01 pm

2 Thu
4th ♏

☽♏☍♅♉	2:01 am	
☽♏△♆♓	3:58 pm	**12:58 pm**
☽♏✶♀♑	5:52 pm	**2:52 pm**
☽♏♂♏	7:45 pm	**4:45 pm**
☽♏✶♀♑	11:26 pm	**8:26 pm**
☽♏□♃≈		9:22 pm ☽ v/c

Fri 3
4th ♏

Solar Eclipse | ● New Moon 12 ♐ 22 (Pacific)

☽♏ □ ♃♒	12:22 am		☽ v/c
☽ enters ♐	7:13 am	**4:13 am**	
☉♐ ⊼ ♅♉	10:14 am	**7:14 am**	
☽♐ △ ⚷♈	8:42 pm	**5:42 pm**	
☽♐ ⚹ ♄♒	9:46 pm	**6:46 pm**	
☽♐ ⊼ ♅♉		**10:35 pm**	
☽♐ ☌ ☉♐		**11:43 pm**	

Sat 4
4th ♐

Solar Eclipse | ● New Moon 12 ♐ 22 (Eastern)

☽♐ ⊼ ♅♉	1:35 am		
☽♐ ☌ ☉♐	2:43 am		
☽♐ ☌ ☿♐	7:43 am	**4:43 am**	
☽♐ □ ♆♓	3:22 pm	**12:22 pm**	
☽♐ ⚹ ♃♒		**9:08 pm**	☽ v/c

OP: After Moon sextiles Jupiter today until Moon enters Capricorn on Sunday. A good opportunity to be enthusiastic with the Moon just out from under-the-beams, if you like staying up late!

Sun 5
1st ♐

☽♐ ⚹ ♃♒	12:08 am		☽ v/c
☽ enters ♑	6:31 am	**3:31 am**	
☽♑ □ ⚷♈	8:03 pm	**5:03 pm**	
☽♑ △ ♅♉		**9:56 pm**	

OP: Two back-to-back OPs: The second OP starts when the Moon enters Capricorn today until v/c Moon on Monday. Use this powerful OP to pursue any interest or goal, from hard work to romance.

Eastern Time plain / **Pacific Time bold**

NOVEMBER

S	M	T	W	T	F	S
	1	2	3	4	5	6
7	8	9	10	11	12	13
14	15	16	17	18	19	20
21	22	23	24	25	26	27
28	29	30				

DECEMBER

S	M	T	W	T	F	S
			1	2	3	4
5	6	7	8	9	10	11
12	13	14	15	16	17	18
19	20	21	22	23	24	25
26	27	28	29	30	31	

JANUARY 2022

S	M	T	W	T	F	S
						1
2	3	4	5	6	7	8
9	10	11	12	13	14	15
16	17	18	19	20	21	22
23	24	25	26	27	28	29
30	31					

December

6 Mon
1st ♏
Hanukkah ends

☽♑ △ ♅♉	12:56 am	
♂♏ ✶ ♀♑	6:41 am	**3:41 am**
☽♑ ✶ ♆♓	3:09 pm	**12:09 pm**
☽♑ ♂ ♀♑	8:21 pm	**5:21 pm**
☽♑ ♂ ☿♑	10:56 pm	**7:56 pm**
☽♑ ✶ ♂♏	11:42 pm	**8:42 pm** ☽ v/c

7 Tue
1st ♑

☽ enters ♒	6:49 am	**3:49 am**
☿♐ □ ♆♓	10:16 am	**7:16 am**
☽♒ ✶ ♃♈	8:56 pm	**5:56 pm**
☽♒ ♂ ♄♒	10:43 pm	**7:43 pm**
♂♏ □ ♃♒		**10:21 pm**
☽♒ □ ♅♉		**11:01 pm**

8 Wed
1st ♒

♂♏ □ ♃♒	1:21 am	
☽♒ □ ♅♉	2:01 am	
☽♒ ✶ ☉♐	10:57 am	**7:57 am**
☽♒ ✶ ☿♐	9:07 pm	**6:07 pm**

9 Thu
1st ♒

☽♒ ♂ ♃♒	3:53 am	**12:53 am**
☽♒ □ ♂♏	5:00 am	**2:00 am** ☽ v/c
☽ enters ♓	9:53 am	**6:53 am**

☽♓ ✶ ♅♉ 6:22 am **3:22 am**
☽♓ □ ☉♐ 8:36 pm **5:36 pm**
☽♓ ☌ ♆♓ 10:50 pm **7:50 pm**

FRI 10
1st ♓
◗ 2nd Quarter 19 ♓ 13

☽♓ ✶ ♀♑ 7:52 am **4:52 am**
☽♓ ✶ ♀♑ 7:56 am **4:56 am**
☽♓ □ ☿♐ 10:33 am **7:33 am**
♀♑ ☌ ♀♑ 11:29 am **8:29 am**
☿♐ ✶ ♃≈ 2:24 pm **11:24 am**
☽♓ △ ♂♏ 2:40 pm **11:40 am** ☽ v/c
☽ enters ♈ 4:46 pm **1:46 pm**
☉♐ □ ♆♓ **10:21 pm**

SAT 11
2nd ♓

OP: After Moon squares Mercury until Moon enters Aries. (Pisces is one of the four signs in which the v/c Moon is a good thing. See page 75.) This OP is excellent for pursuing lofty plans.

☉♐ □ ♆♓ 1:21 am
☽♈ ☌ ♃♈ 8:56 am **5:56 am**
☽♈ ✶ ♄≈ 11:50 am **8:50 am**

SUN 12
2nd ♈

Eastern Time plain / **Pacific Time bold**

NOVEMBER								DECEMBER								JANUARY 2022					
S	M	T	W	T	F	S		S	M	T	W	T	F	S		S	M	T	W	T	F	S
	1	2	3	4	5	6					1	2	3	4								1
7	8	9	10	11	12	13		5	6	7	8	9	10	11		2	3	4	5	6	7	8
14	15	16	17	18	19	20		12	13	14	15	16	17	18		9	10	11	12	13	14	15
21	22	23	24	25	26	27		19	20	21	22	23	24	25		16	17	18	19	20	21	22
28	29	30						26	27	28	29	30	31			23	24	25	26	27	28	29
																30	31					

December

13 Mon
2nd ♈

OP: After Moon squares Venus until v/c Moon. The Moon is between two benefics during this short, lovely OP. A good time to start a project.

♂ enters ♐	4:53 am	**1:53 am**	
☽♈ △ ☉♐	11:03 am	**8:03 am**	
☿ enters ♑	12:52 pm	**9:52 am**	
☽♈ □ ♀♑	6:01 pm	**3:01 pm**	
☽♈ □ ♀♑	7:02 pm	**4:02 pm**	
☽♈ ⚹ ♃≈	9:52 pm	**6:52 pm** ☽ v/c	

14 Tue
2nd ♈

☽ enters ♉	3:11 am	**12:11 am**
☽♉ ⚻ ♂♐	4:33 am	**1:33 am**
☽♉ △ ☿♑	5:20 am	**2:20 am**
☽♉ □ ♄≈	11:36 pm	**8:36 pm**
☽♉ ♂ ♅♉		**10:51 pm**

15 Wed
2nd ♉

OP: After Moon sextiles Neptune today until Moon enters Gemini on Thursday. This OP offers a stable time to work on practical, artistic, or financial matters.

☽♉ ♂ ♅♉	1:51 am	
☽♉ ⚹ ♆♓	8:21 pm	**5:21 pm**

16 Thu
2nd ♉

☽♉ ⚻ ☉♐	4:50 am	**1:50 am**	
☽♉ △ ♀♑	6:29 am	**3:29 am**	
☽♉ △ ♀♑	8:14 am	**5:14 am**	
☽♉ □ ♃≈	11:08 am	**8:08 am** ☽ v/c	
☽ enters ♊	3:43 pm	**12:43 pm**	
☽♊ ☍ ♂♐	8:56 pm	**5:56 pm**	

☽♊ ⊼ ☿♑   3:14 am **12:14 am**
☽♊ ⚹ ♅♈   8:53 am **5:53 am**
☽♊ △ ♄≈   12:57 pm **9:57 am**

FRI 17
2nd ♊

☽♊ ☐ ♆♓   9:24 am **6:24 am**
☽♊ ⊼ ♀♑   7:38 pm **4:38 pm**
☽♊ ⊼ ♀♑   9:35 pm **6:35 pm**
☿♑ ☐ ♅♈   9:35 pm **6:35 pm**
☽♊ ☍ ☉♐   11:36 pm **8:36 pm**

☽♊ △ ♃≈   **10:02 pm** ☽ v/c

SAT 18
2nd ♊
○ Full Moon 27 ♊ 29
OP: After Moon opposes Sun today until v/c Moon today or
Sunday. This Full Moon OP is good for both work and fun.

☽♊ △ ♃≈   1:02 am   ☽ v/c
☽ enters ♋   4:42 am **1:42 am**
♀℞   5:36 am **2:36 am**
♅ D   11:33 am **8:33 am**
☽♋ ⊼ ♂♐   1:43 pm **10:43 am**
☉♐ ⚹ ♃≈   7:32 pm **4:32 pm**
☽♋ ☐ ♅♈   9:45 pm **6:45 pm**
☽♋ ☍ ☿♑   **10:25 pm**
☽♋ ⊼ ♄≈   **11:17 pm**

SUN 19
3rd ♊
VENUS RETROGRADE
CHIRON DIRECT

Eastern Time plain / **Pacific Time bold**

NOVEMBER						
S	M	T	W	T	F	S
	1	2	3	4	5	6
7	8	9	10	11	12	13
14	15	16	17	18	19	20
21	22	23	24	25	26	27
28	29	30				

DECEMBER						
S	M	T	W	T	F	S
			1	2	3	4
5	6	7	8	9	10	11
12	13	14	15	16	17	18
19	20	21	22	23	24	25
26	27	28	29	30	31	

JANUARY 2022						
S	M	T	W	T	F	S
						1
2	3	4	5	6	7	8
9	10	11	12	13	14	15
16	17	18	19	20	21	22
23	24	25	26	27	28	29
30	31					

December

20 Mon
3rd ♋

☽♋ ☌ ☿♑	1:25 am	
☽♋ ⊼ ♄≈	2:17 am	
☽♋ ⚹ ♅♉	3:17 am	**12:17 am**
☿♑ △ ♅♉	3:18 pm	**12:18 pm**
☽♋ △ ♆♓	10:00 pm	**7:00 pm**

21 Tue
3rd ♋
Winter Solstice
Yule
Sun enters Capricorn

☽♋ ☌ ♀♑	8:10 am	**5:10 am**
☽♋ ☌ ♀♑	9:44 am	**6:44 am** ☽ v/c
☉ enters ♑	10:59 am	**7:59 am**
☽♋ ⊼ ♃≈	2:12 pm	**11:12 am**
☽ enters ♌	4:54 pm	**1:54 pm**
☽♌ ⊼ ☉♑	5:26 pm	**2:26 pm**

22 Wed
3rd ♌

☽♌ △ ♂♐	5:24 am	**2:24 am**
☽♌ △ ⚷♈	9:34 am	**6:34 am**
☽♌ ☌ ♄≈	2:28 pm	**11:28 am**
☽♌ □ ♅♉	2:50 pm	**11:50 am**
☽♌ ⊼ ☿♑	9:54 pm	**6:54 pm**

23 Thu
3rd ♌

☽♌ ⊼ ♆♓	9:12 am	**6:12 am**
☽♌ ⊼ ♀♑	7:07 pm	**4:07 pm**
☽♌ ⊼ ♀♑	7:50 pm	**4:50 pm**
☽♌ ☌ ♃≈		**10:39 pm** ☽ v/c
♄≈ □ ♅♉		**11:17 pm**

☽♌ ☍ ♃≈	1:39 am	☽ v/c
♄≈ □ ♅♉	2:17 am	
☽ enters ♍	3:24 am **12:24 am**	
☽♍ △ ☉♑	9:05 am **6:05 am**	
☽♍ □ ♂♐	6:52 pm **3:52 pm**	
☽♍ ⚹ ♅♈	7:28 pm **4:28 pm**	
☽♍ △ ♅♉		**9:24 pm**
☽♍ ⚹ ♄≈		**9:37 pm**

FRI 24
3rd ♌
CHRISTMAS EVE

☽♍ △ ♅♉	12:24 am
☽♍ ⚹ ♄≈	12:37 am
♂♐ △ ♅♈	5:37 am **2:37 am**
♀♑ ☌ ♀♑	7:02 am **4:02 am**
☽♍ △ ☿♑	3:08 pm **12:08 pm**
☽♍ ☍ ♆♓	6:07 pm **3:07 pm**

SAT 25
3rd ♍
CHRISTMAS DAY
OP: After Moon opposes Neptune today until v/c Moon on Sunday. Wait two hours after the opposition, then take advantage of this productive time.

☽♍ △ ♀♑	3:12 am **12:12 am**	
☽♍ △ ♀♑	3:39 am **12:39 am**	☽ v/c
☽♍ ⚹ ♃≈	10:32 am **7:32 am**	
☽ enters ♎	11:24 am **8:24 am**	
☿♑ ⚹ ♆♓	4:29 pm **1:29 pm**	
☽♎ □ ☉♑	9:24 pm **6:24 pm**	
☽♎ ☍ ♅♈		**11:39 pm**

SUN 26
3rd ♍
◐ 4th Quarter 5 ♎ 32
KWANZAA BEGINS
BOXING DAY (CANADA & UK)

Eastern Time plain / **Pacific Time bold**

NOVEMBER						
S	M	T	W	T	F	S
	1	2	3	4	5	6
7	8	9	10	11	12	13
14	15	16	17	18	19	20
21	22	23	24	25	26	27
28	29	30				

DECEMBER						
S	M	T	W	T	F	S
			1	2	3	4
5	6	7	8	9	10	11
12	13	14	15	16	17	18
19	20	21	22	23	24	25
26	27	28	29	30	31	

JANUARY 2022						
S	M	T	W	T	F	S
						1
2	3	4	5	6	7	8
9	10	11	12	13	14	15
16	17	18	19	20	21	22
23	24	25	26	27	28	29
30	31					

27 Mon
4th ♎

☽♎ ☍ ♂ ♈	2:39 am	
☽♎ ⚹ ♂ ♐	5:07 am	**2:07 am**
☽♎ ⚻ ♅ ♉	7:13 am	**4:13 am**
☽♎ △ ♄ ♒	7:55 am	**4:55 am**
☽♎ ⚻ ♆ ♓		**9:04 pm**

28 Tue
4th ♎

OP: After Moon squares Pluto until v/c Moon. Powerful OP for reaching out, socializing, networking, etc.

☽♎ ⚻ ♆ ♓	12:04 am	
☽♎ □ ☿ ♑	3:57 am	**12:57 am**
☽♎ □ ♀ ♑	7:19 am	**4:19 am**
☽♎ □ ♇ ♑	9:06 am	**6:06 am**
☽♎ △ ♃ ♒	4:11 pm	**1:11 pm** ☽ v/c
☽ enters ♏	4:16 pm	**1:16 pm**
♂ ♐ ⚻ ♅ ♉	8:04 pm	**5:04 pm**
♃ enters ♓	11:09 pm	**8:09 pm**

29 Wed
4th ♏

☿♑ ☌ ♀ ♑	5:27 am	**2:27 am**
☽♏ ⚹ ☉ ♑	5:43 am	**2:43 am**
☽♏ ⚻ ♂ ♈	6:39 am	**3:39 am**
☽♏ ☍ ♅ ♉	10:51 am	**7:51 am**
☽♏ □ ♄ ♒	11:58 am	**8:58 am**
☉♑ □ ♂ ♈	6:53 pm	**3:53 pm**
♂ ♐ ⚹ ♄ ♒	7:22 pm	**4:22 pm**
☽♏ △ ♆ ♓		**11:51 pm**

30 Thu
4th ♏

☽♏ △ ♆ ♓	2:51 am	
☿♑ ☌ ♀ ♑	4:54 am	**1:54 am**
☽♏ ⚹ ♀ ♑	8:19 am	**5:19 am**
☽♏ ⚹ ♇ ♑	11:27 am	**8:27 am**
☽♏ ⚹ ☿ ♑	12:10 pm	**9:10 am** ☽ v/c
☽ enters ♐	6:08 pm	**3:08 pm**
☽♐ □ ♃ ♓	6:42 pm	**3:42 pm**

FRI 31
4th ♐
NEW YEAR'S EVE

☽♐ △ ⚷♈ 7:51 am **4:51 am**
☽♐ ⚻ ♅♉ 11:47 am **8:47 am**
☽♐ ⚹ ♄♒ 1:15 pm **10:15 am**
☽♐ ☌ ♂♐ 3:01 pm **12:01 pm**

SAT 1
4th ♐
NEW YEAR'S DAY
KWANZAA ENDS

☽♐ □ ♆♓ 3:16 am **12:16 am** ☽ v/c
☉♑△♅♉ 4:50 am **1:50 am**
☽ enters ♑ 6:02 pm **3:02 pm**
☽♑ ⚹ ♃♓ 7:13 pm **4:13 pm**
☿ enters ♒ **11:10 pm**

SUN 2
4th ♑
● New Moon 12 ♑ 20

☿ enters ♒ 2:10 am
☽♑□ ⚷♈ 7:31 am **4:31 am**
☽♑△ ♅♉ 11:20 am **8:20 am**
☽♑ ☌ ☉♑ 1:33 pm **10:33 am**
☽♑ ⚹ ♆♓ **11:52 pm**

OP: This Cazimi Moon is usable ½ hour before and ½ hour after the Sun-Moon conjunction. If you have something important to start around now, this is a great time to do it.

Eastern Time plain / **Pacific Time bold**

NOVEMBER

S	M	T	W	T	F	S
	1	2	3	4	5	6
7	8	9	10	11	12	13
14	15	16	17	18	19	20
21	22	23	24	25	26	27
28	29	30				

DECEMBER

S	M	T	W	T	F	S
			1	2	3	4
5	6	7	8	9	10	11
12	13	14	15	16	17	18
19	20	21	22	23	24	25
26	27	28	29	30	31	

JANUARY 2022

S	M	T	W	T	F	S
						1
2	3	4	5	6	7	8
9	10	11	12	13	14	15
16	17	18	19	20	21	22
23	24	25	26	27	28	29
30	31					

World Time Zones
Compared to Eastern Standard Time

(R) EST	(D) Add 9 hours
(S) CST/Subtract 1 hour	(D*) Add 9.5 hours
(Q) Add 1 hour	(E) Add 10 hours
(P) Add 2 hours	(E*) Add 10.5 hours
(O) Add 3 hours	(F) Add 11 hours
(Z) Add 5 hours	(F*) Add 11.5 hours
(T) MST/Subtract 2 hours	(G) Add 12 hours
(U) PST/Subtract 3 hours	(H) Add 13 hours
(U*) Subtract 3.5 hours	(I) Add 14 hours
(V) Subtract 4 hours	(I*) Add 14.5 hours
(V*) Subtract 4.5 hours	(K) Add 15 hours
(W) Subtract 5 hours	(K*) Add 15.5 hours
(X) Subtract 6 hours	(L) Add 16 hours
(Y) Subtract 7 hours	(L*) Add 16.5 hours
(A) Add 6 hours	(M) Add 17 hours
(B) Add 7 hours	(M*) Add 18 hours
(C) Add 8 hours	(P*) Add 2.5 hours
(C*) Add 8.5 hours	

Eastern Standard Time = Universal Time (Greenwich Mean Time) + or − the value from the table.

World Map of Time Zones

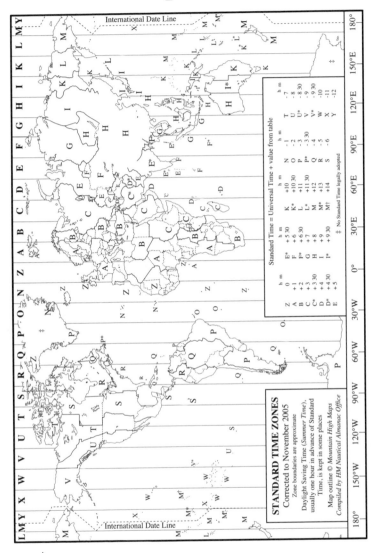

DATE	SID.TIME	SUN	MOON	NODE	MERCURY	VENUS	MARS	JUPITER	SATURN	URANUS	NEPTUNE	PLUTO	CERES	PALLAS	JUNO	VESTA	CHIRON
1 F	6 43 27	10♑46 47	2♌44	19Ⅱ53R	17♑43	20♐25	27♈21	2≈47	1≈37	6♉48R	18♓28	24♑11	12♓00	7≈51	4♐15	20♍09	5♈04
2 Sa	6 47 24	11 47 56	15 55	19 49	19 21	21 40	27 48	3 01	1 44	6 47	18 30	24 13	12 18	8 11	4 34	20 16	5 04
3 Su	6 51 21	12 49 04	29 19	19 46	20 59	22 55	28 14	3 14	1 51	6 47	18 31	24 15	12 37	8 31	4 52	20 24	5 05
4 M	6 55 17	13 50 13	12♍55	19 43	22 37	24 10	28 40	3 28	1 58	6 46	18 32	24 17	12 56	8 51	5 11	20 30	5 06
5 T	6 59 14	14 51 22	26 42	19 40	24 15	25 25	29 07	3 42	2 05	6 46	18 33	24 19	13 15	9 11	5 30	20 37	5 08
6 W	7 3 10	15 52 31	10♎39	19 39D	25 54	26 40	29 34	3 56	2 12	6 45	18 34	24 21	13 34	9 31	5 48	20 43	5 09
7 Th	7 7 7	16 53 40	24 45	19 39	27 32	27 56	0♉02	4 10	2 19	6 45	18 36	24 23	13 53	9 51	6 07	20 49	5 10
8 F	7 11 3	17 54 50	8♏58	19 40	29 11	29 11	0 29	4 24	2 26	6 44	18 37	24 25	14 13	10 11	6 25	20 54	5 11
9 Sa	7 15 0	18 56 00	23 16	19 42	0≈49	0♑26	0 57	4 38	2 33	6 44	18 38	24 27	14 32	10 31	6 43	20 59	5 12
10 Su	7 18 56	19 57 09	7♐38	19 43R	2 27	1 41	1 25	4 52	2 40	6 44	18 40	24 29	14 52	10 51	7 01	21 04	5 14
11 M	7 22 53	20 58 19	21 58	19 44	4 05	2 56	1 54	5 06	2 47	6 44	18 41	24 31	15 11	11 11	7 19	21 08	5 15
12 T	7 26 50	21 59 29	6♑13	19 43	5 43	4 12	2 22	5 20	2 54	6 43	18 42	24 33	15 31	11 31	7 37	21 11	5 16
13 W	7 30 46	23 00 39	20 19	19 40	7 20	5 27	2 51	5 34	3 01	6 43	18 44	24 35	15 51	11 51	7 55	21 14	5 18
14 Th	7 34 43	24 01 48	4≈10	19 35	8 56	6 42	3 20	5 48	3 08	6 43D	18 45	24 37	16 11	12 12	8 13	21 17	5 19
15 F	7 38 39	25 02 57	17 43	19 30	10 30	7 57	3 49	6 02	3 15	6 43	18 47	24 39	16 31	12 32	8 31	21 19	5 21
16 Sa	7 42 36	26 04 05	0♓56	19 23	12 04	9 13	4 19	6 16	3 22	6 43	18 48	24 41	16 52	12 52	8 49	21 21	5 23
17 Su	7 46 32	27 05 12	13 48	19 17	13 35	10 28	4 48	6 30	3 30	6 43	18 50	24 43	17 12	13 12	9 06	21 22	5 24
18 M	7 50 29	28 06 19	26 20	19 11	15 05	11 43	5 18	6 44	3 37	6 44	18 52	24 45	17 32	13 33	9 24	21 23	5 26
19 T	7 54 25	29 07 24	8♈35	19 07	16 32	12 58	5 48	6 59	3 44	6 44	18 53	24 47	17 53	13 53	9 41	21 24R	5 28
20 W	7 58 22	0≈08 29	20 37	19 05D	17 55	14 13	6 18	7 13	3 51	6 44	18 55	24 49	18 14	14 13	9 58	21 24	5 30
21 Th	8 2 19	1 09 34	2♉30	19 04	19 15	15 29	6 49	7 27	3 58	6 44	18 56	24 51	18 34	14 34	10 15	21 23	5 31
22 F	8 6 15	2 10 37	14 19	19 05	20 31	16 44	7 19	7 41	4 05	6 45	18 58	24 53	18 55	14 54	10 32	21 22	5 33
23 Sa	8 10 12	3 11 39	26 10	19 07	21 42	17 59	7 50	7 55	4 12	6 45	19 00	24 55	19 16	15 14	10 49	21 21	5 35
24 Su	8 14 8	4 12 40	8Ⅱ08	19 08R	22 47	19 14	8 21	8 10	4 19	6 46	19 02	24 57	19 37	15 34	11 06	21 19	5 37
25 M	8 18 5	5 13 41	20 17	19 09	23 45	20 30	8 52	8 24	4 27	6 46	19 03	24 59	19 58	15 55	11 23	21 16	5 39
26 T	8 22 1	6 14 40	2♋41	19 07	24 35	21 45	9 23	8 38	4 34	6 47	19 05	25 01	20 19	16 15	11 39	21 13	5 41
27 W	8 25 58	7 15 39	15 23	19 04	25 18	23 00	9 54	8 52	4 41	6 48	19 07	25 03	20 41	16 36	11 56	21 10	5 44
28 Th	8 29 54	8 16 36	28 24	18 59	25 51	24 15	10 26	9 07	4 48	6 48	19 09	25 05	21 02	16 56	12 12	21 06	5 46
29 F	8 33 51	9 17 33	11♌45	18 51	26 14	25 30	10 57	9 21	4 55	6 49	19 10	25 07	21 23	17 16	12 29	21 02	5 48
30 Sa	8 37 48	10 18 28	25 23	18 42	26 27R	26 45	11 29	9 35	5 02	6 50	19 12	25 09	21 45	17 37	12 45	20 57	5 50
31 Su	8 41 44	11 19 23	9♍15	18 33	26 29	28 01	12 01	9 49	5 09	6 51	19 14	25 11	22 07	17 57	13 01	20 52	5 53

Tables are calculated for midnight Greenwich Mean Time

February 2021

DATE	SID.TIME	SUN	MOON	NODE	MERCURY	VENUS	MARS	JUPITER	SATURN	URANUS	NEPTUNE	PLUTO	CERES	PALLAS	JUNO	VESTA	CHIRON
1 M	8 45 41	12≈20 16	23♍17	18♊25Rx	26≈19Rx	29♑16	12♉33	10≈04	5≈17	6♉51	19♓16	25♑13	22♓28	18≈17	13♐17	20♍46Rx	5♈55
2 T	8 49 37	13 21 09	7♎25	18 18	25 59	0≈31	13 05	10 18	5 24	6 52	19 18	25 15	22 50	18 38	13 33	20 40	5 57
3 W	8 53 34	14 22 01	21 36	18 13	25 27	1 46	13 37	10 32	5 31	6 53	19 20	25 16	23 12	18 58	13 48	20 33	6 00
4 Th	8 57 30	15 22 52	5♏45	18 11D	24 45	3 01	14 10	10 46	5 38	6 54	19 22	25 18	23 34	19 19	14 04	20 26	6 02
5 F	9 1 27	16 23 43	19 52	18 10	23 54	4 17	14 42	11 00	5 45	6 56	19 24	25 20	23 56	19 39	14 19	20 18	6 05
6 Sa	9 5 23	17 24 32	3♐56	18 11	22 56	5 32	15 15	11 15	5 52	6 57	19 26	25 22	24 18	19 59	14 34	20 10	6 07
7 Su	9 9 20	18 25 21	17 55	18 12Rx	21 51	6 47	15 47	11 29	5 59	6 58	19 28	25 24	24 40	20 20	14 50	20 02	6 10
8 M	9 13 17	19 26 09	1♑49	18 11	20 42	8 02	16 20	11 43	6 06	6 59	19 30	25 26	25 02	20 40	15 05	19 53	6 12
9 T	9 17 13	20 26 56	15 36	18 08	19 31	9 17	16 53	11 57	6 13	7 00	19 32	25 28	25 24	21 00	15 19	19 43	6 15
10 W	9 21 10	21 27 42	29 15	18 02	18 19	10 32	17 26	12 12	6 20	7 02	19 34	25 30	25 46	21 21	15 34	19 33	6 18
11 Th	9 25 6	22 28 26	12≈43	17 53	17 09	11 48	17 59	12 26	6 27	7 03	19 36	25 31	26 09	21 41	15 49	19 23	6 20
12 F	9 29 3	23 29 09	25 58	17 42	16 03	13 03	18 33	12 40	6 34	7 05	19 38	25 33	26 31	22 01	16 03	19 12	6 23
13 Sa	9 32 59	24 29 51	8♓58	17 30	15 01	14 18	19 06	12 54	6 41	7 06	19 40	25 35	26 53	22 22	16 17	19 01	6 26
14 Su	9 36 56	25 30 31	21 43	17 18	14 05	15 33	19 39	13 08	6 48	7 08	19 42	25 37	27 16	22 42	16 31	18 50	6 29
15 M	9 40 52	26 31 10	4♈11	17 06	13 16	16 48	20 13	13 22	6 55	7 09	19 44	25 39	27 38	23 02	16 45	18 38	6 32
16 T	9 44 49	27 31 47	16 24	16 57	12 35	18 03	20 47	13 36	7 02	7 11	19 47	25 40	28 01	23 22	16 59	18 26	6 35
17 W	9 48 46	28 32 22	28 25	16 50	12 01	19 18	21 20	13 50	7 08	7 13	19 49	25 42	28 24	23 43	17 13	18 13	6 37
18 Th	9 52 42	29 32 56	10♉17	16 46	11 35	20 33	21 54	14 04	7 15	7 14	19 51	25 44	28 46	24 03	17 26	18 00	6 40
19 F	9 56 39	0♓33 28	22 06	16 44D	11 16	21 49	22 28	14 18	7 22	7 16	19 53	25 46	29 09	24 23	17 39	17 47	6 43
20 Sa	10 0 35	1 33 58	3♊55	16 44	11 05	23 04	23 02	14 32	7 29	7 18	19 55	25 47	29 32	24 43	17 52	17 34	6 46
21 Su	10 4 32	2 34 26	15 52	16 44Rx	11 01D	24 19	23 36	14 46	7 36	7 20	19 57	25 49	29 55	25 03	18 05	17 20	6 49
22 M	10 8 28	3 34 52	28 01	16 44	11 05	25 34	24 10	15 00	7 42	7 22	20 00	25 51	0♈18	25 24	18 18	17 06	6 52
23 T	10 12 25	4 35 17	10♋27	16 41	11 14	26 49	24 44	15 14	7 49	7 23	20 02	25 52	0 41	25 44	18 31	16 52	6 55
24 W	10 16 21	5 35 40	23 15	16 37	11 30	28 04	25 19	15 28	7 55	7 25	20 04	25 54	1 04	26 04	18 43	16 37	6 59
25 Th	10 20 18	6 36 00	6♌27	16 29	11 51	29 19	25 53	15 42	8 02	7 28	20 06	25 55	1 27	26 24	18 55	16 22	7 02
26 F	10 24 15	7 36 19	20 03	16 20	12 18	0♓34	26 27	15 56	8 09	7 30	20 09	25 57	1 50	26 44	19 07	16 07	7 05
27 Sa	10 28 11	8 36 36	4♍03	16 08	12 50	1 49	27 02	16 09	8 15	7 32	20 11	25 59	2 13	27 04	19 19	15 52	7 08
28 Su	10 32 8	9 36 52	18 21	15 56	13 26	3 04	27 36	16 23	8 22	7 34	20 13	26 00	2 36	27 24	19 31	15 37	7 11

DATE	SID.TIME	SUN	MOON	NODE	MERCURY	VENUS	MARS	JUPITER	SATURN	URANUS	NEPTUNE	PLUTO	CERES	PALLAS	JUNO	VESTA	CHIRON
1 M	10 36 4	10✶37 05	2♎52	15♊44R	14♒06	4✶19	28♉11	16♒37	8♒28	7♉36	20✶15	26♑02	2♈59	27♒44	19♐42	15♐22R	7♈14
2 T	10 40 1	11 37 17	17 28	15 34	14 51	5 34	28 46	16 50	8 34	7 38	20 17	26 03	3 22	28 04	19 53	15 06	7 18
3 W	10 43 57	12 37 27	2♏02	15 27	15 39	6 49	29 20	17 04	8 41	7 41	20 20	26 05	3 46	28 23	20 04	14 50	7 21
4 Th	10 47 54	13 37 36	16 29	15 23	16 30	8 04	29 55	17 17	8 47	7 43	20 22	26 06	4 09	28 43	20 15	14 35	7 24
5 F	10 51 50	14 37 44	0♐46	15 22	17 25	9 18	0♊30	17 31	8 53	7 45	20 24	26 08	4 32	29 03	20 26	14 19	7 27
6 Sa	10 55 47	15 37 49	14 49	15 21	18 22	10 33	1 05	17 44	9 00	7 48	20 27	26 09	4 56	29 23	20 36	14 03	7 31
7 Su	10 59 44	16 37 54	28 40	15 21	19 23	11 48	1 40	17 58	9 06	7 50	20 29	26 11	5 19	29 43	20 46	13 48	7 34
8 M	11 3 40	17 37 57	12♑18	15 20	20 25	13 03	2 14	18 11	9 12	7 52	20 31	26 12	5 42	0✶02	20 56	13 32	7 37
9 T	11 7 37	18 37 58	25 44	15 16	21 31	14 18	2 50	18 24	9 18	7 55	20 33	26 13	6 06	0 22	21 06	13 16	7 41
10 W	11 11 33	19 37 57	9♒00	15 09	22 38	15 33	3 25	18 38	9 24	7 57	20 36	26 15	6 29	0 42	21 16	13 00	7 44
11 Th	11 15 30	20 37 55	22 04	14 59	23 48	16 48	4 00	18 51	9 30	8 00	20 38	26 16	6 53	1 01	21 25	12 45	7 48
12 F	11 19 26	21 37 51	4✶57	14 47	25 00	18 03	4 35	19 04	9 36	8 03	20 40	26 17	7 16	1 21	21 34	12 29	7 51
13 Sa	11 23 23	22 37 45	17 39	14 33	26 13	19 17	5 10	19 17	9 42	8 05	20 43	26 19	7 40	1 40	21 43	12 14	7 54
14 Su	11 27 19	23 37 37	0♈08	14 19	27 29	20 32	5 45	19 30	9 48	8 08	20 45	26 20	8 04	2 00	21 51	11 59	7 58
15 M	11 31 16	24 37 27	12 26	14 07	28 46	21 47	6 21	19 43	9 53	8 11	20 47	26 21	8 27	2 19	22 00	11 44	8 01
16 T	11 35 13	25 37 15	24 32	13 56	0✶05	23 02	6 56	19 56	9 59	8 13	20 49	26 22	8 51	2 39	22 08	11 29	8 05
17 W	11 39 9	26 37 01	6♉29	13 47	1 26	24 17	7 31	20 09	10 05	8 16	20 52	26 23	9 14	2 58	22 16	11 14	8 08
18 Th	11 43 6	27 36 44	18 19	13 42	2 48	25 31	8 07	20 22	10 10	8 19	20 54	26 25	9 38	3 17	22 23	11 00	8 12
19 F	11 47 2	28 36 26	0♊06	13 39	4 12	26 46	8 42	20 35	10 16	8 22	20 56	26 26	10 02	3 36	22 30	10 46	8 15
20 Sa	11 50 59	29 36 05	11 55	13 38D	5 37	28 01	9 18	20 47	10 21	8 25	20 58	26 27	10 25	3 56	22 38	10 32	8 19
21 Su	11 54 55	0♈35 42	23 50	13 39R	7 04	29 16	9 53	21 00	10 27	8 27	21 01	26 28	10 49	4 15	22 44	10 18	8 22
22 M	11 58 52	1 35 17	5♋56	13 39	8 32	0♈30	10 29	21 12	10 32	8 30	21 03	26 29	11 13	4 34	22 51	10 05	8 26
23 T	12 2 48	2 34 50	18 20	13 37	10 01	1 45	11 05	21 25	10 38	8 33	21 05	26 30	11 37	4 53	22 57	9 52	8 29
24 W	12 6 45	3 34 20	1♌07	13 34	11 32	3 00	11 40	21 37	10 43	8 36	21 07	26 31	12 00	5 12	23 03	9 40	8 33
25 Th	12 10 42	4 33 48	14 20	13 29	13 05	4 14	12 16	21 50	10 48	8 39	21 10	26 32	12 24	5 31	23 09	9 27	8 36
26 F	12 14 38	5 33 14	28 01	13 21	14 38	5 29	12 52	22 02	10 53	8 42	21 12	26 33	12 48	5 49	23 14	9 16	8 40
27 Sa	12 18 35	6 32 37	12♍09	13 11	16 13	6 43	13 27	22 14	10 58	8 45	21 14	26 34	13 12	6 08	23 20	9 04	8 43
28 Su	12 22 31	7 31 58	26 42	13 01	17 50	7 58	14 03	22 26	11 03	8 48	21 16	26 35	13 36	6 27	23 24	8 53	8 47
29 M	12 26 28	8 31 17	11♎32	12 51	19 28	9 13	14 39	22 38	11 08	8 51	21 18	26 36	13 59	6 45	23 29	8 42	8 50
30 T	12 30 24	9 30 34	26 32	12 43	21 07	10 27	15 15	22 50	11 13	8 54	21 21	26 36	14 23	7 04	23 33	8 32	8 54
31 W	12 34 21	10 29 50	11♏30	12 37	22 47	11 42	15 51	23 02	11 18	8 58	21 23	26 37	14 47	7 23	23 37	8 22	8 57

Tables are calculated for midnight Greenwich Mean Time

April 2021

DATE	SID.TIME	SUN	MOON	NODE	MERCURY	VENUS	MARS	JUPITER	SATURN	URANUS	NEPTUNE	PLUTO	CERES	PALLAS	JUNO	VESTA	CHIRON
1 Th	12 38 17	11♈29 03	26♏,20	12♊33R,	24♓29	12♈56	16♊27	23≈14	11≈22	9♉01	21♓25	26♑38	15♈11	7♓41	23♐41	8♍12R,	9♈01
2 F	12 42 14	12 28 14	10♐55	12 32D	26 13	14 11	17 03	23 25	11 27	9 04	21 27	26 39	15 35	7 59	23 45	8 03	9 04
3 Sa	12 46 10	13 27 24	25 12	12 33	27 57	15 25	17 38	23 37	11 32	9 07	21 29	26 40	15 59	8 18	23 48	7 55	9 08
4 Su	12 50 7	14 26 32	9♑07	12 33R,	29 44	16 40	18 14	23 49	11 36	9 10	21 31	26 40	16 22	8 36	23 51	7 47	9 11
5 M	12 54 4	15 25 39	22 44	12 33	1♈31	17 54	18 50	24 00	11 41	9 13	21 34	26 41	16 46	8 54	23 53	7 39	9 15
6 T	12 58 0	16 24 43	6≈02	12 31	3 20	19 08	19 26	24 11	11 45	9 17	21 36	26 42	17 10	9 12	23 55	7 32	9 18
7 W	13 1 57	17 23 46	19 03	12 27	5 11	20 23	20 02	24 23	11 49	9 20	21 38	26 42	17 34	9 30	23 57	7 25	9 22
8 Th	13 5 53	18 22 47	1♓51	12 21	7 03	21 37	20 39	24 34	11 53	9 23	21 40	26 43	17 58	9 48	23 59	7 19	9 25
9 F	13 9 50	19 21 46	14 26	12 12	8 56	22 52	21 15	24 45	11 57	9 27	21 42	26 43	18 22	10 06	24 00	7 13	9 29
10 Sa	13 13 46	20 20 43	26 50	12 03	10 51	24 06	21 51	24 56	12 01	9 30	21 44	26 44	18 46	10 24	24 01	7 08	9 32
11 Su	13 17 43	21 19 39	9♈04	11 53	12 47	25 20	22 27	25 07	12 05	9 33	21 46	26 44	19 10	10 42	24 02	7 03	9 36
12 M	13 21 39	22 18 32	21 09	11 44	14 45	26 35	23 03	25 17	12 09	9 36	21 48	26 45	19 34	10 59	24 02R,	6 58	9 39
13 T	13 25 36	23 17 23	3♉07	11 36	16 44	27 49	23 39	25 28	12 13	9 40	21 50	26 45	19 57	11 17	24 02	6 55	9 43
14 W	13 29 33	24 16 13	14 58	11 31	18 44	29 03	24 15	25 39	12 17	9 43	21 52	26 46	20 21	11 35	24 02	6 51	9 46
15 Th	13 33 29	25 15 00	26 46	11 27	20 46	0♉17	24 52	25 49	12 20	9 47	21 54	26 46	20 45	11 52	24 01	6 48	9 50
16 F	13 37 26	26 13 45	8♊33	11 26D	22 49	1 32	25 28	26 00	12 24	9 50	21 56	26 46	21 09	12 09	24 00	6 46	9 53
17 Sa	13 41 22	27 12 28	20 22	11 26	24 53	2 46	26 04	26 10	12 27	9 53	21 58	26 47	21 33	12 26	23 59	6 44	9 56
18 Su	13 45 19	28 11 09	2♋17	11 28	26 58	4 00	26 40	26 20	12 31	9 57	22 00	26 47	21 57	12 43	23 57	6 43	10 00
19 M	13 49 15	29 09 48	14 24	11 29	29 05	5 14	27 17	26 30	12 34	10 00	22 02	26 47	22 21	13 00	23 55	6 42	10 03
20 T	13 53 12	0♉08 24	26 46	11 30R,	1♉12	6 28	27 53	26 40	12 37	10 04	22 04	26 48	22 44	13 17	23 53	6 42D	10 07
21 W	13 57 8	1 06 59	9♌29	11 30	3 19	7 43	28 29	26 50	12 40	10 07	22 06	26 48	23 08	13 34	23 50	6 42	10 10
22 Th	14 1 5	2 05 31	22 37	11 28	5 27	8 57	29 06	26 59	12 43	10 10	22 08	26 48	23 32	13 51	23 47	6 42	10 13
23 F	14 5 2	3 04 01	6♍13	11 24	7 35	10 11	29 42	27 09	12 46	10 14	22 09	26 48	23 56	14 07	23 44	6 43	10 16
24 Sa	14 8 58	4 02 28	20 18	11 19	9 43	11 25	0♋18	27 18	12 49	10 17	22 11	26 48	24 20	14 24	23 40	6 45	10 20
25 Su	14 12 55	5 00 54	4≏50	11 14	11 50	12 39	0 55	27 28	12 52	10 21	22 13	26 48	24 43	14 40	23 36	6 47	10 23
26 M	14 16 51	5 59 17	19 44	11 09	13 57	13 53	1 31	27 37	12 55	10 24	22 15	26 48R,	25 07	14 57	23 32	6 49	10 26
27 T	14 20 48	6 57 39	4♏,52	11 04	16 02	15 07	2 08	27 46	12 57	10 28	22 17	26 48	25 31	15 13	23 27	6 52	10 30
28 W	14 24 44	7 55 59	20 05	11 02	18 06	16 21	2 44	27 55	13 00	10 31	22 18	26 48	25 55	15 29	23 22	6 56	10 33
29 Th	14 28 41	8 54 17	5♐12	11 00D	20 09	17 35	3 21	28 04	13 02	10 35	22 20	26 48	26 18	15 45	23 17	7 00	10 36
30 F	14 32 37	9 52 34	20 06	11 00	22 10	18 49	3 57	28 13	13 04	10 38	22 22	26 48	26 42	16 01	23 11	7 04	10 39

May 2021

DATE	SID.TIME	SUN	MOON	NODE	MERCURY	VENUS	MARS	JUPITER	SATURN	URANUS	NEPTUNE	PLUTO	CERES	PALLAS	JUNO	VESTA	CHIRON
1 Sa	14 36 34	10♉50 49	4♑39	11♊01	24♉08	20♉03	4♋33	28≈21	13≈07	10♉41	22♓23	26♑48R	27♈06	16♓17	23✗05R	7♍09	10♈42
2 Su	14 40 31	11 49 02	18 48	11 03	26 04	21 17	5 10	28 30	13 09	10 45	22 25	26 48	27 30	16 32	22 59	7 14	10 45
3 M	14 44 27	12 47 14	2≈32	11 04R	27 57	22 31	5 46	28 38	13 11	10 48	22 27	26 48	27 53	16 48	22 52	7 19	10 49
4 T	14 48 24	13 45 25	15 53	11 04	29 47	23 45	6 23	28 46	13 13	10 52	22 28	26 48	28 17	17 03	22 45	7 25	10 52
5 W	14 52 20	14 43 34	28 51	11 04	1♊34	24 58	6 59	28 54	13 14	10 55	22 30	26 48	28 40	17 19	22 38	7 32	10 55
6 Th	14 56 17	15 41 41	11♓32	11 02	3 18	26 12	7 36	29 02	13 16	10 59	22 31	26 48	29 04	17 34	22 30	7 39	10 58
7 F	15 0 13	16 39 47	23 56	10 59	4 58	27 26	8 13	29 10	13 18	11 02	22 33	26 47	29 28	17 49	22 22	7 46	11 01
8 Sa	15 4 10	17 37 52	6♈09	10 55	6 35	28 40	8 49	29 18	13 19	11 06	22 34	26 47	29 51	18 04	22 14	7 54	11 04
9 Su	15 8 6	18 35 55	18 11	10 51	8 08	29 54	9 26	29 25	13 21	11 09	22 36	26 47	0♉15	18 19	22 06	8 02	11 07
10 M	15 12 3	19 33 57	0♉07	10 48	9 38	1♊08	10 02	29 32	13 22	11 13	22 37	26 46	0 38	18 34	21 57	8 10	11 10
11 T	15 16 0	20 31 57	11 57	10 45	11 03	2 21	10 39	29 40	13 24	11 16	22 39	26 46	1 02	18 48	21 48	8 19	11 12
12 W	15 19 56	21 29 56	23 45	10 43	12 25	3 35	11 15	29 47	13 25	11 19	22 40	26 46	1 25	19 03	21 38	8 29	11 15
13 Th	15 23 53	22 27 53	5♊33	10 42D	13 43	4 49	11 52	29 54	13 26	11 23	22 41	26 46	1 49	19 17	21 29	8 38	11 18
14 F	15 27 49	23 25 49	17 22	10 42	14 57	6 03	12 29	0♓00	13 27	11 26	22 43	26 45	2 12	19 31	21 19	8 49	11 21
15 Sa	15 31 46	24 23 43	29 15	10 43	16 06	7 16	13 05	0 07	13 28	11 30	22 44	26 45	2 36	19 45	21 09	8 59	11 24
16 Su	15 35 42	25 21 35	11♋16	10 44	17 12	8 30	13 42	0 13	13 28	11 33	22 45	26 44	2 59	19 59	20 58	9 10	11 27
17 M	15 39 39	26 19 26	23 27	10 46	18 13	9 44	14 19	0 20	13 29	11 36	22 47	26 43	3 22	20 13	20 48	9 21	11 29
18 T	15 43 35	27 17 15	5♌52	10 47	19 10	10 57	14 55	0 26	13 30	11 40	22 48	26 43	3 46	20 26	20 37	9 33	11 32
19 W	15 47 32	28 15 03	18 35	10 47R	20 03	12 11	15 32	0 32	13 30	11 43	22 49	26 42	4 09	20 40	20 25	9 44	11 35
20 Th	15 51 29	29 12 48	1♍40	10 48	20 52	13 24	16 09	0 38	13 30	11 46	22 50	26 42	4 32	20 53	20 14	9 57	11 37
21 F	15 55 25	0♊10 32	15 09	10 47	21 36	14 38	16 46	0 43	13 31	11 50	22 51	26 41	4 55	21 06	20 02	10 09	11 40
22 Sa	15 59 22	1 08 15	29 04	10 47	22 15	15 52	17 22	0 49	13 31	11 53	22 53	26 40	5 18	21 19	19 51	10 22	11 42
23 Su	16 3 18	2 05 55	13♎24	10 46	22 50	17 05	17 59	0 54	13 31R	11 56	22 54	26 40	5 42	21 32	19 39	10 36	11 45
24 M	16 7 15	3 03 35	28 08	10 45	23 20	18 19	18 36	0 59	13 31	12 00	22 55	26 39	6 05	21 44	19 27	10 49	11 47
25 T	16 11 11	4 01 12	13♏09	10 44	23 46	19 32	19 13	1 04	13 31	12 03	22 56	26 38	6 28	21 57	19 14	11 03	11 50
26 W	16 15 8	4 58 49	28 19	10 44D	24 07	20 46	19 49	1 09	13 31	12 06	22 57	26 37	6 51	22 09	19 02	11 17	11 52
27 Th	16 19 4	5 56 24	13✗30	10 43	24 23	21 59	20 26	1 14	13 30	12 09	22 58	26 37	7 14	22 21	18 49	11 32	11 54
28 F	16 23 1	6 53 58	28 31	10 44	24 34	23 12	21 03	1 18	13 30	12 13	22 59	26 36	7 37	22 33	18 36	11 47	11 57
29 Sa	16 26 58	7 51 31	13♑15	10 44	24 41R	24 26	21 40	1 22	13 30	12 16	23 00	26 35	8 00	22 45	18 23	12 02	11 59
30 Su	16 30 54	8 49 04	27 36	10 44	24 43	25 39	22 17	1 27	13 29	12 19	23 00	26 34	8 23	22 57	18 10	12 17	12 01
31 M	16 34 51	9 46 35	11≈31	10 44	24 40	26 53	22 53	1 31	13 28	12 22	23 01	26 33	8 45	23 08	17 57	12 33	12 04

Tables are calculated for midnight Greenwich Mean Time

196

June 2021

DATE	SID.TIME	SUN	MOON	NODE	MERCURY	VENUS	MARS	JUPITER	SATURN	URANUS	NEPTUNE	PLUTO	CERES	PALLAS	JUNO	VESTA	CHIRON
1 T	16 38 47	10♊44 05	25≈00	10♊44R	24♊34R	28♊06	23♋30	1♓34	13≈27R	12♉25	23♓02	26♑33R	9♉08	23♉19	17♐44R	12♍49	12♈06
2 W	16 42 44	11 41 35	8♓02	10 44D	24 22	29 19	24 07	1 38	13 27	12 29	23 03	26 32	9 31	23 30	17 30	13 05	12 08
3 Th	16 46 40	12 39 04	20 43	10 44	24 07	0♋33	24 44	1 41	13 26	12 32	23 04	26 31	9 54	23 41	17 17	13 22	12 10
4 F	16 50 37	13 36 32	3♈05	10 44	23 48	1 46	25 21	1 45	13 25	12 35	23 04	26 30	10 16	23 52	17 03	13 38	12 12
5 Sa	16 54 33	14 33 59	15 12	10 45	23 26	2 59	25 58	1 48	13 23	12 38	23 05	26 29	10 39	24 02	16 50	13 55	12 14
6 Su	16 58 30	15 31 26	27 09	10 45	23 00	4 13	26 34	1 51	13 22	12 41	23 06	26 28	11 02	24 13	16 36	14 13	12 16
7 M	17 2 27	16 28 52	8♉59	10 46	22 32	5 26	27 11	1 53	13 21	12 44	23 06	26 27	11 24	24 23	16 23	14 30	12 18
8 T	17 6 23	17 26 17	20 46	10 46	22 02	6 39	27 48	1 56	13 19	12 47	23 07	26 26	11 47	24 33	16 09	14 48	12 20
9 W	17 10 20	18 23 42	2♊34	10 47R	21 30	7 52	28 25	1 58	13 18	12 50	23 07	26 25	12 09	24 42	15 55	15 06	12 22
10 Th	17 14 16	19 21 06	14 24	10 47	20 57	9 05	29 02	2 00	13 16	12 53	23 08	26 24	12 31	24 52	15 42	15 25	12 23
11 F	17 18 13	20 18 29	26 19	10 46	20 23	10 19	29 39	2 02	13 14	12 56	23 08	26 23	12 54	25 01	15 28	15 43	12 25
12 Sa	17 22 9	21 15 51	8♋21	10 46	19 50	11 32	0♌16	2 04	13 13	12 59	23 09	26 21	13 16	25 10	15 15	16 02	12 27
13 Su	17 26 6	22 13 13	20 33	10 44	19 17	12 45	0 53	2 05	13 11	13 01	23 09	26 20	13 38	25 19	15 01	16 21	12 28
14 M	17 30 2	23 10 33	2♌55	10 43	18 45	13 58	1 30	2 07	13 09	13 04	23 10	26 19	14 00	25 27	14 48	16 40	12 30
15 T	17 33 59	24 7 53	15 31	10 41	18 15	15 11	2 07	2 08	13 07	13 07	23 10	26 18	14 22	25 36	14 34	17 00	12 32
16 W	17 37 56	25 5 12	28 21	10 39	17 47	16 24	2 44	2 09	13 05	13 10	23 10	26 17	14 44	25 44	14 21	17 20	12 33
17 Th	17 41 52	26 2 30	11♍29	10 38	17 22	17 37	3 21	2 10	13 02	13 13	23 11	26 16	15 06	25 52	14 08	17 40	12 35
18 F	17 45 49	26 59 47	24 56	10 38D	17 00	18 50	3 58	2 10	13 00	13 15	23 11	26 14	15 28	25 59	13 55	18 00	12 36
19 Sa	17 49 45	27 57 04	8♎43	10 38	16 41	20 03	4 35	2 11	12 58	13 18	23 11	26 13	15 50	26 07	13 42	18 20	12 37
20 Su	17 53 42	28 54 19	22 50	10 39	16 27	21 16	5 12	2 11R	12 55	13 21	23 11	26 12	16 12	26 14	13 29	18 41	12 39
21 M	17 57 38	29 51 34	7♏17	10 40	16 16	22 29	5 49	2 11	12 53	13 23	23 12	26 11	16 34	26 21	13 16	19 01	12 40
22 T	18 1 35	0♋48 48	22 00	10 41	16 10D	23 42	6 26	2 11	12 50	13 26	23 12	26 09	16 55	26 27	13 04	19 22	12 41
23 W	18 5 32	1 46 02	6♐53	10 42R	16 08	24 55	7 03	2 11	12 47	13 29	23 12	26 08	17 17	26 34	12 52	19 44	12 42
24 Th	18 9 28	2 43 15	21 52	10 41	16 10	26 08	7 40	2 10	12 44	13 31	23 12	26 07	17 38	26 40	12 39	20 05	12 44
25 F	18 13 25	3 40 28	6♑46	10 40	16 18	27 21	8 18	2 09	12 41	13 34	23 12R	26 06	18 00	26 46	12 28	20 26	12 45
26 Sa	18 17 21	4 37 40	21 28	10 38	16 30	28 34	8 55	2 08	12 39	13 36	23 12	26 04	18 21	26 52	12 16	20 48	12 46
27 Su	18 21 18	5 34 52	5≈52	10 34	16 47	29 47	9 32	2 07	12 35	13 38	23 12	26 03	18 43	26 57	12 04	21 10	12 47
28 M	18 25 14	6 32 04	19 52	10 31	17 09	0♌59	10 09	2 06	12 32	13 41	23 12	26 02	19 04	27 02	11 53	21 32	12 48
29 T	18 29 11	7 29 16	3♓26	10 27	17 35	2 12	10 46	2 04	12 29	13 43	23 12	26 00	19 25	27 07	11 42	21 54	12 49
30 W	18 33 7	8 26 28	16 34	10 25	18 06	3 25	11 23	2 03	12 26	13 46	23 12	25 59	19 46	27 11	11 31	22 17	12 49

July 2021

DATE	SID.TIME	SUN	MOON	NODE	MERCURY	VENUS	MARS	JUPITER	SATURN	URANUS	NEPTUNE	PLUTO	CERES	PALLAS	JUNO	VESTA	CHIRON
1 Th	18 37 4	9♋23 40	29♓18	10♊23D	18♊42	4♌37	12♋00	2♓01R	12♒23R	13♉48	23♓12R	25♑58R	20♋07	27♓16	11♋20R	22♍40	12♈50
2 F	18 41 1	10 20 52	11♈41	10 23	19 23	5 50	12 38	1 59	12 19	13 50	23 11	25 56	20 28	27 20	11 10	23 02	12 51
3 Sa	18 44 57	11 18 05	23 47	10 23	20 08	7 03	13 15	1 56	12 16	13 52	23 11	25 55	20 49	27 23	11 00	23 25	12 52
4 Su	18 48 54	12 15 17	5♉43	10 25	20 58	8 15	13 52	1 54	12 12	13 55	23 11	25 53	21 10	27 27	10 50	23 48	12 52
5 M	18 52 50	13 12 30	17 32	10 26	21 52	9 28	14 29	1 51	12 09	13 57	23 11	25 52	21 30	27 30	10 40	24 12	12 53
6 T	18 56 47	14 09 43	29 19	10 28R	22 51	10 41	15 07	1 48	12 05	13 59	23 11	25 51	21 51	27 33	10 31	24 35	12 53
7 W	19 0 43	15 06 56	11♊08	10 28	23 54	11 53	15 44	1 45	12 02	14 01	23 10	25 49	22 12	27 35	10 22	24 59	12 54
8 Th	19 4 40	16 04 10	23 04	10 28	25 01	13 06	16 21	1 42	11 58	14 03	23 10	25 48	22 32	27 37	10 13	25 22	12 54
9 F	19 8 36	17 01 23	5♋07	10 25	26 12	14 18	16 58	1 39	11 54	14 05	23 10	25 46	22 52	27 39	10 05	25 46	12 55
10 Sa	19 12 33	17 58 37	17 22	10 21	27 28	15 31	17 36	1 35	11 50	14 07	23 09	25 45	23 13	27 41	9 57	26 10	12 55
11 Su	19 16 30	18 55 52	29 49	10 15	28 48	16 43	18 13	1 32	11 46	14 09	23 08	25 44	23 33	27 42	9 49	26 35	12 55
12 M	19 20 26	19 53 06	12♌29	10 09	0♋12	17 56	18 50	1 28	11 42	14 11	23 08	25 42	23 53	27 43	9 42	26 59	12 55
13 T	19 24 23	20 50 20	25 23	10 02	1 40	19 08	19 28	1 24	11 38	14 12	23 07	25 41	24 13	27 43	9 34	27 23	12 56
14 W	19 28 19	21 47 34	8♍29	9 56	3 12	20 20	20 05	1 19	11 34	14 14	23 07	25 39	24 33	27 44R	9 28	27 48	12 56
15 Th	19 32 16	22 44 49	21 49	9 50	4 48	21 33	20 43	1 15	11 30	14 16	23 06	25 38	24 53	27 44	9 21	28 13	12 56R
16 F	19 36 12	23 42 03	5♎23	9 47	6 27	22 45	21 20	1 10	11 26	14 18	23 05	25 36	25 12	27 43	9 15	28 38	12 56
17 Sa	19 40 9	24 39 18	19 09	9 46D	8 10	23 57	21 57	1 06	11 22	14 19	23 05	25 35	25 32	27 43	9 09	29 03	12 56
18 Su	19 44 5	25 36 32	3♏09	9 46	9 56	25 10	22 35	1 01	11 18	14 21	23 04	25 34	25 51	27 41	9 03	29 28	12 56
19 M	19 48 2	26 33 47	17 21	9 47	11 46	26 22	23 12	0 56	11 14	14 22	23 03	25 32	26 11	27 40	8 58	29 53	12 56
20 T	19 51 59	27 31 02	1♐44	9 48R	13 39	27 34	23 50	0 50	11 09	14 24	23 03	25 31	26 30	27 38	8 53	0♎19	12 55
21 W	19 55 55	28 28 17	16 15	9 48	15 34	28 46	24 27	0 45	11 05	14 25	23 02	25 29	26 49	27 36	8 49	0 44	12 55
22 Th	19 59 52	29 25 33	0♑51	9 46	17 32	29 58	25 05	0 39	11 01	14 27	23 01	25 28	27 08	27 34	8 45	1 10	12 55
23 F	20 3 48	0♌22 49	15 25	9 42	19 32	1♍10	25 42	0 34	10 56	14 28	23 00	25 26	27 27	27 31	8 41	1 35	12 54
24 Sa	20 7 45	1 20 05	29 53	9 36	21 34	2 22	26 20	0 28	10 52	14 30	22 59	25 25	27 46	27 28	8 37	2 01	12 54
25 Su	20 11 41	2 17 22	14♒06	9 29	23 37	3 34	26 57	0 22	10 48	14 31	22 59	25 23	28 04	27 25	8 34	2 27	12 54
26 M	20 15 38	3 14 40	28 00	9 20	25 42	4 46	27 35	0 16	10 43	14 32	22 58	25 22	28 23	27 21	8 31	2 54	12 53
27 T	20 19 34	4 11 58	11♓32	9 11	27 47	5 58	28 13	0 10	10 39	14 33	22 57	25 21	28 41	27 17	8 29	3 20	12 53
28 W	20 23 31	5 09 17	24 40	9 04	29 54	7 10	28 50	0 03	10 34	14 34	22 56	25 19	29 00	27 12	8 26	3 46	12 52
29 Th	20 27 28	6 06 37	7♈25	8 58	2♌00	8 22	29 28	29♒57	10 30	14 36	22 55	25 18	29 18	27 07	8 25	4 13	12 51
30 F	20 31 24	7 03 58	19 49	8 55	4 07	9 33	0♌05	29 50	10 26	14 37	22 54	25 16	29 36	27 02	8 23	4 39	12 51
31 Sa	20 35 21	8 01 21	1♉56	8 53D	6 13	10 45	0 43	29 44	10 21	14 38	22 53	25 15	29 54	26 57	8 22	5 06	12 50

Tables are calculated for midnight Greenwich Mean Time

DATE	SID.TIME	SUN	MOON	NODE	MERCURY	VENUS	MARS	JUPITER	SATURN	URANUS	NEPTUNE	PLUTO	CERES	PALLAS	JUNO	VESTA	CHIRON
1 Su	20 39 17	8♌58 44	13♋52	8♊53	8♌19	11♍57	1♍21	29♒37℞	10♒17℞	14♉39	22♓52℞	25♑14℞	0♊12	26♓51℞	8♈21℞	5♎33	12♈49℞
2 M	20 43 14	9 56 08	25 41	8 54	10 24	13 08	1 58	29 30	10 12	14 40	22 51	25 11	0 29	26 44	8 20D	5 59	12 48
3 T	20 47 10	10 53 34	7♌29	8 54℞	12 28	14 20	2 36	29 23	10 08	14 40	22 49	25 09	0 47	26 38	8 21	6 26	12 47
4 W	20 51 7	11 51 01	19 22	8 53	14 31	15 32	3 14	29 16	10 03	14 41	22 48	25 08	1 04	26 31	8 21	6 54	12 46
5 Th	20 55 3	12 48 29	1♍22	8 51	16 33	16 43	3 52	29 09	9 59	14 42	22 47	25 07	1 21	26 24	8 22	7 21	12 45
6 F	20 59 0	13 45 58	13 35	8 46	18 34	17 55	4 29	29 01	9 54	14 43	22 46	25 05	1 39	26 16	8 23	7 48	12 44
7 Sa	21 2 57	14 43 28	26 02	8 39	20 34	19 06	5 07	28 54	9 50	14 43	22 45	25 04	1 55	26 08	8 25	8 15	12 43
8 Su	21 6 53	15 40 59	8♎46	8 29	22 32	20 17	5 45	28 47	9 46	14 44	22 44	25 03	2 12	25 59	8 26	8 43	12 42
9 M	21 10 50	16 38 32	21 47	8 18	24 28	21 29	6 23	28 39	9 41	14 45	22 42	25 01	2 29	25 51	8 29	9 10	12 41
10 T	21 14 46	17 36 05	5♏03	8 07	26 24	22 40	7 01	28 32	9 37	14 45	22 41	25 00	2 45	25 42	8 31	9 38	12 40
11 W	21 18 43	18 33 39	18 32	7 56	28 17	23 51	7 39	28 24	9 32	14 46	22 40	24 59	3 02	25 32	8 34	10 06	12 38
12 Th	21 22 39	19 31 15	2♐13	7 47	0♍10	25 03	8 17	28 16	9 28	14 46	22 39	24 58	3 18	25 23	8 37	10 34	12 37
13 F	21 26 36	20 28 51	16 03	7 41	2 00	26 14	8 55	28 09	9 24	14 46	22 37	24 56	3 34	25 13	8 40	11 02	12 36
14 Sa	21 30 32	21 26 28	29 59	7 37	3 50	27 25	9 33	28 01	9 19	14 47	22 36	24 55	3 49	25 02	8 44	11 30	12 34
15 Su	21 34 29	22 24 06	14♑01	7 36D	5 37	28 36	10 11	27 53	9 15	14 47	22 34	24 55	4 05	24 52	8 48	11 58	12 33
16 M	21 38 26	23 21 45	28 07	7 35℞	7 24	29 47	10 49	27 45	9 11	14 47	22 33	24 54	4 20	24 41	8 52	12 26	12 31
17 T	21 42 22	24 19 25	12♒17	7 35	9 08	0♎58	11 27	27 37	9 06	14 47	22 32	24 53	4 36	24 29	8 57	12 54	12 30
18 W	21 46 19	25 17 07	26 28	7 34	10 52	2 09	12 05	27 30	9 02	14 47	22 30	24 51	4 51	24 18	9 02	13 23	12 28
19 Th	21 50 15	26 14 49	10♓40	7 31	12 34	3 19	12 43	27 22	8 58	14 48	22 29	24 50	5 06	24 06	9 07	13 51	12 26
20 F	21 54 12	27 12 32	24 49	7 25	14 14	4 30	13 21	27 14	8 54	14 48℞	22 27	24 49	5 20	23 54	9 13	14 20	12 25
21 Sa	21 58 8	28 10 17	8♈53	7 17	15 53	5 41	13 59	27 06	8 50	14 48	22 26	24 48	5 35	23 41	9 18	14 48	12 23
22 Su	22 2 5	29 08 02	22 45	7 06	17 31	6 52	14 37	26 58	8 46	14 47	22 25	24 47	5 49	23 29	9 24	15 17	12 21
23 M	22 6 1	0♍05 49	6♉23	6 54	19 07	8 02	15 15	26 50	8 42	14 47	22 23	24 46	6 03	23 16	9 31	15 46	12 19
24 T	22 9 58	1 03 38	19 43	6 42	20 42	9 13	15 53	26 42	8 38	14 47	22 22	24 45	6 17	23 03	9 37	16 15	12 18
25 W	22 13 55	2 01 28	2♊43	6 31	22 15	10 23	16 31	26 35	8 34	14 47	22 20	24 43	6 31	22 49	9 44	16 44	12 16
26 Th	22 17 51	2 59 19	15 23	6 22	23 47	11 33	17 10	26 27	8 30	14 47	22 18	24 42	6 44	22 36	9 51	17 13	12 14
27 F	22 21 48	3 57 13	27 44	6 15	25 18	12 44	17 48	26 19	8 26	14 46	22 17	24 41	6 58	22 22	9 59	17 42	12 12
28 Sa	22 25 44	4 55 08	9♋51	6 11	26 47	13 54	18 26	26 11	8 23	14 46	22 15	24 40	7 11	22 08	10 07	18 11	12 10
29 Su	22 29 41	5 53 05	21 46	6 10	28 15	15 04	19 04	26 04	8 19	14 46	22 14	24 39	7 23	21 53	10 15	18 40	12 08
30 M	22 33 37	6 51 03	3♌36	6 09	29 42	16 14	19 43	25 56	8 15	14 45	22 12	24 38	7 36	21 39	10 23	19 09	12 06
31 T	22 37 34	7 49 04	15 24	6 09	1♎07	17 24	20 21	25 48	8 12	14 45	22 11	24 37	7 48	21 24	10 23	19 38	12 04

September 2021

DATE	SID.TIME	SUN	MOON	NODE	MERCURY	VENUS	MARS	JUPITER	SATURN	URANUS	NEPTUNE	PLUTO	CERES	PALLAS	JUNO	VESTA	CHIRON
1 W	22 41 30	8♍47 07	27♊17	6♊08℞	2♎30	18♎34	20♍59	25≈41℞	8≈08℞	14♉44℞	22♓09℞	24♑36℞	8♊01	21♓09℞	10♐31	20♎08	12♈01℞
2 Th	22 45 27	9 45 11	9♋21	6 06	3 52	19 44	21 38	25 34	8 05	14 43	22 07	24 35	8 12	20 54	10 40	20 37	11 59
3 F	22 49 24	10 43 17	21 39	6 01	5 13	20 54	22 16	25 26	8 01	14 43	22 06	24 35	8 24	20 39	10 49	21 07	11 57
4 Sa	22 53 20	11 41 26	4♌15	5 53	6 32	22 04	22 55	25 19	7 58	14 42	22 04	24 34	8 36	20 24	10 58	21 37	11 55
5 Su	22 57 17	12 39 36	17 12	5 43	7 50	23 13	23 33	25 12	7 55	14 41	22 03	24 33	8 47	20 09	11 08	22 06	11 53
6 M	23 1 13	13 37 47	0♍31	5 31	9 05	24 23	24 12	25 05	7 51	14 41	22 01	24 32	8 58	19 53	11 18	22 36	11 50
7 T	23 5 10	14 36 01	14 08	5 19	10 20	25 32	24 50	24 58	7 48	14 40	21 59	24 31	9 08	19 38	11 27	23 06	11 48
8 W	23 9 6	15 34 16	28 03	5 07	11 32	26 42	25 29	24 51	7 45	14 39	21 58	24 30	9 19	19 22	11 38	23 36	11 46
9 Th	23 13 3	16 32 33	12♎09	4 58	12 42	27 51	26 07	24 44	7 42	14 38	21 56	24 30	9 29	19 06	11 48	24 06	11 43
10 F	23 16 59	17 30 52	26 23	4 50	13 51	29 00	26 46	24 37	7 39	14 37	21 54	24 29	9 39	18 51	11 59	24 35	11 41
11 Sa	23 20 56	18 29 12	10♏40	4 46	14 57	0♏10	27 25	24 31	7 36	14 36	21 53	24 28	9 48	18 35	12 10	25 06	11 38
12 Su	23 24 53	19 27 34	24 55	4 44D	16 02	1 19	28 03	24 24	7 34	14 35	21 51	24 27	9 58	18 19	12 21	25 36	11 36
13 M	23 28 49	20 25 58	9♐07	4 44℞	17 03	2 28	28 42	24 18	7 31	14 34	21 49	24 27	10 07	18 03	12 32	26 06	11 34
14 T	23 32 46	21 24 23	23 14	4 44	18 03	3 37	29 21	24 12	7 28	14 32	21 48	24 26	10 15	17 47	12 44	26 36	11 31
15 W	23 36 42	22 22 49	7♑15	4 43	19 00	4 45	0♏00	24 06	7 26	14 31	21 46	24 26	10 24	17 32	12 56	27 06	11 29
16 Th	23 40 39	23 21 17	21 09	4 41	19 54	5 54	0 38	24 00	7 24	14 30	21 44	24 25	10 32	17 16	13 08	27 37	11 26
17 F	23 44 35	24 19 47	4≈56	4 35	20 45	7 03	1 17	23 54	7 21	14 29	21 43	24 24	10 40	17 00	13 20	28 07	11 23
18 Sa	23 48 32	25 18 19	18 34	4 27	21 33	8 11	1 56	23 48	7 19	14 27	21 41	24 24	10 47	16 45	13 32	28 37	11 21
19 Su	23 52 28	26 16 52	2♓01	4 17	22 17	9 20	2 35	23 43	7 17	14 26	21 40	24 23	10 55	16 29	13 45	29 08	11 18
20 M	23 56 25	27 15 26	15 16	4 06	22 58	10 28	3 14	23 37	7 15	14 25	21 38	24 23	11 01	16 14	13 58	29 38	11 16
21 T	0 0 22	28 14 03	28 17	3 55	23 34	11 36	3 53	23 32	7 13	14 23	21 36	24 22	11 08	15 58	14 11	0♏09	11 13
22 W	0 4 18	29 12 42	11♈02	3 44	24 06	12 44	4 32	23 27	7 11	14 22	21 35	24 22	11 14	15 43	14 24	0 40	11 10
23 Th	0 8 15	0♎11 22	23 31	3 36	24 33	13 52	5 11	23 22	7 09	14 20	21 33	24 22	11 20	15 28	14 37	1 10	11 08
24 F	0 12 11	1 10 05	5♉46	3 30	24 56	15 00	5 50	23 18	7 07	14 18	21 31	24 21	11 26	15 13	14 51	1 41	11 05
25 Sa	0 16 8	2 08 50	17 49	3 26	25 13	16 07	6 29	23 13	7 06	14 17	21 30	24 21	11 31	14 59	15 05	2 12	11 03
26 Su	0 20 4	3 07 37	29 42	3 25D	25 24	17 15	7 08	23 09	7 04	14 15	21 28	24 21	11 36	14 44	15 19	2 43	11 00
27 M	0 24 1	4 06 26	11♊30	3 25	25 28℞	18 22	7 47	23 04	7 03	14 13	21 26	24 20	11 41	14 30	15 33	3 13	10 57
28 T	0 27 57	5 05 18	23 18	3 26	25 26	19 30	8 26	23 00	7 01	14 12	21 25	24 20	11 45	14 16	15 47	3 44	10 54
29 W	0 31 54	6 04 11	5♋11	3 26℞	25 17	20 37	9 05	22 57	7 00	14 10	21 23	24 20	11 49	14 02	16 01	4 15	10 52
30 Th	0 35 51	7 03 07	17 14	3 26	25 01	21 44	9 44	22 53	6 59	14 08	21 22	24 20	11 53	13 48	16 16	4 46	10 49

Tables are calculated for midnight Greenwich Mean Time

October 2021

DATE	SID.TIME	SUN	MOON	NODE	MERCURY	VENUS	MARS	JUPITER	SATURN	URANUS	NEPTUNE	PLUTO	CERES	PALLAS	JUNO	VESTA	CHIRON
1 F	0 39 47	8≏02 06	29♋32	3♊23Rₓ	24≏37Rₓ	22♏51	10≏24	22≈49Rₓ	6≈58Rₓ	14♉06Rₓ	21♓20Rₓ	24♈19Rₓ	11♊56	13♊34Rₓ	16♈31	5♏17	10♈46Rₓ
2 Sa	0 43 44	9 01 06	12♌11	3 19	24 06	23 58	11 03	22 46	6 57	14 04	21 19	24 19	11 59	13 21	16 46	5 48	10 44
3 Su	0 47 40	10 00 09	25 13	3 12	23 27	25 04	11 42	22 43	6 56	14 03	21 17	24 19	12 01	13 08	17 01	6 20	10 41
4 M	0 51 37	10 59 14	8♍40	3 04	22 40	26 11	12 22	22 40	6 55	14 01	21 15	24 19	12 03	12 55	17 17	6 51	10 38
5 T	0 55 33	11 58 22	22 32	2 55	21 47	27 17	13 01	22 37	6 55	13 59	21 14	24 19	12 05	12 43	17 32	7 22	10 36
6 W	0 59 30	12 57 31	6≏45	2 47	20 47	28 23	13 40	22 35	6 54	13 57	21 12	24 19D	12 06	12 31	17 48	7 53	10 33
7 Th	1 3 26	13 56 42	21 14	2 40	19 43	29 29	14 20	22 32	6 54	13 55	21 11	24 19	12 07	12 19	18 04	8 25	10 30
8 F	1 7 23	14 55 56	5♏54	2 35	18 34	0✗35	14 59	22 30	6 53	13 53	21 09	24 19	12 08	12 07	18 20	8 56	10 27
9 Sa	1 11 19	15 55 11	20 36	2 33D	17 24	1 40	15 39	22 28	6 53	13 50	21 08	24 19	12 08Rₓ	11 56	18 36	9 27	10 25
10 Su	1 15 16	16 54 28	5✗14	2 32	16 13	2 46	16 18	22 27	6 53	13 48	21 07	24 19	12 08	11 45	18 52	9 59	10 22
11 M	1 19 13	17 53 48	19 43	2 33	15 04	3 51	16 58	22 25	6 53D	13 46	21 05	24 19	12 08	11 34	19 08	10 30	10 19
12 T	1 23 9	18 53 08	4♑00	2 34	13 58	4 56	17 37	22 24	6 53	13 44	21 04	24 19	12 07	11 24	19 25	11 02	10 17
13 W	1 27 6	19 52 31	18 02	2 35Rₓ	12 58	6 01	18 17	22 23	6 53	13 42	21 02	24 19	12 05	11 14	19 42	11 33	10 14
14 Th	1 31 2	20 51 56	1≈50	2 35	12 05	7 05	18 57	22 22	6 53	13 40	21 01	24 20	12 04	11 04	19 59	12 05	10 11
15 F	1 34 59	21 51 22	15 23	2 32	11 21	8 10	19 36	22 21	6 53	13 37	20 59	24 20	12 01	10 55	20 16	12 36	10 09
16 Sa	1 38 55	22 50 49	28 42	2 28	10 46	9 14	20 16	22 20	6 54	13 35	20 58	24 20	11 59	10 46	20 33	13 08	10 06
17 Su	1 42 52	23 50 19	11♓48	2 22	10 23	10 18	20 56	22 20	6 54	13 33	20 57	24 20	11 56	10 38	20 50	13 40	10 03
18 M	1 46 48	24 49 50	24 40	2 16	10 10D	11 21	21 36	22 20D	6 55	13 31	20 55	24 21	11 53	10 29	21 08	14 11	10 01
19 T	1 50 45	25 49 23	7♈19	2 09	10 08	12 25	22 16	22 20	6 56	13 28	20 54	24 21	11 49	10 22	21 25	14 43	9 58
20 W	1 54 42	26 48 58	19 47	2 03	10 18	13 28	22 55	22 20	6 57	13 26	20 53	24 21	11 45	10 14	21 43	15 15	9 56
21 Th	1 58 38	27 48 35	2♉02	1 58	10 38	14 31	23 35	22 21	6 58	13 24	20 52	24 22	11 40	10 07	22 01	15 46	9 53
22 F	2 2 35	28 48 14	14 08	1 55	11 08	15 33	24 15	22 21	6 59	13 21	20 50	24 22	11 36	10 00	22 19	16 18	9 51
23 Sa	2 6 31	29 47 56	26 04	1 54D	11 47	16 36	24 55	22 22	7 00	13 19	20 49	24 23	11 30	9 54	22 37	16 50	9 48
24 Su	2 10 28	0♏47 39	7♊54	1 54	12 35	17 38	25 35	22 23	7 01	13 16	20 48	24 23	11 25	9 48	22 55	17 22	9 46
25 M	2 14 24	1 47 25	19 41	1 55	13 30	18 39	26 15	22 24	7 02	13 14	20 47	24 24	11 19	9 42	23 13	17 54	9 43
26 T	2 18 21	2 47 12	1♋29	1 57	14 32	19 41	26 55	22 26	7 04	13 12	20 46	24 24	11 12	9 37	23 32	18 26	9 41
27 W	2 22 17	3 47 02	13 21	1 58	15 40	20 42	27 35	22 27	7 05	13 09	20 45	24 25	11 05	9 32	23 50	18 58	9 38
28 Th	2 26 14	4 46 54	25 22	2 00Rₓ	16 53	21 43	28 16	22 29	7 07	13 07	20 44	24 26	10 58	9 28	24 09	19 30	9 36
29 F	2 30 11	5 46 48	7♌38	2 00	18 10	22 43	28 56	22 31	7 09	13 04	20 43	24 26	10 51	9 24	24 28	20 02	9 33
30 Sa	2 34 7	6 46 45	20 13	1 59	19 32	23 43	29 36	22 34	7 11	13 02	20 41	24 27	10 43	9 20	24 47	20 34	9 31
31 Su	2 38 4	7 46 43	3♍12	1 57	20 56	24 42	0♏16	22 36	7 13	12 59	20 40	24 28	10 35	9 17	25 06	21 06	9 29

November 2021

DATE	SID.TIME	SUN	MOON	NODE	MERCURY	VENUS	MARS	JUPITER	SATURN	URANUS	NEPTUNE	PLUTO	CERES	PALLAS	JUNO	VESTA	CHIRON
1 M	2 42 0	8♏46 44	16♍37	1♊55R	22≏23	25♐42	0♏56	22≈39	7≈15	12♉57R	20♓39R	24♑28	10♐26R	9♓14R	25♐25	21♏38	9♈27R
2 T	2 45 57	9 46 47	0≏29	1 51	23 53	26 41	1 37	22 42	7 17	12 54	20 39	24 29	10 17	9 11	25 44	22 10	9 24
3 W	2 49 53	10 46 52	14 47	1 48	25 24	27 39	2 45	22 45	7 19	12 52	20 38	24 30	10 08	9 09	26 03	22 42	9 22
4 Th	2 53 50	11 46 58	29 28	1 46	26 57	28 37	2 58	22 48	7 21	12 50	20 37	24 31	9 58	9 07	26 23	23 14	9 20
5 F	2 57 46	12 47 07	14♍24	1 44	28 31	29 34	3 38	22 51	7 24	12 47	20 36	24 31	9 48	9 06	26 42	23 46	9 18
6 Sa	3 1 43	13 47 18	29 27	1 43D	0♏06	0♑31	4 19	22 55	7 26	12 45	20 35	24 32	9 38	9 04	27 02	24 18	9 16
7 Su	3 5 40	14 47 30	14♐29	1 44	1 41	1 28	4 59	22 59	7 29	12 42	20 34	24 33	9 27	9 04	27 22	24 51	9 13
8 M	3 9 36	15 47 45	29 21	1 45	3 17	2 24	5 40	23 03	7 32	12 40	20 33	24 34	9 16	9 03D	27 41	25 23	9 11
9 T	3 13 33	16 48 00	13♑57	1 46	4 54	3 20	6 20	23 07	7 34	12 37	20 33	24 35	9 05	9 03	28 01	25 55	9 09
10 W	3 17 29	17 48 17	28 13	1 47	6 31	4 15	7 01	23 11	7 37	12 35	20 32	24 36	8 53	9 04	28 21	26 27	9 07
11 Th	3 21 26	18 48 36	12≈06	1 48R	8 07	5 09	7 42	23 16	7 40	12 32	20 31	24 37	8 42	9 05	28 42	26 59	9 05
12 F	3 25 22	19 48 56	25 38	1 48	9 44	6 03	8 22	23 21	7 43	12 30	20 31	24 38	8 30	9 06	29 02	27 32	9 04
13 Sa	3 29 19	20 49 17	8♓48	1 47	11 21	6 56	9 03	23 25	7 47	12 27	20 30	24 39	8 17	9 07	29 22	28 04	9 02
14 Su	3 33 15	21 49 39	21 41	1 46	12 58	7 48	9 44	23 31	7 50	12 25	20 29	24 40	8 05	9 09	29 43	28 36	9 00
15 M	3 37 12	22 50 03	4♈17	1 45	14 35	8 40	10 25	23 36	7 53	12 22	20 29	24 41	7 52	9 11	0♑03	29 09	8 58
16 T	3 41 9	23 50 28	16 39	1 44	16 12	9 31	11 05	23 41	7 57	12 20	20 28	24 42	7 39	9 14	0 24	29 41	8 56
17 W	3 45 5	24 50 55	28 51	1 43	17 48	10 22	11 46	23 47	8 00	12 18	20 28	24 43	7 26	9 17	0 44	0♐13	8 55
18 Th	3 49 2	25 51 23	10♉53	1 42	19 24	11 11	12 27	23 53	8 04	12 15	20 27	24 45	7 13	9 20	1 05	0 46	8 53
19 F	3 52 58	26 51 53	22 49	1 42D	21 00	12 00	13 08	23 59	8 07	12 13	20 27	24 46	7 00	9 24	1 26	1 18	8 51
20 Sa	3 56 55	27 52 25	4♊40	1 41	22 36	12 48	13 49	24 05	8 11	12 10	20 26	24 47	6 46	9 27	1 47	1 50	8 50
21 Su	4 0 51	28 52 57	16 28	1 42	24 12	13 35	14 30	24 11	8 15	12 08	20 26	24 48	6 32	9 32	2 08	2 23	8 48
22 M	4 4 48	29 53 32	28 15	1 42	25 48	14 21	15 11	24 18	8 19	12 06	20 26	24 50	6 19	9 36	2 29	2 55	8 47
23 T	4 8 44	0♐54 08	10♋05	1 42R	27 23	15 06	15 52	24 24	8 23	12 03	20 25	24 51	6 05	9 41	2 50	3 28	8 45
24 W	4 12 41	1 54 46	22 00	1 42	28 58	15 50	16 33	24 31	8 27	12 01	20 25	24 52	5 51	9 46	3 11	4 00	8 44
25 Th	4 16 38	2 55 25	4♌03	1 42	0♐33	16 34	17 15	24 38	8 31	11 59	20 25	24 54	5 37	9 52	3 33	4 32	8 43
26 F	4 20 34	3 56 06	16 19	1 42	2 08	17 16	17 56	24 45	8 36	11 57	20 25	24 55	5 23	9 58	3 54	5 05	8 41
27 Sa	4 24 31	4 56 48	28 50	1 42D	3 43	17 57	18 37	24 52	8 40	11 54	20 24	24 56	5 09	10 04	4 15	5 37	8 40
28 Su	4 28 27	5 57 32	11♍42	1 42	5 17	18 37	19 18	25 00	8 44	11 52	20 24	24 58	4 55	10 10	4 37	6 10	8 39
29 M	4 32 24	6 58 18	24 58	1 42	6 52	19 15	20 00	25 07	8 49	11 50	20 24	24 59	4 40	10 17	4 58	6 42	8 38
30 T	4 36 20	7 59 05	8≏40	1 42	8 26	19 53	20 41	25 15	8 53	11 48	20 24	25 01	4 26	10 24	5 20	7 15	8 37

Tables are calculated for midnight Greenwich Mean Time

DATE	SID.TIME	SUN	MOON	NODE	MERCURY	VENUS	MARS	JUPITER	SATURN	URANUS	NEPTUNE	PLUTO	CERES	PALLAS	JUNO	VESTA	CHIRON
1 W	4 40 17	8♐59 53	22≏49	1Ⅱ43	10♏00	20♑29	21♏23	25≈23	8≈58	11♉46R	20♓24D	25♑02	4Ⅱ12R	10♓31	5♑42	7♐47	8♈36R
2 Th	4 44 13	10 00 43	7♏23	1 44	11 35	21 04	22 04	25 31	9 03	11 44	20 24	25 04	3 58	10 39	6 04	8 20	8 35
3 F	4 48 10	11 01 35	22 18	1 44R	13 09	21 37	22 46	25 39	9 08	11 42	20 24	25 05	3 44	10 47	6 26	8 52	8 34
4 Sa	4 52 7	12 02 27	7♐28	1 44	14 43	22 09	23 27	25 48	9 13	11 39	20 24	25 07	3 31	10 55	6 47	9 25	8 33
5 Su	4 56 3	13 03 21	22 43	1 44	16 17	22 40	24 09	25 56	9 17	11 37	20 24	25 08	3 17	11 04	7 09	9 57	8 32
6 M	5 0 0	14 04 16	7♑52	1 43	17 51	23 08	24 50	26 05	9 23	11 35	20 25	25 10	3 03	11 13	7 32	10 29	8 31
7 T	5 3 56	15 05 12	22 47	1 41	19 25	23 36	25 32	26 13	9 28	11 34	20 25	25 11	2 50	11 22	7 54	11 02	8 31
8 W	5 7 53	16 06 09	7≈21	1 39	20 59	24 01	26 14	26 22	9 33	11 32	20 25	25 13	2 36	11 31	8 16	11 34	8 30
9 Th	5 11 49	17 07 06	21 28	1 37	22 33	24 25	26 55	26 31	9 38	11 30	20 25	25 15	2 23	11 41	8 38	12 07	8 29
10 F	5 15 46	18 08 04	5♓08	1 36	24 07	24 47	27 37	26 41	9 43	11 28	20 25	25 16	2 10	11 50	9 00	12 39	8 29
11 Sa	5 19 43	19 09 03	18 21	1 36D	25 41	25 07	28 19	26 50	9 49	11 26	20 26	25 18	1 58	12 01	9 23	13 12	8 28
12 Su	5 23 39	20 10 02	1♈11	1 36	27 16	25 25	29 01	26 59	9 54	11 24	20 26	25 20	1 45	12 11	9 45	13 44	8 28
13 M	5 27 36	21 11 01	13 40	1 37	28 50	25 40	29 43	27 09	10 00	11 23	20 26	25 21	1 33	12 22	10 08	14 17	8 27
14 T	5 31 32	22 12 01	25 53	1 39	0♑24	25 54	0♐25	27 19	10 05	11 21	20 27	25 23	1 21	12 33	10 30	14 49	8 27
15 W	5 35 29	23 13 02	7♉54	1 41	1 58	26 06	1 07	27 28	10 11	11 19	20 27	25 25	1 09	12 44	10 53	15 22	8 27
16 Th	5 39 25	24 14 03	19 48	1 42	3 33	26 15	1 49	27 38	10 16	11 17	20 28	25 27	0 57	12 55	11 15	15 54	8 26
17 F	5 43 22	25 15 05	1Ⅱ37	1 42R	5 07	26 22	2 31	27 48	10 22	11 16	20 28	25 28	0 46	13 07	11 38	16 26	8 26
18 Sa	5 47 18	26 16 08	13 25	1 42	6 42	26 27	3 13	27 59	10 28	11 14	20 29	25 30	0 35	13 19	12 01	16 59	8 26
19 Su	5 51 15	27 17 11	25 13	1 40	8 16	26 29R	3 55	28 09	10 34	11 13	20 29	25 32	0 25	13 31	12 23	17 31	8 26D
20 M	5 55 12	28 18 14	7♋05	1 37	9 50	26 29	4 37	28 19	10 40	11 11	20 30	25 34	0 14	13 43	12 46	18 04	8 26
21 T	5 59 8	29 19 19	19 01	1 32	11 25	26 26	5 19	28 30	10 46	11 10	20 31	25 35	0 04	13 56	13 09	18 36	8 26
22 W	6 3 5	0♑20 24	1♌04	1 27	12 59	26 21	6 01	28 41	10 52	11 09	20 31	25 37	29♉55	14 08	13 32	19 08	8 26
23 Th	6 7 1	1 21 29	13 15	1 21	14 33	26 14	6 44	28 51	10 58	11 07	20 32	25 39	29 45	14 21	13 55	19 41	8 26
24 F	6 10 58	2 22 35	25 37	1 16	16 06	26 04	7 26	29 02	11 04	11 06	20 33	25 41	29 36	14 34	14 18	20 13	8 27
25 Sa	6 14 54	3 23 42	8♍12	1 13	17 40	25 51	8 08	29 13	11 10	11 05	20 34	25 43	29 28	14 48	14 41	20 46	8 27
26 Su	6 18 51	4 24 49	21 03	1 10	19 13	25 36	8 51	29 24	11 16	11 03	20 35	25 45	29 19	15 02	15 04	21 18	8 27
27 M	6 22 47	5 25 57	4≏12	1 09D	20 45	25 18	9 33	29 35	11 22	11 02	20 35	25 47	29 12	15 15	15 27	21 50	8 28
28 T	6 26 44	6 27 05	17 43	1 10	22 16	24 59	10 16	29 47	11 29	11 01	20 36	25 48	29 04	15 29	15 50	22 22	8 28
29 W	6 30 41	7 28 14	1♏36	1 11	23 47	24 37	10 58	29 58	11 35	11 00	20 37	25 50	28 57	15 44	16 13	22 55	8 29
30 Th	6 34 37	8 29 24	15 53	1 12	25 17	24 12	11 41	0♓09	11 41	10 59	20 38	25 52	28 50	15 58	16 36	23 27	8 29
31 F	6 38 34	9 30 34	0♐32	1 13R	26 45	23 46	12 23	0 21	11 48	10 58	20 39	25 54	28 44	16 13	17 00	23 59	8 30

The Planetary Hours

The selection of an auspicious time for starting any activity is an important matter. Its existence tends to take on a nature corresponding to the conditions under which it was begun. Each hour is ruled by a planet, and the nature of any hour corresponds to the nature of the planet ruling it. The nature of the planetary hours is the same as the description of each of the planets. Uranus, Neptune, and Pluto are considered here as higher octaves of Mercury, Venus, and Mars.

Sunrise Hour	Sun	Mon	Tue	Wed	Thu	Fri	Sat
1	☉	☽	♂	☿	♃	♀	♄
2	♀	♄	☉	☽	♂	☿	♃
3	☿	♃	♀	♄	☉	☽	♂
4	☽	♂	☿	♃	♀	♄	☉
5	♄	☉	☽	♂	☿	♃	♀
6	♃	♀	♄	☉	☽	♂	☿
7	♂	☿	♃	♀	♄	☉	☽
8	☉	☽	♂	☿	♃	♀	♄
9	♀	♄	☉	☽	♂	☿	♃
10	☿	♃	♀	♄	☉	☽	♂
11	☽	♂	☿	♃	♀	♄	☉
12	♄	☉	☽	♂	☿	♃	♀

Sunset Hour	Sun	Mon	Tue	Wed	Thu	Fri	Sat
1	♃	♀	♄	☉	☽	♂	☿
2	♂	☿	♃	♀	♄	☉	☽
3	☉	☽	♂	☿	♃	♀	♄
4	♀	♄	☉	☽	♂	☿	♃
5	☿	♃	♀	♄	☉	☽	♂
6	☽	♂	☿	♃	♀	♄	☉
7	♄	☉	☽	♂	☿	♃	♀
8	♃	♀	♄	☉	☽	♂	☿
9	♂	☿	♃	♀	♄	☉	☽
10	☉	☽	♂	☿	♃	♀	♄
11	♀	♄	☉	☽	♂	☿	♃
12	☿	♃	♀	♄	☉	☽	♂

Table of Rising and Setting Signs

To find your approximate Ascendant, locate your Sun sign in the left column and determine the approximate time of your birth. Line up your Sun sign with birth time to find Ascendant. Note: This table will give you the approximate Ascendant only. To obtain your exact Ascendant you must consult your natal chart.

Sun Sign	6–8 a.m.	8–10 a.m.	10 a.m.–12 p.m.	12–2 p.m.	2–4 p.m.	4–6 p.m.
Aries	Taurus	Gemini	Cancer	Leo	Virgo	Libra
Taurus	Gemini	Cancer	Leo	Virgo	Libra	Scorpio
Gemini	Cancer	Leo	Virgo	Libra	Scorpio	Sagittarius
Cancer	Leo	Virgo	Libra	Scorpio	Sagittarius	Capricorn
Leo	Virgo	Libra	Scorpio	Sagittarius	Capricorn	Aquarius
Virgo	Libra	Scorpio	Sagittarius	Capricorn	Aquarius	Pisces
Libra	Scorpio	Sagittarius	Capricorn	Aquarius	Pisces	Aries
Scorpio	Sagittarius	Capricorn	Aquarius	Pisces	Aries	Taurus
Sagittarius	Capricorn	Aquarius	Pisces	Aries	Taurus	Gemini
Capricorn	Aquarius	Pisces	Aries	Taurus	Gemini	Cancer
Aquarius	Pisces	Aries	Taurus	Gemini	Cancer	Leo
Pisces	Aries	Taurus	Gemini	Cancer	Leo	Virgo

Sun Sign	6–8 p.m.	8–10 p.m.	10 p.m.–12 a.m.	12–2 a.m.	2–4 a.m.	4–6 a.m.
Aries	Scorpio	Sagittarius	Capricorn	Aquarius	Pisces	Aries
Taurus	Sagittarius	Capricorn	Aquarius	Pisces	Aries	Taurus
Gemini	Capricorn	Aquarius	Pisces	Aries	Taurus	Gemini
Cancer	Aquarius	Pisces	Aries	Taurus	Gemini	Cancer
Leo	Pisces	Aries	Taurus	Gemini	Cancer	Leo
Virgo	Aries	Taurus	Gemini	Cancer	Leo	Virgo
Libra	Taurus	Gemini	Cancer	Leo	Virgo	Libra
Scorpio	Gemini	Cancer	Leo	Virgo	Libra	Scorpio
Sagittarius	Cancer	Leo	Virgo	Libra	Scorpio	Sagittarius
Capricorn	Leo	Virgo	Libra	Scorpio	Sagittarius	Capricorn
Aquarius	Virgo	Libra	Scorpio	Sagittarius	Capricorn	Aquarius
Pisces	Libra	Scorpio	Sagittarius	Capricorn	Aquarius	Pisces

Blank Horoscope Chart

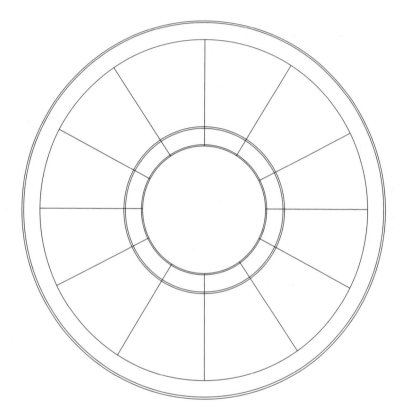

Address Book

Name

Address

City, State, Zip

Phone   Phone

Email

Name

Address

City, State, Zip

Phone   Phone

Email

Name

Address

City, State, Zip

Phone   Phone

Email

Name

Address

City, State, Zip

Phone   Phone

Email

Name

Address

City, State, Zip

Phone   Phone

Email

Address Book

Name

Address

City, State, Zip

Phone   Phone

Email

Name

Address

City, State, Zip

Phone   Phone

Email

Name

Address

City, State, Zip

Phone   Phone

Email

Name

Address

City, State, Zip

Phone   Phone

Email

Name

Address

City, State, Zip

Phone   Phone

Email